THE DIARIES OF
Lady Anne Clifford

EDITED BY D.J.H. CLIFFORD

LADY ANNE CLIFFORD (1590–1676) at the age of thirty, by an unknown
artist (1620)

THE DIARIES OF
Lady Anne Clifford

EDITED BY D.J.H. CLIFFORD

ALAN SUTTON

First published in the United Kingdom in 1990 by
Alan Sutton Publishing Ltd · Phoenix Mill · Far Thrupp · Stroud · Gloucestershire

First published in the United States of America in 1991 by
Alan Sutton Publishing Inc · Wolfeboro Falls · NH 03896–0848

Reprinted 1990
Paperback edition, with corrections, first published 1992
Reprinted 1994

British Library Cataloguing in Publication Data

Clifford, Lady, Anne *1590–1676*
The diaries of Lady Anne Clifford.
1. England. Clifford, Lady, Anne 1590–1676
I. Title II. Clifford, D.J.H.
942.061092

ISBN 0-86299-560-4 (cased)
ISBN 0-75090-163-2 (paperback)

Library of Congress Cataloguing in Publication Data

Pembroke. Anne Clifford Herbert, Countess of, 1590–1676.
The diaries of Lady Anne Clifford/edited by D.J.H. Clifford.
p. cm.
Includes bibliographical references and index.
ISBN 0-86299-560-4 (h/b)
ISBN 0-75090-163-2 (pbk)
1. Pembroke. Anne Clifford Herbert, Countess of, 1590–1676 – Diaries.
2. England – Social life and customs – 17th century.
3. Great Britain – Court and courtiers – Diaries.
4. Great Britain – Nobility – Diaries.
I. Clifford, D.J.H. (David J.H.)
II. Title.
DA378. P4A3 1991
942.06′1092–dc20
[B]
90–9903
CIP

Cover illustration:

Left- and right-hand panels of *The Great Picture*, showing Lady Anne Clifford at the ages of
fifteen and fifty-six. Attributed to Jan van Belcamp, 1646. (By courtesy of Abbot Hall Art
Gallery, Kendal, Cumbria; *The Great Picture* is on display in the Great Hall at Appleby
Castle from May to September)

Typesetting and origination by
Alan Sutton Publishing Limited.
Printed in Great Britain by
Redwood Books, Trowbridge.

To
Lady Anne

Contents

List of Illustrations   viii

Introduction and Acknowledgements   x

Prologue   1

The Knole Diary, 1603–1619   19

The Years Between, 1620–1649   83

The Kendal Diary, 1650–1675   103

The Last Months, 1676   229

Epilogue   269

Appendix 1: The Knole Catalogue   274

Appendix 2: Some Places to Visit   277

Bibliography   279

Index   281

List of
Illustrations

PLATES

Frontispiece: Lady Anne Clifford, aged thirty (H. Fattorini Esq)
1   George Clifford, 3rd Earl of Cumberland (H. Fattorini Esq)   12
2   Lady Margaret Russell, Countess of Cumberland (H. Fattorini Esq)   13
3   Richard Sackville, 3rd Earl of Dorset (English Heritage: Ranger's House, Blackheath)   34
4   Francis Clifford, 4th Earl of Cumberland (H. Fattorini Esq)   46
5   Knole House, Kent (Author's collection)   58
6   Margaret Sackville, aged four (Lord Sackville: Knole House, Kent)   63
7   Francis Russell, 4th Earl of Bedford (Author's collection)   77
8   Isabella Sackville (Lord Sackville: Knole House, Kent)   86
9   Philip Herbert, 4th Earl of Pembroke and Montgomery (Author's collection)   90
10   Wilton House, Wiltshire (Author's collection)   93
11   *The Great Picture*, showing Lady Anne Clifford at the ages of fifteen and fifty-six (By courtesy of Abbot Hall Art Gallery, Kendal, Cumbria; *The Great Picture* is on display in the Great Hall at Appleby Castle from May to September)   98–9
12   Appleby Castle, Westmorland (Author's collection)   111
13   Castle Ashby, Northamptonshire (Northamptonshire Record Office)   117
14   Margaret Sackville, Countess of Thanet (Sackville College)   129
15   Hothfield House, Kent (Kent County Libraries)   134
16   Brough Castle, Westmorland (Author's collection)   145
17   Pendragon Castle, Westmorland (Author's collection)   153
18   Skipton Castle, Yorkshire (Author's collection)   163

List of Illustrations

19 John Tufton, 2nd Earl of Thanet, and his wife, Lady Margaret Sackville (H. Fattorini Esq)   167
20 Thanet House, London (Guildhall Library)   170
21 Barden Tower, Yorkshire (Author's collection)   186
22 Bolebrooke House, Sussex (Author's collection)   214
23 Brougham Castle, Westmorland (Author's collection)   236
24 Lady Anne Clifford, aged fifty-six (National Portrait Gallery, London)   247
25 A page from the manuscript of the 'Last Months' diary (Mrs S. and Mr. R.B. Hasell McCosh, Dalemain)   264

MAP

Location of sites in Westmorland and Yorkshire mentioned in the diaries, showing also the routes taken by Lady Anne   107

GENEALOGICAL TABLES

1 The Clifford descent to Lady Anne   16–17
2 The divided inheritance   272–3

Introduction and Acknowledgements

'It is but seldom that any personage who is not of first class historical importance has succeeded in impressing his or her personality upon a whole countryside or has transmitted, however superficially, a personal tradition through succeeding generations of a rural population. This is, however, the case with the Lady Anne Clifford.' This comment from the introduction to the Royal Commission on Historical Monuments' 1936 inventory of Westmorland monuments is as valid today, four hundred years after Lady Anne's birth, as it has ever been. Indeed, the impress of her character and her actions can still be felt in the rural areas of Westmorland and Craven as if she had been alive just a few years ago. Yet this remarkable woman died in 1676.

Lady Anne, as she is always referred to in Appleby and Skipton, was the last of the illustrious northern branch of the Cliffords to bear the name. From her earliest years she appears to have been imbued with all the traditions of her family and that pride of race which a long descent from a medieval stock afforded. She had a passion for the pomp of her family history, making continual notes from documents that had been found telling of even the minor doings of her ancestors, among whom were numbered the 'Butcher' Lord who fell at Towton, and 'The Shepherd Lord' who spent much of his youth as a fugitive tending sheep among the Lakeland fells.

Anne Clifford was the only surviving daughter – as she is careful to tell us – of George Clifford, 3rd Earl of Cumberland. She married successively Richard, 3rd Earl of Dorset, and Philip, 4th Earl of Pembroke. In spite of frequent quarrels over the disposal of her inheritance, her first marriage was hardly so unhappy as the second, which was an inevitable failure.

The Clifford lands in the north of England had, in accordance with her father's iniquitous will, to pass through the male line before reverting to herself; so it was not until the deaths of her uncle and cousin, the fourth and fifth earls, without further male heirs, that in 1643 she entered into her inheritance. Even then it was not for another six years that she at length found it possible to move from London to the north. From that time, when she was almost sixty, until her death in 1676, she never again left her northern estates, and the picture of this great lady, hereditary Sheriffess of Westmorland residing in one or other of her castles, and gathering round about her a little court, becomes increasingly distinct.

This picture is at once attractive and intimate, and displays in all its phases a character which combined a masculine determination with a very feminine affection for her family and dependants. A determined lady, pursuing her course of action regardless of its effects on her health or even its dangers to life itself, all the while hosting rounds of visits from her daughters and numerous grandchildren, and regularly presenting little gifts to her servants, tenants and friends. Her love of the countryside, especially within the bounds of her lands, was a ruling passion; and there even survives a word-picture of Lady Anne in her country clothes – a black tweed – 'her dress, not disliked by any, was as yet imitated by none'.

The details of this picture are to be found in Lady Anne's diaries, which she kept for most of her long life. They have come down to us, not, unfortunately, as a complete record, but as four separate and distinct manuscripts, located in four different places.

The first, regrettably fragmented, manuscript is a late eighteenth-century transcript which now forms part of the Sackville Collection at Kent County Record Office, Maidstone. It seems to have originated during the time of Anne's first marriage to Richard Sackville. His country seat was at Knole, near Sevenoaks in Kent, and it was here that she probably made most of her notes. This 'Knole Diary' covers in fact only some four years between 1603 and 1619, at which time it abruptly ends. The first section covers Anne's childhood, and includes an on-the-spot account of the funeral of Queen Elizabeth through very young eyes, followed by a day-by-day description of the royal progress made by the newly crowned James Stuart and his somewhat ineffectual wife, Anne of Denmark. There is then a gap until 1616. Anne Clifford is now Countess of Dorset, and on almost every page appear her reactions to the running battle she is waging with her wayward, spendthrift husband, her Uncle Francis, and King James himself, over the inheritance of the northern estates. That there are regular rows between Anne and Richard comes through only too clearly, but her allusions to these are delicate in the extreme, and it may be argued that though this is essentially a very personal diary, Lady Anne chooses her words with care for fear of the pages falling into the wrong hands. The whole of the year 1618 is unaccounted for in the surviving manuscript, and family legend would have it that these entries were deliberately suppressed by a later member of the family.

Richard Sackville, 3rd Earl of Dorset, died in 1624, leaving his wife with two surviving daughters and still fighting her case. In 1630 she married, not without some considerable misgiving, the ageing Philip Herbert. He proved, if anything, a far worse choice than Sackville, and for most of their married life they lived apart. Thankfully for Anne, he died in 1650, but by this time she had won her case and was already resident in the north.

For the period from 1620 to 1649 two further sources, although very incomplete, nevertheless keep us in touch with Anne's fortunes. The first, the Books of Record, which form part of the Hothfield manuscripts, are discussed below. The second is a slim volume, located in the British Library, which is in itself a transcript made in 1727 by Henry Fisher. On first inspection it appears to be a précis from the Books of Record, containing as it does summaries of the genealogies which comprise most of those documents, but there are also reminiscences by Lady Anne on her life. Moreover, Fisher also includes entries covering the important years of Anne's second marriage, which appear nowhere else. These I have included in the section entitled 'The Years Between'.

The second main diary begins in 1650. It is preserved in the third volume of the Books of Record, or the Great Books, as Anne liked to call them. She arranged for three almost identical copies of these books to be made; two sets of which are to be found in Kendal in the care of Cumbria Record Office.

The first two volumes contain vast amounts of genealogical information about the early ancestors of the Cliffords, acquired painstakingly by Anne and her mother as evidence to present to the courts on the inheritance matter. They contain extracts from deeds, wills and the like, some of which have only survived in this way, and which she must have had to call upon during her thirty-eight year long fight. What makes these books so fascinating is that they are original, and include regular notes and alterations in Anne's own hand.

The third volume contains what I have for convenience called the 'Kendal Diary', a continuous record taking us right up to within three months of Lady Anne's death. Here we have the private thoughts of an ageing, stubborn and 'Proud Northern Lady' as Martin Holmes has so aptly called her. Anne is now largely at peace with the world; her

daughters are happily married, and have produced many grandchildren, of whom she is obviously very fond. They visit her regularly,
and she is often in touch with them by letter. Their births, marriages and
deaths are all minutely recorded. Anne hardly makes any mention of the
world outside her own domain. There is scant mention of international
or even national events, in contrast to the records made by her
contemporaries Pepys and Evelyn. A passing reference to the Great Fire
of London, the visit of a foreign nobleman, and her unconcealed
contempt for life at the court of King Charles II, which it should be
remembered she did not once attend, are practically the only comments
she makes on the world outside her own circle of interest. Instead she
passes on a vivid tapestry of her life among the Westmorland fells which
she had loved so much since that first time she set eyes on them, as a
girl, and which now at last, she could call her very own.

The Great Books were clearly written down in several different hands
at Lady Anne's dictation. Principal among her scribes must have been
Edward Langley, who served for many years as her secretary; there is a
letter still in existence in which she says: 'Take care thatt there may be
some greatt paper be bought for Ed. Langley to writt in, for the finishing
of my 3 greatt written hand-books. One of them, which is the first parte
was brought well to mee withein this few days hither, and I pray you,
haste the 2 partes, which is the Biggest of them, done hither to mee as
soon as Langley hath done it.'

The Great Books at Kendal are indeed large by modern standards; the
pages measure 17 in × 14 in. And it is the final half of the third volume
that contains the day-by-day notes that form the bulk of the diary. Lady
Anne calls it 'A Summary of my Life', and the fact that it starts in 1650,
implies that it was only a part of a larger project.

One can only speculate as to where the remainder of her diaries may
be; it has been said that the 6th Earl of Thanet, a grandson of Anne's,
was responsible for their destruction. T.D. Whitaker, in his *History of
Craven* (1805), recalls that he saw at Skipton several references to large
parcels of notes that may possibly have been destroyed by the earl.
Whatever the truth of this claim, it is still the case that these valuable
original documents have, so far, never been recovered.

Fortunately, however, the original manuscript of Lady Anne's 'Last
Months' has survived intact, in the care of the Hasell McCosh family of
Dalemain, Cumbria, descendants of Edward Hasell, Lady Anne's private
secretary. It is of great interest in that it records Lady Anne's diary entries
until the day before she died, and in these last few pages we are able to
glimpse perhaps as never before the endearing qualities of her character.

She welcomes a continual stream of local worthies to her favourite castle of Brougham, giving away small gifts to those deserving recognition and reprimanding others for their misdemeanours. Although her health cannot have been of the best – she continually mentions that she was confined to her room – yet she seems to have retained a wonderful mental awareness right up until the very end.

A brief note on the texts. The 'Knole Diary' in particular includes many marginal annotations made by Lady Anne. These I have shown as numbered footnotes where they occur; in this I have largely followed the format used by Vita Sackville-West (*The Diary of the Lady Anne Clifford*, ed. 1923). I have also added further explanatory notes from time to time, indicated in the text by * and †. The original spelling has been faithfully preserved, and, particularly in the case of the 'Kendal Diary', the variations in spelling should interest the lexicographer. The only liberties I have taken, in the interests of clarity, are to extend abbreviated titles and names ('K' to 'King', 'Ld Jn' to 'Lord John', etc.), to introduce some punctuation, so helping to break up those sentences which would otherwise have appeared unreasonably long, and to make Biblical references consistent in style.

As an aid to identifying some of the 'personae', I have included in the appendices a list of the Dorset household at Knole during Lady Anne's time there. The genealogical tables on pp. 16–17 and 272–3 indicate her ancestry and some of her closer relations mentioned in the text.

This volume is not intended to be a biography of Lady Anne, neither is there any critical assessment of her character; this is left for the reader to determine. However, should the diaries encourage a greater depth of study, then I unhesitatingly recommend Dr G.C. Williamson's *Lady Anne Clifford*, published by Titus Wilson of Kendal in 1922 . For a lighter examination of her life there is also *Proud Northern Lady* by Martin Holmes, which is still available from Messrs Phillimore. Further relevant material is suggested in the bibliography.

Inevitably, when one is engaged in research, and particularly into family history, untold numbers of kind folk contribute in varied ways in supplying the titbits of information which add further pieces to the jigsaw. I am very conscious that the help I have received from all these, be they country vicars, archivists, librarians, friends or relations, may have been taken far too much for granted. In this present exercise I have no excuse.

In particular I would like to thank Lord Sackville and Mr Hugh

Introduction and Acknowledgements

Sackville-West at Knole, for their initial encouragement and support, and also Lord Hothfield for his permission to publish the 'Kendal Diary' from the original manuscript. My thanks are also due to Mr Nigel Nicolson for allowing me to follow his mother's footsteps. I am also extremely grateful to the staff of the record offices at Maidstone and Kendal for their commendable patience despite my sometimes outrageous demands upon their resources. The author is also indebted to those who kindly subscribed to the first edition of this book.

This book, my first on such a scale, could not possibly have reached publication without the tremendous and unstinting help I have received from Alan Sutton Publishing. I found that the editor appointed as my 'minder', Roger Thorp, had Cumbrian connections himself, and was already imbued in all the folklore that the memories of Lady Anne have evoked. He has certainly, through his own interest in the subject, enabled me to avoid several pitfalls. I am deeply indebted to him.

Finally, I shall always be in debt to my very good friend, 'cousin', and accomplice, Dick Clifford, who knows far more about our great family than I shall ever hope to. He it was who made sure I got my history right, and kindly checked that all was in order on the family tree.

David Clifford

Prologue

Westminster, Thursday 8 April 1603. The funeral procession of Queen Elizabeth is passing down Whitehall on its way to the Abbey. Among the watching crowd is a young girl of thirteen. Her mother, the Countess of Cumberland, is one of the pallbearers, and her aunt, the Countess of Warwick, is another. This girl later noted, somewhat plaintively, that, 'I was not allowed to be one because I was not high enough, which did much trouble me'. And she had to be content with watching the funeral service from another part of the Abbey.

The girl's name was Anne Clifford, and little could she have realized as she watched the last of the Tudor monarchs being laid to rest, that she too, after almost outliving the three Stuart kings who succeeded Elizabeth, would, in her turn, be the last of the illustrious north country line of her family to bear the proud name of Clifford.

Anne Clifford was born at Skipton Castle in Yorkshire on 30 January 1590. Her father was George, 3rd Earl of Cumberland, and her mother, the beautiful and talented Margaret Russell, a daughter of the Earl of Bedford. She was taken to London early on in her life, and placed in the care of her 'Aunt Warwick', a great lady at court, whose task it was to train the little girl in courtly manners, preparing her for a position in the Queen's Household when she was old enough.

The Cumberlands had had two sons before Anne was born, but both had died young; indeed she was only fourteen months old when the second boy died at North Hall in Hertfordshire, and she relates that, 'ever after that time I continewed to bee the onely Childe of my parents, nor had they any other Daughter but myself'.

In her Great Books she reflects on her childhood: 'I was verie happie in my first Constitution, both in my mynd and Bodye. Both for internall and externall Endowments, for never was there Childe more equallie resembleing both Father and Mother than myself. The Collour of myne eyes was Black lyke my father's, and the form and aspect of them was quick and lively like my Mother's. The haire of myne head,' she goes on, 'was Browne and thick, and so long that it reached to the Calfe of my Legges when I stood upright, with a peake of haire on my forehead and

1

a Dimple in my Chynne lyke my Father, full Cheekes and round face lyke my Mother, and an exquisite shape of Bodie resembling my Father.'

From the age of eleven, Anne had as tutor the poet and writer Samuel Daniel. He must have had a tremendous influence on her, as she became a great lover of poetry, with a particular affection for the writings of Edmund Spenser. Anne never ceased to venerate Daniel, and sometime after his death in 1619, she caused, at her own expense, a monument to be erected to his memory in the tiny church at Beckington in Somerset where he is buried.

Shortly after Anne's birth in 1590, George Clifford had been appointed the Queen's Champion, and in 1592, he was admitted to the Most Noble Order of the Garter. He had now become one of Elizabeth's most trusted advisers, and what little time he spent in England he preferred to spend at court, rather than returning to one or other of his properties to stay with his family.

George Clifford's lands, acquired over the centuries by means of judicious marriages and from grateful sovereigns, covered a sizeable area of north-west England; he also owned or leased country seats in the south, as well as at least two properties in London.

He was lavish with his wealth, both in England and abroad. He equipped no less than eleven expeditions to various parts of the world – as far East as Madagascar, and west to the Azores and the Caribbean. Some of these trips were on her majesty's service, but others appear to have had a distinctly buccaneering connection; as we can gather from documents of the time, not all the booty that the earl gained from his forays necessarily ended up in the royal coffers. From 1586 almost until his death he was rarely at home, and although his letters to his wife – 'swete Meg' – show some affection, he treated her very badly, and so far as their daughter was concerned he remained a very remote figure indeed.

George Clifford outlived his queen by only two years, dying at the fairly young age of forty-seven. Anne was legally his sole heir, her two brothers having died young. Her father, however, neglectful of his family to the last, although leaving Anne the not inconsiderable sum of £15,000, willed the entire estates to his brother Francis, who succeeded to the earldom.

To be fair, George must have realized when he made out his will in 1603 that he was unlikely to have a son to succeed at that time, and wished to save his daughter the responsibilities attached to running such a vast enterprise. After all, she was hardly fifteen when he died. None the less, it was a cruel move, and was in fact in direct opposition to an entail made by King Edward II to an earlier Clifford, in which it was clearly stated that the Clifford lands should always descend to the direct heir, whatever the sex. After George's death, his wife almost immediately started to contest the will on her daughter's behalf, and then, a year or two later, Anne was taken north to view her inheritance.

The Clifford estates covered most of the old historic county of Westmorland, together with that part of North Yorkshire known as Craven; in all, an area estimated in size as almost 90,000 acres. The northern boundary was marked by Brougham Castle, near Penrith, the southern by Skipton Castle. In between, at strategic points, were the castles of Appleby, Brough and Pendragon. All these castles had, in days gone by, seen action against Scottish raiders, and all, especially Skipton, were to see more during the Civil War.

Anne herself relates that she and her mother were 'forced for their owne good' to visit Westmorland, and that they arrived at Appleby Castle on 22 July 1607, 'which was the first time that I had been in the Countie since my father's death'. Lady Cumberland had already decided upon the course of action she should adopt over the estates, and began to instigate a very careful search of all relevant papers which would enable them to make out a strong enough case in support of the claim. In the ensuing years, an enormous collection of documents was amassed, many of them family papers, which were laboriously copied down. Covering over three hundred years of Clifford family history, it was a collection which, in the words of John Baynes, writing a century later, 'no other noble family in the world can show'.

Mother and daughter stayed for a time at Appleby, and then moved on to Brougham, and then after three or four nights at Naworth, home of a relative, they returned back to London, intending to call at Skipton on the way. But here they were barred from entering the castle where Anne had been born, by order of the new earl. Disappointed by such abrupt treatment they stayed at nearby Beamsley, where her mother had been engaged in building a hospital for the elderly ladies of the district. From here they toured the Craven lands, which included Barden Tower and Bolton Abbey, where several of Anne's ancestors lay buried. They arrived back in London in April 1608, and shortly afterwards Lady Cumberland started proceedings in the court of ward concerning the lands of her daughter's inheritance.

The Countess of Cumberland died in 1616, and Anne, still only twenty-six, took up the challenge with a determination and stubbornness that completely belied her youth and small stature. Mention of this 'Great Business' that she was engaged upon occurs frequently in the pages of the 'Knole Diary', and so as to more easily understand the disputes and their background, in which Lady Anne had to deal against two unsympathetic husbands, her 'Uncle Cumberland', and indeed King James himself, it would be useful to look at the earlier history of the family.

Using as a guide the sequence employed by Lady Anne in her Great Books, the first ancestor to mention is Robert de Viteripont, whose grandfather came over to England with William the Conqueror. Robert was a great favourite of King John, and by reason of the royal favour, as well as his own abilities, which gained him marriage with an heiress, he became a man of immense power and wealth. The king gave him possession of Westmorland, creating him baron and hereditary sheriff of that county. These grants gave him the lordship of the castles at Brougham, Brough, Appleby and Pendragon, together with the considerable income these estates would attract. Moreover, he later became sheriff of four other counties, Custodian of Windsor Castle and one of the country's Law Lords.

Some of these lands were subsequently sold off by Robert de Viteripont's son, John, and there must be many families in the north today who perhaps owe their present landholdings to the fortunate circumstance that John de Viteripont made it possible for their forebears to purchase, a rare occurrence in those times.

John's son, Robert, proved to be a great warrior; he married Isobel Fitz-Geoffrey and was killed fighting against King Henry III in the Barons' Wars. He left two daughters as co-heiresses – Isabella, ten years of age, and Idonea, a baby of just twelve months. This Robert was the last of the Viteriponts in Westmorland, and with him the family connection with the county had almost ended, for the king had seized his estates on account of treason. Fortunately, however, he later restored them to the two girls, whom he put into the guardianship of two of his faithful adherents; Idonea with Sir Roger de Leybourne, and Isabella with Sir Roger de Clifford. Both these worthy knights decided that they could best fulfil their charge by marrying off their respective wards to their own children, which was quite possibly what King Henry had intended.

Roger de Clifford's son, another Roger, had to wait only four or five years for his ward to reach the then marriageable age of fifteen, but the younger Leybourne had three times as long to wait, and eventually acquired through Idonea's dowry the castles of Brough and Pendragon. Idonea de Leybourne outlived her husband, married again, outlived her second husband, and finally died at the good age of eighty-six. Her share of the Viteripont inheritance then reverted to her sister's grandson.

And now to the origins of the Cliffords.

Domesday Book records that five brothers named Pons, sons of William Pons, a kinsman of King William, are found with lands in Gloucestershire and Herefordshire. One of these brothers, Richard, married Maud Fitz-Walter daughter of Milo, Sheriff of Gloucester. Richard had established himself at Llandovery in South Wales, and had built a castle there. The couple had four sons and a daughter. One of the boys, Walter, in due time married Margaret de Toeni, whose grandfather had carried William's standard at the battle of Hastings. Her uncle, William Fitz-Osbern, Earl of Hereford, was the first Warden of the Welsh Marches, and his priority was to build a chain of castles along the border as protection against Welsh incursions. One of these, a motte and bailey, he had passed to Ralph de Toeni, Margaret's father. It was perched upon a cliff overlooking a ford in the River Wye. The story goes that this castle of Clifford was given to Walter and his bride, causing the young man to take the name of de Clifford.

The newly named de Cliffords had seven children ; four boys and three girls. One of the daughters may have been something of a handful to her parents. Her name was Jane, but she claimed the attention of King Henry II, and has become better known as 'The Fair Rosamund'.

Walter, the eldest son, became the second lord of Clifford Castle on his father's death, and can certainly be said to be the ancestor of Lady Anne. He married Agnes de Cundy, an heiress from Covenby in Lincolnshire, and by him she had six sons and two daughters. Again, the eldest was called Walter, and he married Margaret, daughter of Llewelyn, Prince of Wales, and left an only daughter, Maud. The title and lordship therefore devolved on to the second son, Roger, who married Sibilla, daughter of Robert Ewyas, a neighbouring landowner in Herefordshire. It was their son, Roger, who became the guardian, and later the father-in-law of Isabella de Viteripont, when his son, Roger, married her in 1269.

All three Rogers were active men and great soldiers of the time, and for services in the wars in France, Ireland and in England, the youngest of them was well rewarded by Henry III with grants of valuable lands in the Vale of Monmouth to add to his already sizeable holdings in Herefordshire and Worcestershire. When the time came for him to move north when he married, he was already a wealthy man. The Monmouth estates were later exchanged for the Craven lands, including Skipton Castle, which estates have remained with Lady Anne's descendants in the female line until this present century.

In 1282 Sir Roger Clifford III was drowned attempting to cross the Menai Straits while in action against the Welsh. He was forty-six. Isabella was left a widow of twenty-nine with their only son, Robert, aged nine. This Robert later became a true man of war. As Lord of Westmorland he was able to muster, as indeed he was required to, a sizeable private army to be put at the disposal of the king. He was frequently engaged in fighting against the Scots, and took part in the siege of Caerlaverock in 1298. He was ultimately slain leading the English cavalry at Bannockburn in 1314. He was also responsible for building up the defences of Skipton Castle, and they were sturdy enough to survive until Cromwell's troops destroyed them in 1645.

Robert Clifford was succeeded by his eldest son, another Roger, who however enjoyed only some eight years of manhood. He supported the Lancastrian campaign against Piers Gaveston, and at the battle of Boroughbridge in 1322 he was severely wounded in the head and was captured by the royalist forces. Whereas the Lancastrian leaders were executed, Roger appears to have been reprieved on account of his injury and lived a further five years. His estates however were confiscated, although fortunately for the Clifford cause they were restored again to his younger brother, Robert. Most sources make no mention of this Roger having married; some allege that he had a romance with a woman named Julian, who lived in a house in Whinfell Forest not far from Brougham. Here he used to visit her, in much the same way as King Henry II met Rosamund Clifford one hundred and fifty years earlier. But there is an interesting note in the *Chronicles of Lanercost*, written not many years afterwards, which states that Roger did in fact marry one of the daughters of Humphrey de Bohun, 4th Earl of Hereford. No matter what the truth may have been, Roger died, without any apparent issue, and was succeeded by his younger brother Robert. Robert proved to be a model lord and a home-loving gentleman. He was a great builder and repairer of his castles, and he also had a great passion for the chase.

These were quieter times, and in 1333 King Baliol of Scotland paid a visit to Brougham, and it was on this occasion that a famous stag hunt took place. It is related that a hound named Hercules pursued a fine hart from Whinfell to the Scottish border and back again. The hart came to a high wall, gave one last desperate leap to clear it, and collapsed and died on the other side. The hound failed to follow, and also died from exhaustion. To commemorate this strange event, the hart's horns were nailed to a nearby tree, which for ever after was called the Hartshorn Tree. It was still there in Lady Anne's time, still retaining its trophy, and she makes several references to it.

We are told, somewhat significantly, that this Robert Clifford died in his bed. Unlike his father and grandfather before him, or so many Lord Cliffords afterwards.

He was succeeded by Robert, his eldest son, in whom blazed out afresh all the military fire of his race. He served in the French Wars under Edward III and the Black Prince, and was at the battle of Crécy when only sixteen. He was killed, still in France, at an early age sometime around 1349.

Another Roger, his brother, succeeded to the inheritance, and he actually survived to be a grandfather. Yet he was by no means a peace-loving man, and played his fair share in the king's campaigns in Scotland and in France. But fighting to this Roger was a duty not a passion. He too was a builder, and extended Brougham Castle to its present size. His wife, Maud Beauchamp, survived him for many years, and lived on at Brougham, which was made her jointure.

They unaccountably produced a wild and headstrong son named Thomas. For some as yet unknown reason he was banished from parliament and from serving the king, so by way of working off his surplus energies he joined up with a French force engaged in quelling a Hun uprising in Germany, where he was killed in his twenty-eighth year.

Thomas survived his father by only two years, and left a son, John, who in due course married, went away to the wars, and died in battle – a practice which was all too fast becoming a habit with these Clifford lords. John's wife was Elizabeth Percy, daughter of Hotspur. Lord John Clifford fell in the French wars in 1390, when he was about thirty-four. His widow later married Ralph Neville of Raby Castle who was lord also of Penrith.

Lady Anne says of Elizabeth: 'This Elizabeth Percy was one of the greatest women of her time, both for her birth and her marriages; but the mis-fortunes of the wars so followed her that in her time her grand-father the Earl of Northumberland was beheaded, and his son, her father slain in battle [at Shrewsbury]; her first husband was slain in France; and after her decease her son, Thomas, Lord Clifford, and her son John, Lord Neville, and her grandson John, Lord Clifford were all slain in battle.' Elizabeth lies buried in Staindrop Church, near Raby, County Durham.

Young Thomas Clifford, son of John and Elizabeth, went early to the

French wars, where he soon became a distinguished commander. One of his most interesting exploits was the capture of the strongly held town of Pontoise in winter-time. One snowy night, he and his men, all clad in white, surprised the garrison by their audacity, and in so doing brought about the surrender of the town with hardly any casualties. Arctic camouflage is certainly not a modern invention!

After a long period of service in France, Thomas returned to England, where he almost immediately got involved in the Wars of the Roses, taking the side of the Lancastrians. He was killed at the first battle of St Albans and lies buried in the abbey precincts. He left a son John, who although only twenty, was already fiercely engaged in the same conflict. This John occupies an unhappy niche in the history books for his cold-blooded murder of Edmund, the young Earl of Rutland, son of the Duke of York.

The story is well known, but is worth recounting, if only in brief. After the battle of Wakefield in which the Duke of York was slain, the young Edmund, not yet eighteen years old, was captured and taken before Lord John Clifford. While on his knees begging for mercy, John is said to have exclaimed, 'Thy father slew mine, and I will slay thee!' He then stabbed him to death, and for this deed carried the nickname of 'The Butcher'. Lady Anne disputes this, the generally accepted version of the event, claiming that Edmund was killed honourably in battle. But the well-accredited chronicles of the time appear to make the more unsavoury version incontestable. 'The Black-faced Clifford', as Shakespeare describes him, was himself killed by a stray arrow on the eve of the battle of Towton, claimed to be the bloodiest battle ever fought on English soil. With victory going to the Yorkists, the Lancastrian faction was crushed, and Edward IV was confirmed on the English throne.

John Clifford left a widow, Margaret, daughter and heiress of Henry, Lord Bromflete and Baron Vesci, and these titles thus came into the Clifford family. However, because of her husband's deeds, the vengeance of the Yorkists fell heavily upon her and her two sons. The estates were seized, the family attainted, and the boys were hunted to stand trial for their father's crimes. Margaret succeeded in smuggling them to the east coast, intending them to find safety in the Low Countries. Only the younger boy, Richard, apparently went over to Holland, where, according to Lady Anne, he 'died young'. However, recent research has shown that he was still alive in around 1490, in his thirties, as a deed has come to light naming him as heir of part of his mother's lands, which parts were to revert to him on her death. Margaret herself died in 1493. Research is currently in progress which points to the possibility that this Richard may have settled down in Norfolk, and that a line stemming from him still survives to this day.

The elder son, Henry, appears to have first been taken to the Bromflete seat at Londesborough, in the Yorkshire Wolds, where for his safety he was brought up by a shepherd family. This location was not deemed safe enough, and so he was moved up to the Cumbrian fells, where other shepherds cared for him under the cliffs of Blencathra. His mother had meanwhile remarried, to Sir Lancelot Threlkeld of nearby Yanwath, and was therefore conveniently near him. It has been said that he was completely ignorant of his true identity and was not taught how to read or write. After twenty years of this existence came the battle of Bosworth in 1485, when Henry Tudor wrested the English throne from the Yorkist Richard III. One of the new king's first actions was to pardon all adherents to the Lancastrian cause, and this included the Cliffords. Henry Clifford, now dubbed 'The Shepherd Lord' had all his estates and honours restored to him as the rightful heir to his father. Wordsworth has given us a fine tribute with his poem 'The Song at the Feast at Brougham Castle', which recounts the story vividly.

Henry, Lord Clifford and Baron Vesci, must have quickly remedied his earlier lack of education, for Lady Anne tells us:

He did exceedingly delight in astronomy and the contemplation of the stars. He built the great part of Barden Tower, where he lived much, because in that place he had furnished himself with instruments. . . . He was a plain man, and lived for the most part a country life, and seldom came to Court or to London; but when he was called thither to sit as Peer of the Realm, he behaved himself wisely and like a good English Gentleman.

It appears that Henry's astronomical studies also included astrology, for Lady Anne relates that in her time, 'there was a tradition that by his skill, he, on the birth of a grandson, read the stars and foretold that this grandson would have two sons, between whom and their posterity there should be great suits at law, and that the heirs male of the line should end with these two sons, or soon after them,' which, whatever one is to believe, actually came to pass.

The Shepherd Lord married twice, and left two or three sons and several daughters. Despite the simple manner of his upbringing and his hobby of stargazing, he was still able to assume a command at the age of sixty at the battle of Flodden in 1513. He died ten years later, to be succeeded by his son Henry, a contemporary of Henry VIII. The two

Henrys virtually grew up together and by their twenties had become close friends. It will therefore come as no surprise to learn that the young king created Henry Clifford first Earl of Cumberland, and a Knight of the Garter. He was also appointed Lord President of the North of England and Lord Warden of the Marches. Henry died at Skipton in 1542 and is buried in the parish church there.

He was succeeded by his eldest son, Henry, who in the early part of his life followed his father's skills in military and other matters. He married Lady Eleanor Brandon, niece to the king and a granddaughter of Henry VII. It was a magnificent wedding, King Henry VIII himself being present. To provide a suitably regal place for the reception of such a bride, the earl undertook an extensive and sumptuous addition to the castle at Skipton, which was completed within three months! Eleanor, alas, only lived for another ten years, leaving just one daughter. She had had two sons, but both had died young. Had one of these boys survived to succeed his father, history might have taken a very different course, as there is an interesting codicil in Henry VIII's will stating that, should none of his own children produce male heirs, then the Crown of England should pass to a son of Eleanor Clifford.

Immediately after Eleanor's death, Henry was stricken with an illness so serious that many believed he too would die. For weeks he was fed as a baby, on asses' milk, and wrapped up in soft blankets. He recovered, after some months, to perfect health, and took as his second wife Anne, daughter of Lord Dacre of Greystoke, Gilsland and Kirkoswald. It was a much quieter wedding, and Anne seems to have been a quiet, homely sort of girl. We are told that 'never did she go to London or anywhere near to it'.

Henry, like his father, studied astronomy, but also became a 'great distiller of waters and maker of chemical extractions, and very studious in all manner of learning; he had an excellent library of books, both hand-written and printed, to which he was addicted exceedingly, especially towards his latter end'. He died at Brougham in 1570, and was also buried at Skipton. He left two sons by Anne Dacre, George and Francis, and thus far the alleged astrological forecast of his grandfather, the Shepherd Lord, was fulfilled.

The eldest son, George, 3rd Earl of Cumberland, had been born at Brougham in 1558, just three months before the death of Queen Mary. He married, as has already been stated, Lady Margaret Russell, and Anne was their daughter.

We have seen that this long line of northern Cliffords consisted, almost without exception, of men of mark, ever to the forefront of the leading events of their time, and Anne's father was no exception to this pattern. The medieval brand of chivalry had passed with the demise of feudalism, but the spirit of chivalry was now needed more than ever. Not in the conflict of factions within the realm, but in national defence, something not contemplated in England since 1066.

The would-be hero in Elizabeth's time had to win his spurs through commerce or on the high seas; for the Elizabethan Age saw the birth of English naval supremacy, as well as English colonization, and there arose the new passion for foreign voyaging. It was to this in particular that George Clifford gave his wealth and energy so unreservedly.

Academically he was brilliant only in mathematics; indeed he graduated at Cambridge University, and then gained his Master's degree in the subject at Oxford, but from its study came a taste for navigation, and in this he became most proficient. While his ancestors had spent their wealth in building castles and maintaining private armies, George's resources went into providing ships and funding crews to sail in them. His eleven expeditions to the West Indies and as far as the Indian Ocean make up a book on their own, and indeed Dr G.C. Williamson published such a book in 1922 (*George Clifford, Third Earl of Cumberland*), narrating the earl's adventures in great detail.

George Clifford was one of the witnesses at the execution of Mary Queen of Scots, and a year later a signatory to the document that sanctioned the launching of the tiny English fleet against the Armada in 1588. He himself commanded the *Elizabeth Bonaventure* during the action in the Channel, this ship being one of the largest in the navy at the time. It is no small claim to say that this Earl of Cumberland stands in our maritime archives alongside the names of Drake, Frobisher, Hawkins and Raleigh.

When George was home from the sea he did not rest; he was forever at court, being one of the Queen's favourites in her later years. He wore her glove in his hat, embellished with jewels collected on his voyages; and he had special suits of armour made for his appearances as her Champion.

But although he was one of England's heroes, he was far from being so within his family for, in short, he was a bad husband and father. His final act of unkindness – disinheriting his daughter from all the titles and possessions of the Cliffords – hit her hard enough to toughen her resolve to fight all she could to right the wrong done in his name. Yet we find Anne, who loved and venerated her mother almost to idolatry, remarkably cool in her comments about her father. We read no words of

GEORGE CLIFFORD (1558–1605), 3rd Earl of Cumberland, Lady Anne's
father, by Nicholas Hilliard

LADY MARGARET RUSSELL (1560–1616), Countess of Cumberland, Lady Anne's mother, by an unknown artist

bitterness against him, though she must surely have thought that his interpretation of the fifth commandment was somewhat perplexing. Anne makes reference to her last meeting with him:

> . . . in the open air, for then I took my leave of him on Greenwich Heath in Kent, as hee had brought mee so farre on my way towards Sutton-in-Kent, where my Mother then lay, after I had bene and stayed the space of a month in the ould Howse at Grafton in Northamptonshire, where my father lived, by reason of some unhappie unkindness towards my Mother. Which was a tyme of great sorrow to my Saintlyke Mother, till I returned back againe to her from my father, the sayd first daie of September.

George Clifford died shortly afterwards, with Anne recording the event as follows:

> My nouble and brave father died in the Duchy House by the Savoy in London nere the River of Thames when he was about three months past fortie seven yeares old. My Mother and I being present with him at his death, I being then just fifteen yeares and nyne months ould at the same date. When a little before his death Hee expressed with much affection to my Mother and me, and a great Beliefe that hee had that his Brother's sonne would dye without issue male, and thereby all his Landes would come to be myne . . .

The 3rd Earl of Cumberland was buried at Skipton, next to his father and grandfather. His tomb, magnificently provided by his daughter, has been justly described as the grandest monument ever built for someone not of royal blood. There are heraldic shields in profusion, tracing his ancestral links with the many families with which the House of Clifford had become connected; but one tends to suspect that not a little of this splendour was rooted in Lady Anne's own interest and pride in her forebears.

After the funeral, Margaret, his countess, commenced an action at law to contest the will on behalf of her daughter. It was argued that the Viteripont estates were, by the royal grant of Edward II, to descend to the heirs, whether male or female, in the direct line, so long as there was an heir. If the law was to uphold this, then Anne's father had clearly made an illegal will; and with this law suit commenced the fulfilment of the second part of the Shepherd Lord's prediction.

In 1609 Anne Clifford was married to Richard Sackville; she has described this as follows:

The 25th day of February in 1609, I was married to my first Lord, Richard Sackville, then but Lord Buckhurst, in my mother's house and her own chamber in Augustine Fryers in London, which was part of a chappell there formerly, she being then present at my marriage.

Two days after the wedding, Sackville's father, the 2nd Earl of Dorset, died, and so Anne immediately became a countess and mistress of the Sackville family seat at Knole in Kent. Anne goes on to relate:

About two yeares after I was married to my said Lord he went to travel in France and the Low Countries for a year, upon a pre-ingagement to his grandmother and others of his friends before he married me. He stayed beyond the seas about a year and came to me at Knowle the 8th April 1612.

And in the time that I after lived his wife I had by him five children, viz. three sons and two daughters. The three sons all dyed young at Knowle where they were born; but my first child the Lady Margaret, who was born at Dorsett House the 2nd July 1614, is now Countess of Thanett, and is mother to ten children.

And for the most part, while I was his wife, I lived either in his houses at Knowle, or at Bowlebrook, or in Great Dorset House or Little Dorset House; but Great Dorset House came not to be his till the decease of his good grand-mother, Cicely Baker, Countess Dowager of Dorset, whose jointure house it was. She dyed the 1st October 1615. And the 22nd September 1618 dyed his mother-in-law, Anne Spencer, Countess Dowager of Dorset.

The above notes, made by Lady Anne, are for some unknown reason preserved neither in her 'Knole Diary' nor in the larger diary incorporated in the Hothfield papers, as they have come down to us. The originals, however, date from about 1650, when Lady Anne was compiling her Great Books. These are now lost, but happily were transcribed by a Mr Henry Fisher in February 1727 and are now in the British Library under Harleian MS. 6177. There are a few more entries on this manuscript, not available elsewhere, which will be quoted later on in context.

Richard Sackville, rather like Anne's father, fancied himself as a great courtier, and spent much of his time there. He was intelligent and

THE CLIFFORD DESCENT TO LADY ANNE

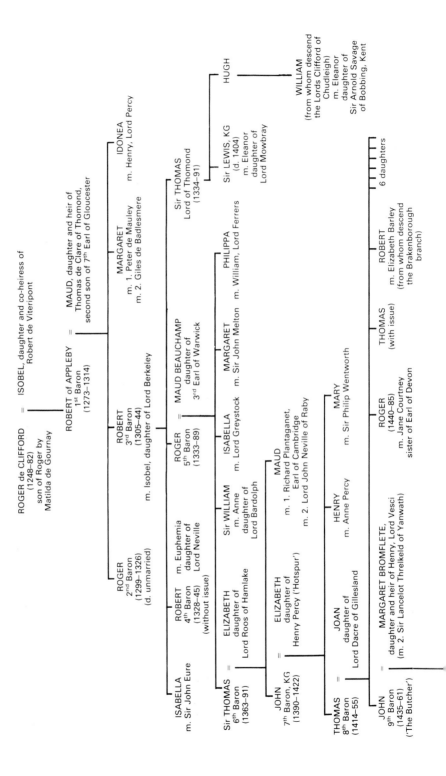

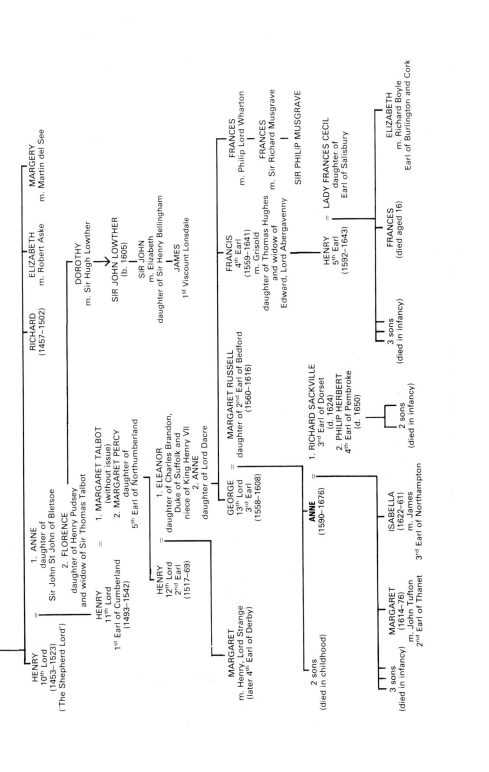

learned, but was also abounding in extravagance. He soon showed to his bride that he had little sympathy for her endeavours, unless he could benefit from so doing, and indeed sided with the king in trying to persuade Anne to give up her case. Twice Anne was taken before King James and urged to yield up her claim, but, though the king and her husband coerced, the brave lady held out in resolute defiance.

The countess, her mother, was still in possession of the estates in Westmorland, and in 1616 Anne, after seven years of stormy marriage, went up to see her for what transpired to be the last time. The parting after the final meeting of these two ladies on the Appleby road, just a few minutes' walk from Brougham Castle, is made the more poignant from Anne's description of it. Indeed it made such a lasting impression on her that forty years later she consecrated the spot with a memorial, known thereafter as 'the Countess' Pillar'.

The Appleby road is a busy trunk-road these days, but the monument can still be seen above it on the southern side. On its north face are two heraldic shields. One shows Clifford impaling Viteripont, the other Clifford impaling Russell; the one being the most remote, the other being the most recent of Lady Anne's forebears.

Margaret, Countess of Cumberland, was buried in a sumptuous tomb provided by her daughter in St Lawrence's Church in Appleby.

Shortly after her mother's death, King James procured an order against Anne; her husband signed away his claim to her estates, and royal letters patent were issued, completing her disinheritance. Almost immediately afterwards we find the new earl (Uncle Cumberland) entertaining the king at Brougham.

At this point, however, let us go back in time again to 1603 and the beginning of Lady Anne's diaries.

THE KNOLE
DIARY
1603–1619

1603

In Christmas I used to go much to the Court & sometimes I did lie at my Aunt Warwick's Chamber on a Pallet, to whom I was much bound for her continual care & love of mee, in so much as if Queen Elizabeth had lived she intended to prefer me to be of the Privy Chamber for at that time there was much hope and expectation of me as of any other young Ladie whatsoever. A little after the Queen removed to Richmond she began to grow sicklie. My Lady used to go often thither and carry me with her in the Coach and using to wait in the Coffee Chamber, & many times we came home very late.

About the 21st or 22nd of March my Aunt of Warwick sent my Mother word about 9 a clock at night – she living then at Clerkenwell – that she should remove to Austin Friars her House for fear of some Commotions, then God in His Mercy did deliver us from it. The 20th March Mr Flocknall, my Aunt Warwick's man, brought us word from his lady that the Queen died about 2.30 a clock in the morning. This Message was delivered to my Mother & me in the same chamber where afterwards I was married.[1]

About 10 o'clock King James was proclaimed in Cheapside by all the Council with great joy and triumph.[2] I went to see and hear. This peacable coming in of the King was unexpected of all parts of the people. Within 2 or 3 days we returned to Clerkenwell again.

A little after this Q.E.'s Corps came by night in a Barge from Richmond to Whitehall, my Mother & a great Company of Ladies attending it where it continued a great while standing in the Drawing Chamber, where it was watched all night by several Lords & Ladies. My Mother sitting up with it two or three nights, but my Lady would not give me leave to watch by reason I was held too young.

---

1 I was at Q. Elizabeth's death 13 yrs & 2 months old, & Mr R. Sackville was 14 yrs old, he being then at Dorset House with his Grandfather & that great family. At the death of this worthy Queen my Mother & I lay at Austin Friars in the same chamber.
2 The first time that the K. sent to the Lds in England he gave command that the Earls of Northumberland, Cumbd, Ld Thos Howard & Ld Mountjoy should be bidden to the Council.

At this time we used very much to go to Whitehall and walked much in the Garden which was frequented by Lords & Ladies. My Mother being all full of hopes every Man expecting Mountains & finding Molehills, excepting Sir R. Cecil and the House of the Howards who hated my Mother & did not much love my Aunt Warwick.

About this time my Lord Southampton was enlarged of his Imprisonment out of the Tower.

When the Corps of Q.E. had continued at Whitehall as the Council thought fit, it was carried with great solemnity to Westminster, the Lords & Ladies going on foot to attend it. My Mother & my Aunt Warwick being Mourners, but I was not allowed to be one because I was not high enough, which did much trouble me then, but yet I stood in the Church at Westminster to see the Solemnities performed.[3]

A little after this my lady & a great deal of other Company as Mrs Elizabeth Bridges, Lady Newton & her daughter Lady Finch went down with my Aunt Warwick to North Hall and from thence we all went to Tibbalds* to see the King who used my Mother & Aunt very graciously. But we all saw a great change between the fashion of the Court as it is now and that in the Queen's time, for we were all lousy by sitting in the chamber of Sir Thomas Erskine.

As the King came out of Scotland when he lay at York, there was a strife between my Father & Lord Burleigh,[†] who was the President and who should carry the Sword, but it was adjudged on my Father's side because it was an office by inheritance, and so is lineally descended to me.

From Tibbalds the King went to Charter House where Lord T. Howard was created Earl of Suffolk and Lord Mountjoy Earl of Devonshire, and restored Lords Southampton & Essex who stood attainted. Likewise he created many Barons among which my Uncle Russell was made Lord Russell of Thorney, & for Knights, they were innumerable. All this Spring I had my health very well. My Father used to come to us sometimes at Clerkenwell but not often, for he had at this time as it were wholly left my Mother, yet the House was kept still at her charge.

About this time my Aunt of Bath and her Lord came to London and

---

3 Q.E.'s funeral was on Thursday April 8th.

* Theobalds, a royal lodge (now a conference centre) on the border between Hertfordshire and Middlesex.

† William Cecil of Burghley (1521–98) was created Lord High Treasurer and Chief Secretary of State by Queen Elizabeth I.

The Knole Diary, 1603–1619

brought them my Lord Fitz-Warren & my Cousin Frances Bourchier, whom I met at Bagshot where I lay all night with my Cousin, & Mrs Mary Carey, which was the first beginning of the greatness between us. About 5 miles from London there met my Mother, my Lord of Bedford and his Lady, my Uncle Russell & much other Company so that we were in number about 300 which did all accompany them to Bath House, where they continued most of that summer. Whither I went daily & visited them & grew daily more inward with my Cozen Frances & Mrs Carey.

About this time my Aunt Warwick went to meet the Queen,[*] having Mrs Bridges with her & my Aunt Vavasour.[†] My Mother & I should have gone with them, but that her Horse (which she borrowed from Mr Elmes) and old Mr Stickley were not ready. Yet I went the same night & overtook my Aunt at Tittinhanger, Lady Blunt's House where my Mother came the next day to me at noon – my Aunt being gone before. Then my Mother & I went on our journey to overtake her, & killed three Horses that day with extremities of heat, & came to Wrest, my Lord of Kent's, where we found the Doors shut & none in the House, but one Servant who only had the Keys of the Hall, so that we were forced to lie in the Hall all night till towards morning, at which time came a Man and let us into the Higher Rooms where we slept 3 or 4 hours.

This morning we hasted away betimes & came that night to Rockingham Castle where we overtook my Aunt Warwick & her Company where we continued a day or two with old Sir Edward Watson & his Lady. Then we went to Lady Needham's who once served my Aunt of Warwick, & from thence to a sister of hers whose name I have forgotten.

Thither came my Lady of Bedford who was so great a Woman with the Queen as everybody much respected her, she having attended the Queen out of Scotland. The next day we went to Mr Griffin's at Dingleys which was the first time I ever saw the Queen & Prince Henry when she kissed us all & used us kindly. Hither also came my Lady of Suffolk, my young Lady Derby & Lady Walsingham, which three Ladies were the great Favourites of Sir Robert Cecil. That night we went along with the Queen's Train, there being an infinite number of Coaches, &, as I take it, my Aunt & my Mother & I lay at Sir Rd. Knightley's, where Lady

---

[*] Anne of Denmark, wife of King James I.
[†] Anne Vavasour, in her youth one of Queen Elizabeth's maids of honour, had caused a minor sensation by giving birth to an illegitimate child in one of the royal rooms at court in 1581. This did not, however, prevent her from frequenting court circles some thirty years later, during Lady Anne's time.

Elizabeth Knightley made exceedingly much of us. The same night my Mother & I & only Aunt Vavasour rid on Horseback thro' country & went to a Gentleman's House where the Lady Elizabeth, her Grace,* lay, which was the first time I ever saw her; my Lady Kildare & the Lady Harrington being her Governesses. The same night we returned to Sir Rd. Knightley's.

The next day we went along with the Queen to Althorp, Lord Spencer's House, where my Mother saw my Cousin Henry Clifford,† my Uncle's Son, which was the first time we ever saw him.[4] From thence, the 27th being Monday, the Queen went to Hatton, where the King met her, where there were an infinite number of Lords & Ladys & other people that the County could scarce lodge them.

From thence the Court removed & were banqueted with great Royalty by my Father at Grafton where the King & Queen were entertained with Speeches and delicate presents at which time my Lord & the Alexanders did run a Course at the field where he hurt Henry Alexander very dangerously. Where the Court lay this night I am uncertain. At this time of the King's being at Grafton my Mother was there, but not held as Mistress of the House by reason of the Difference between my Lord & her which was grown to a great height.

The night after, my Aunt of Warwick, my Mother & I, as I take it, lay at Dr Challoner's, where my Aunt of Bath & my Uncle Russel met us, which house my G. Father of Bedford used to lie much at, being in Amersham. The next day the Queen went to a Gentleman's House whose name I cannot remember, where there met her many great Ladies to kiss her hand, as the Marchioness of Winchester, my Lady of Northumberland, my Lady Southampton &c.

From thence the Sovereign removed to Windsor where the Feast of St George was solemnised tho' it should have been done before. There I stood with my Lady Elizabeth's Grace in the Shrine of the Great Hall at Windsor to see the King and all the Knights sit at dinner. Thither came the Archduke's Ambassador, who was received by the King & Queen in the Great Hall where there was an infinite Company of Lords

---

4 The Queen & Prince came to Althorp the 25th June on Saturday. My Mother, A. Warwick & I not till the next day, which Sunday was kept with great solemnitie, there being an infinite number of Lds & Ladies. There we saw the Queen's favour to Ly Hatton & Ly Cecil, for she shewed no favour to the elderly Ladies but to Ly Rich & such like Company.

* Princess Elizabeth, eldest daughter of King James I.

† Afterwards the 5th (and last) Earl of Cumberland.

& Ladies & so great a Court as I think I shall never see the like again.

From Windsor the Court removed to Hampton Court, where my Mother & I lay at Hampton Court in one of the Round Towers, round which were Tents where they died 2 or 3 in a day of the Plague. There I fell extremely sick of a Fever, so as my mother was in some doubt it might turn to the Plague, but within 2 or 3 days I grew reasonably well and was sent away to my Cousin Stiddolph's for Mrs Taylor was newly put away from me, her husband dying of the Plague shortly after.

A little before this my Mother & I, my Aunt of Bath & my Cousin Frances* went to North Hall, my Mother being extreme angry with me for riding before with Mr Mene, where my Mother in her Anger commanded that I should lie in a Chamber alone, which I could not endure. But my Cousin Frances got the Key of my Chamber & lay with me which was the first time I loved her so well. The next day Mr Minerill as he went abroad fell down suddenly & died, so as most thought it was the Plague which was then very rife; it put us all in great fear & amazement, for my Aunt had then a suit to follow in Court & my Mother to attend the King about the business between my Father & her.

My Aunt of Warwick sent us Medicines from a House near Hampton Court where she then lay with Sir Moyle Finch and his Lady. Now was the Master of Orkney and the Lord Tilliburne much in love with Mrs Carey, and came there to see us with George Murray in their Company, who was of the King's Bed Chamber.

Within 9 or ten days we were allowed to come to the Court again, which was before I went to my Cozen Stiddulph's. Upon the 25th of July the King & Queen were crowned at Westminster. My Father & Mother both attended in their Robes, and my Aunt of Bath & my Uncle Russell, which solemn sight my Mother would not let me see because the Plague was hot in London. Therefore I continued at Norburie where my Coz did so feed me with Breakfasts & Pear Pies and such things as shortly after I fell into sickness.

After the Coronation the Court returned to Hampton Court,[5] where my Mother fetched me from Norburie & so we lay at a little House near Hampton Court about a fortnight, & my Aunt of Bath lay in Huggins' lodgings where my Coz. Frances & I & Mary Carey did use to walk much about the House & Gardens when the King and Queen were

---

5   My Coz. Frances Bourchier stood to see the Coronation tho' she had not robes & went not among the Company.

*   Frances Bourchier, daughter of Lord and Lady Bath.

gone. About this time my Cozen Anne Vavasour was married to Sir Richard Warburton.

From Hampton Court my Mother went to Lancilwell, Sir Francis Palmer's House, with my Aunt of Bath, myself and all our Companie, where we continued as long as the Court lay at Basingstoke and I went often to the Queen & my Lady Arabella. Now was my Lady Rich grown great with the Queen, in so much as my Lady of Bedford was something out with her, and when she came to Hampton Court was entertained but even indifferently, and yet continued to be of the Bed Chamber. One day the Queen went from Basingstoke and dined at Sir Hy. Wallop's where my Lady, my Aunt and I had lain 2 or 3 nights before and did help to entertain her. As we rode from my Lady Wallop's to Lancilwell, riding late by reason of our stay at Basingstoke, we saw a strange Comet in the night like a Canopie in the air which was a thing observed all over England.

From Lancilwell we went to Mr Dutton's where we continued a week & had great Entertainments, & at that time kept a fast by reason of the Plague which was generally observed all over England. From Mr Dutton's we went to Barton, one Mr Dormer's, where Mrs Humphrie, her Mother & she entertained us with great kindness – from thence we went often to the Court at Woodstock where my Aunt of Bath followed her suit to the King and my Mother wrote Letters to the King, and her means were by my Lord of —— [blank in manuscript] and to the Q. by my Lady of Bedford.

My Father at this time followed his suit to the King about the Border lands so that sometimes My Mother & he did meet, when their countenance did shew the dislike they had one of the other, yet he would speak to me in a slight fashion & give me his Blessing. While we lay there we rid thro' Oxford once or twice but whither we went I remember not. There we saw the Spanish Ambassador who was then new come to England about the Peace.[6]

While we lay at Barton I kept so ill a Diet with Mrs Carey & Mrs Kinson on eating Fruit so that I shortly fell into the same sickness. From this place my Aunt of Bath, having little hope of her suit, took her leave

---

6 Not long before this Michaelmas myself, my cousin Frances, Mrs Goodwin & Mrs Howbridge waiting on us, went in my Mother's Coach from Barton to Cookham where my Uncle Russell, his wife and son then lay. The next day we went to Nonsuch where Prince Henry & Her Grace lay where I staid for a week, & left my Coz. there who was proposed to continue with Her Grace, but I came back by Cookham and came to Barton where my A. of Bath went into the country.

of my Mother and returned into the West Country. While they lay at Barton, my Mother and my Aunt paid for charge of the House equally.

Some week or a fortnight after my Aunt was gone – which was about Michaelmas – my Lady went from Barton to Green's Norton & lay one night at my Coz. Thomas Sellinger's where we saw old Mr Hicklin, where he & his Daughter proffer'd Wm. Pond to serve my Lady at this place, where we came about 10 a clock at night, & I was so weary as I could not tell whether I should eat or sleep first.

The next day we went to North Hall where we found my A. of Warwick something ill & melancholy. She herself had not been there passing a month, but lay at Sir Moyle Finch's in Kent by reason of the great Plague which was then much about North Hall.

Not long after Michaelmas my Uncle & Aunt Russell & their son, my Lady Bedford, my mother & I gave ale allowance to Mr Chambers my Aunt's Steward, in which sort the House was kept. During our being there I used to wear my Hair color'd velvet every day & learned to sing & play on the Bass Viol of Jack Jenkins my Aunt's Boy. Before Xmas my Coz. Frances was sent for from Nonsuch to North Hall by reason that Her Grace was to go from thence to be brought up with the Lady Harrington in the Country. All this time we were merry at North Hall. My Coz. Frances Bourchier & my Coz. Francis Russell & I did use to walk much in the Garden & were great one with another. Now there was much talk of a Mask which the Queen had at Winchester, & how all the Ladies about the Court had gotten such ill names that it was grown a scandalous place, & the Queen herself was much fallen from her former greatness & reputation she had in the world.

1616

JANUARY

Upon New Year's Day[7] I kept to my chamber all day, my Lady Rich* and my Sister Sackville† supping with me, but my Lord and all the Company at Dorset House went to see the Mask at the Court. Upon the 6th, being the Twelfth day, I supped with my Lady of Arundel & sat with her in the Ladyship's Box to see the Mask which was the second time it was presented before the King & Queen.

Upon the 8th went to see Lady Raleigh at the Tower.‡

Upon the 21st my Lord & I went to church at Sevenoaks to grace the Bishop of St David's Prayers.

FEBRUARY

All the time I stayed in the Country I was sometimes merry & sometimes sad, as I had news from London.

Upon the 8th day of February I came to London, my Lord Bishop of St David's riding with me in the Coach and Mary Neville. This time I was sent up for by my Lord about the composition with my Uncle of Cumberland.§

Upon Monday the 12th my Lord Rous was married to Mrs Ann Lake the Secretary's Daughter.

---

7 Jan. 1616. the 1st day Sir Geo. Villiers was made Master of the Horse & my Lord Worcester Privy Seal.

* Wife of Sir Robert Rich.

† Wife of Sir Edward Sackville, the brother of Lady Anne's first husband, Richard Sackville, 3rd Earl of Dorset.

‡ Sir Walter Raleigh had been imprisoned in the Tower of London with his wife and family since 1603 on a charge of treason, and was released in January 1616 to seek gold in South America.

§ Francis Clifford (1559–1641), 4th Earl of Cumberland.

The Knole Diary, 1603–1619

Upon the 14th, my Lord supp'd at the Globe – upon the 15th my Lord & I went to see the young Lady Arundel, & in the afternoon my Lady Willoughby* came to see me. My Lady Gray brought my Lady Carr to play at Glecko† with me, when I lost £15 to them; they two & my Lady Grantham‡ & Sir Geo. Manners supping with me.

Upon the 16th my Lady Grantham & Mrs Newton came to see me – the next day, she told me, the Archbishop of Canterbury would come to see me, & she persuaded me very earnestly to agree to this Business which I took as a great argument of her Love.

My Coz. Russell came to me the same day & chid me & told me of all my Faults & errors in this business – he made me weep bitterly; then I spoke a prayer of Owens & went to see my Lady Wotten at Whitehall, where we walked 5 or 6 turns but spoke nothing of this Business, tho' her heart & mine were full of it – from hence I went to the Abbey of Westminster where I saw the Queen of Scots, her Tomb and all the other Tombs, and came home by Water where I took an extream cold.

Upon the 17th my Lord Archbishop of Canterbury, my Lord William Howard, my Lord Roos, my Coz. Russell, my brother Sackville & a great Company of Men of note were all in the Gallery at Dorset House, where the Archbishop took me aside & talked with me privately one Hour & half, & persuaded me both by Divine & human means to set my Hand to their Arguments. But my answer to his Lordship was that I would do nothing till my Lady & I had conferred together. Much persuasion was used by him & all the Company, sometimes terrifying me & sometimes flattering me, but at length it was concluded that I should have leave to go to my Mother & send an answer by the 22nd of March next whether I will agree to the Business or not, & to this Prayer my Lord of Canterbury & the rest of the Lords have set their Hands.

Next day was a marvellous day to me through the mercy of God, for it was generally thought that I must either have sealed to the Argument or else have parted with my Lord.

Upon the 19th I sent Tobias & Thomas Bedding to most of the Ladies in town of my Acquaintance to let them know of my Journey into the North.

---

* Wife of William, 3rd Lord Willoughby.
† Glecko (derived from 'gleeko') was a popular card game of the sixteenth to eighteenth centuries for two or three players.
‡ Wife of Sir Thomas Grantham of Lincoln.

Upon the 20th came my Lord of Russell & my Cousin George [Clifford]. In all this time of my Troubles my Coz. Russell was exceeding careful and kind to me.

Upon the 21st my Lord and I began our journey Northward – the same day my Lord Willoughby came & broke his fast with my Lord. We had 2 Coaches in our Company with Four Horses a piece and about 26 Horsemen. I having no women to attend me, but Willoughby and Judith, Thomas Glenham going with my Lord.

Upon the 26th going from Litchfield to Croxall, & about a mile from Croxall my Lord & I parted, he returning to Litchfield & I going into Derby. I came to my Lodgings with a Heavy Heart considering how many things stood between my Lord & I. I had in my Company 10 Persons & 13 Horses.

MARCH

Upon the 1st we went from the Parson's House near the Dangerous Moors, being 8 miles, & afterwards by Ways so dangerous the Horses were fain to be taken out of the Coach to be lifted down the Hills. This day Rivers' Horse fell from a Bridge into the River. We came to Manchester about ten at night.

Upon the 20th in the morning my Lord William Howard with his son, my Coz. William Howard & Mr John Dudley came hither to take the answer of my Mother & myself which was a direct denial to stand to the Judges' award. The same day came Sir Timothy Whittington hither who did all he could to mitigate the anger between my Lord William Howard & my Mother, so at last we parted all good friends, and it was agreed my Men and Horses should stay, & we should go up to London together after Easter.

Upon the 22nd, my Lady & I went in a Coach to Whingfield and rode about the park and saw all the woods.[8]

Upon the 27th my Cousin Wm. Howard sent me a Dapple Gray Nag for my own Saddle. Upon the 31st being Easter day I received with my Mother in the Chapel at Broome.

---

8 Upon the 24th my Lady of Somerset was sent by water from Blackfriars as Prisoner to the Tower.

APRIL

Upon the 1st came my Coz. Charles Howard and Mr John Dudley with Letters to shew that it was my Lord's pleasure that the Men and Horses should come away without me, & so after much falling out betwixt my Lady & them, all my folks went away there being a paper drawn to shew that they went away by my Lord's direction, & contrary to my Will.

At night I sent two Messengers to my Folks to entreat them to stay. For some 2 nights my Mother & I lay together & had much talk about this Business.[9]

Upon the 2nd I went after my Folks in my lady's Coach, she bringing me a Quarter of a mile in the Way, where she & I had a grevious & heavy Parting. Most part of the way I rid behind Mr Hodgson.[10]

Upon the 10th we went from Ware to Tottenham where my Lord's Coach with his men & Horses met me & [we] came to London to the lesser Dorset House.

Upon the 11th I came from London to Knowle where I had but a cold welcome from my Lord. My lady Margaret met me in the outermost gate & my Lord came to me in the Drawing Chamber.

Upon the 12th I told my Lord how I had left those Writings which the Judges and my Lord would have me sign & seal behind with my Mother.

Upon the 13th my Lord & Thomas Glenham went up to London.

Upon the 17th came Tom Woodyatt from London, but brought me no news of my going up which I daily look for.[11]

Upon the 18th Baskett[*] came hither & brought me a letter from my Lord to let me know this was the last time of asking me whether I would set my Hand to this Award of the Judges.

Upon the 19th I returned my Lord for answer that I would not stand to the Award of the Judges what Misery soever it cost me. This morning the Bishop of St David's & my little Child were brought to speak to me.

---

9   April 1616. As I came I heard that Sir John Digby, late Ambassador to Spain was made Vice-Chamberlain and sworn of the Privy Council.

10   Not long after this my Coz. Sir John Oliver was made Lord Deputy of Ireland in place of Sir Arthur Chichester.

11   Upon the 17th my Mother sickened as she came from Prayers, being taken with a cold chillness in the manner of an Ague which after wards turned to great heats and pains in her side, so as when she was opened it was plainly seen she had an Imposthume [i.e. an abscess].

*   Peter Basket, gentleman of the horse to the Earl of Dorset, see Appendix 1.

About this time I used to rise early in the Morning & go to the Standing in the garden, & taking my Prayer Book with me beseech God to be merciful to me in this & to help me as He always hath done.

MAY

Upon the 1st, Rivers came from London in the Afternoon & brought me word that I should neither live at Knole or Bolebrooke.

Upon the 2nd came Mr Legg* & told divers of the Servants that my Lord would come down & see me once more, which would be the last time that I should see him again.

Upon the 3rd came Baskett down from London & brought me a Letter from my Lord by which I might see it was his pleasure that the Child should go the next day to London, which at first was somewhat grievous to me, but when I considered that it would both make my Lord more angry with me & be worse for the Child, I resolved to let her go. After, I had sent for Mr Legg and talked with him about that and other matters and wept bitterly.[12]

Upon the 4th being Saturday, between 10 & 11 the Child went into the Litter to go to London, Mrs Bathurst & her two maids with Mr Legge & a good Company of the Servants going with her. In the afternoon came a man called Hilton, born in Craven, from my Lady Willoughby to see me which I took as a great Argument of her Love being in the midst of all my Misery.[13]

Upon the 8th I dispatched a Letter to my Mother.

Upon the 9th I received a letter from Mr Bellasis how extreme ill my Mother had been, & in the afternoon came Humphrey Godding's Son with Letters that my Mother was exceeding ill, & as they thought, in some danger of Death, so as I sent Rivers presently to London with Letters to be sent to her & certain Cordials and Conserves.

At night was brought to me a letter from my Lord to let me know his determination was [that] the Child should live at Horseley, & not come hither any more, so as this was a very grievous and sorrowful day to me.

---

12 My Lady Margaret lay in the Great Dorset House, for now my Lord and his whole Company was removed from the Lesser Dorset House where I lay when I was first married.

13 About this time my Lord Shrewsbury died at his House in Broad Street.

* Edward Legge, steward to the Earl of Dorset, see Appendix 1.

The Knole Diary, 1603–1619

Upon the 10th Rivers came from London & brought me word from Lord William that she was not in such danger as I fear'd; the same day came the Stewards from London whom I expected would have given warning to many of the Servants to go away because the Audits was newly come up.[14]

Upon the 11th being Sunday, before Mr Legge went away I talked with him an hour or two about all this Business & matters between me & my Lord, so as I gave him better satisfaction & made him conceive a better opinion of me than ever he did.

A little before Dinner came Matthew[*] down from London, my Lord sending me by him the Wedding Ring that my Lord Treasurer & my old Lady were married withall, & a message that my Lord would be here the next week, & that the Child would not as yet go down to Horsley, & I sent my Lord the Wedding Ring that my Lord & I was married with. The same day came Mr Marsh from London & persuaded me much consent to this Agreement.

The 12th at night, Grosvenor[†] came hither & told me how my Lord had won £200 at the Cocking Match, and that my Lord of Essex & Lord Willoughby who was on my Lord's side won a great deal & how there were some unkind words between my Lord and his side, & Sir William Herbert & his side. This day my Lady Grantham sent me a letter about these Businesses between my Uncle Cumberland & me, & returned me an answer.

All this time my Lord was in London where he had all and infinite great resort coming to him. He went much abroad to Cocking, to Bowling Alleys, to Plays and Horse Races, & [was] commended by all the World. I stayed in the Countrey having many times a sorrowful & heavy Heart & being condemned by most folks because I would not consent to the Agreement, so as I may truly say, I am like an Owl in the Desert.

Upon the 13th being Monday, my Lady's Footman Thomas Petty brought me letters out of Westmoreland by which I perceived how very sick and full of grevious pains my dear Mother was, so as she was not able to write herself to me, & most of her people about her feared she would hardly recover this sickness. At night I went out and pray'd to God my only Helper that she might not die in this pitiful case.

---

14 Upon the 10th, early in the morning I wrote a very earnest letter to beseech him that I might not go to the little House that was appointed for me, but that I might go to Horsley and sojurn with my Child, and to the same effect I wrote to my sister Beauchamp.

*   Matthew Caldicott, the Earl of Dorset's secretary and confidante.

† Mr Graverner, gentleman usher to the Earl of Dorset, see Appendix 1.

RICHARD SACKVILLE (1589–1624), 3rd Earl of Dorset, whom Lady Anne
married in 1609, by William Larkin

The 14th. Richard Jones came from London to me & brought a letter with him from Matthew, the effect whereof was to persuade me to yield to my Lord's desire in this Business at this time, or else I was undone for ever.

Upon the 15th my Lord came down from London & my Coz. Cecily Neville;* my Lord lying in Leslie Chamber & I in my own.

Upon the 17th my Lord & I after Supper had some talk about these Businesses, Matthew being in the room, where we all fell out & so parted for that night.

Upon the 18th, being Saturday, in the morning my Lord & I having much talk about these Businesses, we agreed that Mr Marsh should go presently down to my Mother & that by him I should write a letter to persuade her to give over her jointure presently to my Lord, & that he would give her yearly as it was worth.

This day my Lord went from Knole to London.[15] Upon the 20th being Monday I dispatch'd Mr Marsh with letters to my Mother about the Business aforesaid. I sent them unsealed because my Lord might see them.

My Brother Compton[†] & his Wife kept the House at West Horsley, & my Brother and my sister his wife sojourned with them, so as the Child was with both her Aunts.[16]

Upon the 22nd Mr Davy came down from London & brought me word that my Mother was very well recovered from her dangerous sickness; by him I writ a Letter to my Lord that Mr Amherst[‡] & Mr Davy might confer together about my Jointure to free it from the payment of Debts & all other Incumbrances.

Upon the 24th my Lady Somerset[§] was arraigned & condemned at Westminster hall where she confessed her fault and asked the King's Mercy, & was much pitied by all beholders.[17]

---

15 My Lord was at London when my Mother died, but he went to Lewes before he heard of her death.

16 Upon the 20th my Child went to W. Horsley with Mary Neville and Mrs Bathurst from London. Mary Hicken was with her, for she still lain in bed with Lady Margaret.

17 Upon the 24th, being Friday, between the hours of 6 and 9 at night died my dear Mother at Brougham, in the same Chamber where my father was born, 13 years and 2 months after the death of Queen Elizabeth and ten years and 7 months after the death of my Father. I being 26 years and five months, and the Child 2 years wanting a month.

* Daughter of Lady Abergavenny, who was sister to the 2nd Earl of Dorset, Lady Anne's father-in-law.

† Sir Henry Compton of Brambletye House, Sussex. He married Lady Cecily Sackville.

‡ Sergeant-at-law.

§ Daughter of Lord Treasurer Suffolk and cousin to Richard Sackville.

Upon the 25th my Lord of Somerset was arraigned & condemned in the same place & stood much upon his innocency.

Upon the 27th being Monday, my Lord came down to Buckhurst. My Lord Vaux & his Uncle Sir Henry Neville & divers others came with him, but the Lords that promised to go with him stayed behind agreeing to meet him the next day at Lewes.[18]

Upon the 28th my Lady Selby* came hither to see me & told me that she had heard some Folks say that I have done well in not consenting to the Composition.

Upon the 29th Kendal came and brought me the heavy news of my Mother's death, which I held as the greatest & most lamentable Cross that could have befallen me.

Also he brought her Will along with him, wherein she appointed her body should be buried in the Parish Church of Alnwick, which was a double Grief to me when I consider'd her Body should be carried away & not interr'd at Skipton; so as I took that as a sign that I should be dispossessed of the Inheritance of my Forefathers.

The same night I sent Hamon away with the Will to my Lord who was then at Lewes.

Upon the 30th the Bishop of St David's came to me in the morning to comfort me in these afflictions, & in the afternoon I sent for Sir William Selby to speak to him about the conveyance of my dear Mother's body into Northumberland, & about the building of a little Chapel.[19]

Upon the 31st came Mr Amherst from my Lord & brought me word that my Lord would be here on Saturday. The same day Mr James brought me a letter from Mr Woolrich wherein it seem'd it was my Mother's pleasure her Body should be convey'd to what Place I appointed which was some contentment to my aggrieved Soul.†

---

18 At this great meeting at Lewes, my Lord Compton, my Lord Mordaunt and all that crew with Wat. Raleigh, Jack Laurie and a multitude of such company were there. There was much Bull Baiting, Bowling, Cards and Dice, with suchlike sports to entertain.

19 On the 30th at night or the 31st my Lord was told the news of my Mother's death, he being then at Lewes.

* Lady Selby lived at the Moat, Ightham. This property is now owned by the National Trust.

† This was in effect a codicil to the original will.

JUNE

Upon the 1st being Saturday, my Lord left all the Company at Buckhurst & came hither about 7 a clock in the morning & so went to Bed & slept till 12, when I made Rivers write my letters to Sir Christopher Pickering, Mr Woolrich, Mr Dombvill and Ralph Conniston, wherein I told him that my Lord was determined to take possession for my Right & to desire that the Body might be wrapp'd in Lead till they heard from me. About 4 my Lord went to London.

Upon the 4th, Marsh & Rivers came from London & gave me to understand how my Lord, by the knowledge & consent of Sir William Howard & the advice of his learned Counsel had sent a letter down into Westmoreland to my Lady's Servants and Tenants to keep possession for him & me, which was a thing I little expected, but gave me much contentment for I thought my Lord of Cumberland had taken possession of the Jointure quietly.

Upon the 8th being Saturday, Rivers & Mr Burridge were sent down into Westmoreland from the Council for restoring the possession of Appleby Castle as it was at my Lady's decease.[20]

At this time my Lord desired to have me pass my Rights of the Lands of Westmoreland to him & my Child, & to this end he brought my Lord William Howard to persuade me, & then my Lord told me I should go presently to Knole, & so I was sent away upon half an hour's warning, leaving my Coz. Cecily Neville & Willoughby behind me at London, & so went down alone with Kath. Buxton about 8 a clock at night, so as it was 12 before we came to Knole.

Upon the 15th came the Steward to Knole with whom I had much talk at this time. I wrought very hard & made an end of one of my Cushions of Irish Stitch Work.

Upon the 17th came down Dr Layfield, Ralph Couniston & Basket, D.L. bringing with him the conveyance which Mr Walter had drawn, & persuaded me to go up & set my Hand to it which I refused because my Lord had sent me down so suddenly 2 days before.

Upon the 19th my Lord came down for me & Dr Layfield with him, when my Lord persuaded me to consent to his Business & assured me how kind & good a Husband he would be to me.

Upon the 20th my Lord & I, Dr Layfield & K. Baston went up to

---

20 About this time came Lady Elizabeth Cavendish, Sir R. Yateley & Mr Watson to see me and comfort me after the loss of my Mother, and persuaded me much to consent to the Agreement.

London, & the same day I passed (by fine before my Lord Hubbard) the Inheritance of Westmoreland to my Lord if I had no heirs of my own Body, & upon the 21st, being Friday, my Lord wrote his Letters to my Lord William & gave directions to Mr Marsh to go with them and that the possession of Brougham Castle should be very carefully looked to – the same day he went to Horseley to see the Child at his Sisters.[21]

Upon Sunday the 23rd my Lord & I went to St Bride's Church and heard a Sermon.

Upon the 24th my Lord, Lord —— [blank in manuscript], my Coz. Cicely Neville went by Barge to Greenwich & waited on the King and Queen to Chapel & dined at my Lady Bedford's where I met Lady Hume, my old acquaintance. After dinner we went up to the Gallery where the Queen used me exceeding well.

Upon the 28th came Kendall with Letters so as my Lord determined I should go presently into the North.

Upon the 30th, Sunday, presently after Dinner my Lady Robert Rich, my Coz. Cecily Neville & I went down by Barge to Greenwich where in the Gallery there passed some unkind words between my Lady Knolles & me. I took my leave of the Queen & all my Friends here.

About this time it was agreed between my Lord & me that Mrs Bathurst should go away from the Child & that Willoughby should have charge of her till I should appoint it otherwise. He gave me his faithful promise that he would come after me into the North as soon as he could, & that the Child should come out of Hand so that my Lord & I were never greater Friends than at this time.

JULY

Upon the 1st, Lord Hobart came to Dorset House where I acknowledged a Fine to him of a great part of my Third[*] in my Lord's Land, but my Lord gave me his faithful word & promise that in Michaelmas Term next he would make me a Jointure of the full thirds of his Living. About one

---

21 About this time I went into the Tiltyard to see my Lord Knol[l]es where I saw Lady Somerset's little Child, being the first time I ever saw it.

* A share or apportionment, not necessarily one third, of a bequest.

o'clock I set forward on my Journey. My Lord brought me down to the Coach side where we had a loving and kind parting.[22]

Upon the 11th, Ralph brought me word that it[*] could not be buried at Appleby, so I sent Rivers away presently who got their consents. About 5 o'clock came my Coz. William Howard & 5 or 6 of his. About 8 we set forward, the Body going in my Lady's own Coach with 4 Horses, & myself following it in my own Coach with two Horses & most of the Men & Women on Horseback, so as there were about 40 in the Company, & we came to Appleby about ½ an hour after eleven, & about 12 the Body was put into the Ground. About 3 o'clock in the morning we came home, where I shew'd my Coz. Howard the Letter I writ to my Lord.

Upon the 17th I rid into Whinfield park, & there I willed the Tenants that were carrying of hay at Billians Town that they should keep the money in their own Hands till it were known who had a right to it.

Upon the 25th I signed a Warrant for the killing of a Stag in Stainmore, being the 1st I ever had signed of that kind.

Upon the 29th I sent my Folks into the Park to make Hay, where they being interrupted by my Unkle Cumberland's people, 2 of my Unkle's people were hurt by Mr Kidd – the one in the leg, the other in the Foot, whereupon complaint was made to the Judges at Carlisle, & a Warrant sent forth for the apprehending of all my Folks that were in the Field at that time, to put in surety to appear at Kendal at the Assizes.

AUGUST

Upon the 1st day came Baron Bromley & Judge Nichols to see me as they came from Carlisle and ended the Matter about the hurting of my Uncle's Men & have released my Folks that were bound to appear at the Assizes.

Upon the 4th my Coz. John Dudley supped here & told me that I had given very good satisfaction to the Judges & all the Company that was with them.

Upon the 11th came Mr Marsh & brought a Letter of the King's Hand

---

22   About this time Acton [Acton Curvett, Dorset's chief footman] lost his race to my Ld Salisbury and my Lord lost 200 shilling pieces by betting on his side.

*   The body of Margaret, Countess of Cumberland, Lady Anne's mother.

in it that I should not be molested in Brougham Castle, & with all how all things went well & that my Lord would be here very shortly.[23]

Upon the 22nd I met my Lord at Appleby Town's end where he came with a great Company of Horses, Lord William Howard he & I riding in the Coach together, and so we came that night to Brougham. There came with him Thomas Glenham, Coventry, Grosvenor, Grey Dick etc etc. The same night Prudence [Bucher], Bess, Penelope [Tutty] & some of the men came hither, but the Stuff was not yet come so they were fain to lie 3 or 4 in a Bed.[24]

Upon the 24th in the afternoon I dressed the Chamber where my Lady died & set up the Green Velvet Bed, where the same night we went to lie there.

Upon the 26th came my Coz. Clifford to Appleby, but with a far less Train than my Lord.

Upon the 27th our Folks being all at —— [blank in manuscript] there passed some ill words between Matthew, one of the Keepers & William Durin, whereupon they fell to blows, & Grosvenor, Grey Dick, Thos. Todd & Edwards drawing their Swords made a great Uproar in the Town, & 3 or 4 were hurt, & the Men went to ring the Bell [and] fell from a ladder and was sore hurt.

Upon the 28th we made an end of Dressing the House in the Forenoon, & in the Afternoon I wrought Stitch Work and my Lord sat and read by me.

SEPTEMBER

Upon the 11th Mr Sandford went to London by whom I sent a very earnest Letter to my Lord that I might come up to London.[25]

Upon the 21st was the 1st Day I put on my Black Silk Grogram Gown. Upon the same day came Rivers down to Brougham & brought me word that I could not go to London this winter.

---

23 About this time my lady Exeter was brought to bed of a Daughter, and my lady Montgomery of a son, being the first Son.
24 Upon a Saturday my Lord shewed me his Will, whereby he had given all his land to the Child saving £3,500 per annum to my Brother Sackville, £1,500 per annum which is appointed payment of his Debts, and my Jointure excepted, which was a matter I little expected.
25 Upon the 18th died my Lady Margaret's old Beagle.

Upon the 31st I rid into Whinfield in the Afternoon. This Month I spent in working & reading. Mr Dumbell read a great part of the History of the Netherlands.*

NOVEMBER

Upon the 1st I rose by times in the morning and went up to the Pagan Tower to my prayers & saw the sun rise.

Upon the 4th I sat in the Drawing Chamber all the day at my work.[26]

Upon the 9th I sat at my Work & heard Rivers and Marsh read Montaigne's *Essays*, which Book they have read almost this fortnight.

Upon the 12th I made an end of my cushion of Irish Stitch which my Coz. C. Neville began when she went with me to the Bath, it being my chief help to pass away the time to work.

Upon the 19th William Punn came down from London with Letters from my Lord whereby I perceived there had passed a Challenge between him and my Coz. Clifford, which my Lord sent by my Coz. Cheyney. The Lords of the Council sent for them both & the King made them Friends, giving my Lord marvellous good words & willed him to send for me because he meant to make an Agreement himself between us.

This going up to London of mine at this time I little expected. By him I also heard that my Sister Sackville was dead.

Upon the 20th I spent most of the day in playing at Tables. All this time since my Lord went away I wore my Black Taffety Night Gown & a Yellow Taffety Waist Coat, & used to arise betime in the morning, & walk upon the Leads and afterwards hear Reading.

Upon the 23rd I did string the Pearls & Diamonds left me by my Mother into a necklace.

Upon the 23rd I went to Mr Blentre's House in Cumberland where I

---

26 Upon the 4th Prince Charles was created Prince of Wales in the Great Hall at Whitehall where he had been created Duke of York about 13 years before. There was banners and running at the Ring, but it was not half so great a Pomp as was at the creation of Prince Henry. Not long after this Lord Chancellor was created Viscount Brakely, and my Lord Knollys, Viscount Wallingford. My Lord Cork was displaced, and Montague made Lord Chief Justice in his stead.

* Perhaps *A Tragicall Historie of the Troubles and Civil Warres of the Low Countries, 1559–1581*, translated by Thomas Stock and published in 1583.

stay'd an hour or two & heard Music & saw all the House and Gardens.[27]

Upon the 26th Thomas Hilton came hither & told me of some Quarrels that would be between some Gentlemen that took my Lord's part, & my Coz. Clifford's, which did much trouble me.

Upon the 29th I bought of Mr Clebom who came to see me a Cloak & a saveguard of Cloth laced with Black Lace to keep me warm on my Journey.

DECEMBER

Upon the 4th came Basket with all the Horses to carry me to London, but he left the Coach at Roses.*

Upon the 9th I set out from Brougham Castle towards London. About 3 o'clock in the afternoon we came to Roses. All this day I rode on Horseback on Rivers' mare, 27 miles that day.

Upon the 11th I went to York. 3 of Lord Sheffield's Daughters & Mrs Matthews the Bishop's wife came to see me. This night Mrs Matthews lay with me. About this time died Mr Marshall, my Lord's Auditor & Surveyor, & left me a Purse of 10 Angels as a remembrance of his Love.[28]

Upon the 18th I alighted at Islington where my Lord, who came in My Lady Withy Pole's Coach which he borrowed, my Lady Effingham, the Widow, my Sister Beauchamp† & a great many more came to meet me, so that we were in all 10 or 11 Coaches, & so I came to Dorset House where the Child met me in the Gallery. The House was well dressed up against [when] I came.

Upon the 23rd my Lady Manners came in the morning to dress my head. I had a new Black wrought Taffety Gown which my Lady St John's

---

27 Upon the 23rd Baker, Hookfield, Harry the caterer and Tom Fool went from hence to London. Upon the 24th Baskett set out from London to Brougham Castle to fetch me up.
28 Upon the 12th William Punn overtook us at Wantbridge having found the Diamond Ring at Roos which I was very glad of. The 15th was Mr John Tufton just 8 years, being he that was afterwards married to my 1st Child in the Church of St Bartholomew's. The Child was brought to me in the gallery, being the first time I had seen her since my Mother died.
* At Bowes, Yorkshire (now in County Durham).
† Frances Devereux, first cousin to Richard Sackville and sister to Robert Devereux, 3rd Earl of Essex, was the second wife of William Seymour, Lord Beauchamp (later 6th Duke of Somerset), whom she married in March 1616.

Taylor made me. She used often to come to me and I to her and was very kind one to another. About 5 o'clock in the evening my Lord and I and the Child went in the Great Coach to Northampton House where my Lord Treasurer & all the Company commended her, & she went down & kissed her, but I stayed with my Lady Suffolk.

All this time of my being at London I was much sent to and visited by many, being unexpected that ever matters should have gone so well with me & my Lord, everybody persuading me to hear & make an end, since the King had taken the matter in hand so as now.

Upon the 27th I dined at my Lady Elizabeth Gray's Lodgings at Somerset House where I met my Lady Compton & Lady Fielding & spoke to them about my coming to the King. Presently after Dinner came my Lord thither & we went together to my Lady Arundel's where I saw all the Pictures & Statues in the Lower Rooms.

Upon the 28th I dined above in my Chamber & wore my Night Gown because I was not very well, which day and yesterday I forgot it was Fish day and ate Flesh at both Dinners. In the afternoon I play'd at Glecko with my Lady Gray & lost £27 and odd money.

Upon the 31st I sent Thomas Woodgate with a sweet bag to the Queen for a New Year's Gift, & a Standish to Mrs Hanns, both cost me about 16 or 17 pounds.

1617

JANUARY

Upon New Year's Day, presently after Dinner, I went to the Savoy to my Lady Carey [and] from thence she and I went to Somerset House to the Queen where I met Lady Derby, my Lady Bedford, my Lady Montgomery & a great deal of Company that came along with the King & the Prince. My Lady Arundel had much talk with me about the Business & persuaded me to yield to the King in all things. From Somerset House we went to Essex House to see my Lady of Northumberland. From thence I went to see my Lady Rich & so came home. After Supper I went to see my Sister Beauchamp & stay'd with her an hour or two for my Lord was at the Play at Whitehall that night.[29]

Upon the 2nd I went to the Tower to see my Lord and my Lady Somerset.* This was the first time I saw them since the arraignment.

Upon the 5th I went into the Court. We went up into the King's Chamber where my Lord Villiers was created Earl of Buckingham. My Lord, my Lord of Buckingham & divers other Lords bringing him up to the King. I supped with my Lord & Lady Arundel, & after Supper I saw the Play of the Mad Lover in the Hall.

Upon the 6th being Twelfth Day, I went about 4 o'clock to the Court with my Lord. I went up with my Lady Arundel & ate a scrambling supper with her & my Lady Pembroke at my Lord Duke's Lodgings. We stood to see the Masque in the box with my Lady Ruthven.

Upon the 8th we came from London to Knowle. This night my Lord & I had a falling out about the Land.

---

29   As the King passed by he kiss'd me. Afterwards the Queen came out into the Drawing Chamber when she kissed me and used me very kindly. This was the 1st time I ever saw the King, Queen or Prince since they came out of the North.

*   Robert Ker, 6th Earl of Somerset (1587–1632), and his wife, Frances (1590–1672), were arrested in 1615 for the murder of Sir Thomas Overbury in 1613 – he had allegedly threatened to reveal his knowledge of the affair they were conducting prior to Lady Somerset's divorce from Robert Devereux, 3rd Earl of Essex. They were imprisoned in the Tower of London from 1615 to 1621.

The Knole Diary, 1603–1619

Upon the 9th I went up to see the things in the Closet & began to have Mr Sandy's Book read to me about the Government of the Turks, my Lord sitting the most part of the Day reading in his Closet.

Upon the 10th my Lord went up to London upon the sudden, we not knowing it till the Afternoon.

Upon the 16th I received a Letter from my Lord that I should come up to London the next day because I was to go before the King on Monday next. Upon the 17th when I came up, my Lord told me I must resolve to go to the King the next day.

Upon the 18th being Saturday, I went presently after Dinner to the Queen to the Drawing Chamber where my Lady Derby told the Queen how my Business stood, & that I was to go to the King; so she promised me she would do all the good in it she could. When I had stay'd but a little while there I was sent for out, my Lord & I going through my Lord Buckingham's Chamber, who brought us into the King, being in the Drawing Chamber. He put out all that were there, & my Lord and I kneeled by his chair side, when he persuaded us both to Peace, & to put the whole Matter wholly into his hands. Which my Lord consented to, but I beseech'd His Majesty to pardon me for that I would never part with Westmoreland while I lived upon any Condition whatsoever.

Sometimes he used fair means & persuasions, & sometimes foul means, but I was resolved before so as nothing would move me.

From the King we went to the Queen's side & brought my Lady St John to her Lodgings, and so we went Home. At this time I was much bound to my Lord for he was far kinder to me in all these Businesses than I expected, & was very unwilling that the King should do me any Publick Disgrace.[30]

Upon the 19th my Lord & I went to the Court in the Morning thinking the Queen would have gone to the Chapel, but she did not, so my Lady Ruthven & I and many others stood in the Closet to hear the Sermon. I dined with my Lady Ruthven. Presently after Dinner she & I went up to the Drawing Chamber where my Lady D., my Lady Montgomery, my Lady Burleigh, persuaded me to refer these Businesses to the King.

About 6 o'clock my Lord came for me, so he & I & Lady St John went home in her Coach. This night the Masque was danced at the Court, but I would not stay to see it because I had seen it already.

---

30 The Queen gave me a warning not to trust my matters absolutely to the King lest he should deceive me.

For Lawyers there were my Lord Chief Justice Montague and Hobart Yelverton the King's Solicitor & Sir Randal Crewe that was to speak for my Lord & I.

FRANCIS CLIFFORD (1559–1641), 4th Earl of Cumberland, Lady Anne's paternal uncle, from whom she sought to regain the inheritance left him by her father, by an unknown artist

The Knole Diary, 1603–1619

Upon the 20th, I & my Lord went presently after Dinner to the Court; he went up to the King's side about his Business, I went to my Aunt Bedford in her Lodging where I stay'd in Lady Ruthven's Chamber till towards 8 o'clock, about which time I was sent for up to the King in his Drawing Chamber, when the door was lock'd & nobody suffered to stay here but my Lord & I, my Uncle Cumberland, my Coz. Clifford, my Lords Arundel, Pembroke, Montgomery & Sir John Digby.

For Lawyers there were my Lord Chief Justice Montagu & Hobart Yelverton, the King's Sollicitor Sir Randal Crewe that was to speak for my Lord & I.

The King asked us all if we would submit to his Judgement in this Case. My Uncle Cumberland, my Coz. Clifford & my Lord answered they would, but I would never agree to it without Westmoreland, at which the King grew in a great Chaffe, my Lord of Pembroke & the King's Sollicitor speaking much against me. At last when they saw there was no Remedy, my Lord fearing the King would do me some Publick Disgrace, desired Sir John Digby would open the door, who went out with me & persuaded me much to yield to the King. My Lord Hay came to me to whom I told in brief how this Business stood. Presently, after my Lord came from the King when it was resolved that if I would not come to an Agreement, there should be an Agreement made without me. We went down, Sir Robert Douglas, and Sir George Chaworth bringing us to the Coach. By the way my Lord & I went in at Worcester House to see my Lord and Lady & so came home.

This Day I may say I was led miraculously by God's Providence, & next to that I trust all my Good to the worth & nobleness of my Lord's Disposition for neither I nor anybody else thought I should have passed over this Day so well as I have done.

Upon the 22nd the Child had her 6th Fit of the Ague in the morning. Mr Smith went up in the Coach to London to my Lord to whom I wrote a Letter to let him know in what case the Child was, & to give him humble Thanks for his noble usage towards me in London. The same day my Lord came down to Knole to see the Child.

Upon the 23rd my Lord went up betimes to London again. The same day the Child put on her Red Baize Coats.

Upon the 25th I spent most of my Time in working & in going up & down to see the Child. About 5 or 6 o'clock the Fit took her which lasted 6 or 7 hours.

Upon the 28th at this time I wore a plain Green Flannel Gown that William Punn made me, & my Yellow Taffety Waistcoat. Rivers used to read to me in Montaigne's *Plays* and Moll Neville in *The Fairy Queen*[*].

Upon the 30th Mr Amherst the Preacher[†] came hither to see me with whom I had much talk. He told me that now they began to think at London that I had done well in not referring this Business to the King, & that everybody said God had a hand in it.[31]

FEBRUARY

Upon the 4th should have been the Child's Fit, but she miss'd it. Achin came presently after Dinner with a Letter to Tom the Groom to meet my Lord at Hampton Court with his hunting horses. At night Thomas Woodyat came from London & brought a Squirrel to the Child, & my Lord wrote me a Letter by which I perceived my Lord was clean out with me, & how much my Enemies have wrought against me.

Upon the 6th the Child had a grudging of her Ague again at night. Mr Orberton came from London & told me that the Baron de Joeniers came out of France, & had great Entertainment both of the King & the Queen, & was lodged at Salisbury House.

Upon the 7th, presently after Dinner Mr Orberton & I had a great deal of Talk, he telling me how much I was condemned in the World, & what strange censures most Folks made of my Courses. So as I kneeled down to my Prayers & desired God to send a good end to these troublesome Businesses, my Trust being wholly in Him that always helped me.

Upon the 12th the Child had a bitter Fit of her Ague again, insomuch I

---

31 All this time of my being in the Country there was much ado in London about my Business, in so much that my Lord, my Uncle Cumberland, my Coz. Clifford with the Chief Justice and the Council of both sides, on divers times with the King about it, and then the King hearing it go so directly for me he said there was a Law in England to keep me from the Land. There was during this time much Cock-Fighting at the Court where my Lord's Cocks did fight against the King's. Although this Business was somewhat chargeable to my Lord, yet it brought him into great grace and favour with the King, so as he useth him very kindly and speaketh very often and better of him than of any other man. My Lord grew very great with my Lord of Arundel.

* *The Fairie Queene* by Edmund Spenser (1552?–99), was first published between 1590 and 1596. Both Montaigne and Spenser were strong influences on the poetry of Lady Anne's tutor Samuel Daniel. Sharing his enthusiasm, in 1620 she 'mad a monument for Mr. Spenser the pouett and set it up at Westmester'. Spenser's works can be seen on the shelves behind the young Lady Anne on the left-hand panel of *The Great Picture*.

† Dr Jeffrey Amherst, Rector of Horsmonden, Kent, and brother of the serjeant-at-law.

was fearful of her that I could hardly sleep all night. So I beseeched God Almighty to be Merciful to me & spare her Life. Rivers came down presently from London & told me that the Judge had been with the King divers times about my Business, but as yet the award is not published, but it is thought that it will be much according to the award that was formerly set down by the Judges. He told me that he had been with Lord William who, as he thought, did not well like the Agreement considering how he had heretofore shewn himself in the Business.[32]

After Supper the Child's Nose bled, which I think was the chief cause she was rid of her Ague.

Upon the 13th the King made a Speech in the Star Chamber about Duels and Combats, my Lord standing by his Chair where he talked with him all the while, being on extraordinary Grace & Favour with the King.[33]

Upon the 14th I sent Mr Edward's man to London with a Letter to my Lord to desire him to come down hither. All this Day I spent with Marsh,[*] who did write the Chroonicles of 1607,[†] who went in afterwards to my Prayers, desiring God to send me some End of my Troubles, that my Enemies might not still have the upper hand of me.

Upon the 16th my Lord came hither from London before Dinner, & told me how the whole state of my Business went & how things stood at Court.[34]

Upon the 17th about 8 o'clock in the morning my Lord returned to London.[35] At night Mr Asken came & brought me a Letter from Lady Grantham, & told me a great deal of news from London, & I signed a Bill to give him 7 pound at his return from Jerusalem. This day I gave the Child's old clothes to Legge for his wife.

Upon the 21st the Child had an extreme Fit of the Ague & the Doctor sat by her all the Afternoon & gave her a Salt Powder to put in her beer.

32　My Sister Compton and her Husband were now upon terms of parting, so as they left Horsley, she lying in London it was agreed she should have £100 a year, and he to take the Child from her.

33　My Lord did not so often come to Lord William as heretofore, the Friendship between them grew cold, my Lord beginning to harbour some ill opinion of him.

34　He told me the E. of Buckingham was sworn of the Privy Council and that my Lord Willoughby's Brother Mr H. Burtie was put into the Inquisition at Ancona.

35　About this time there was much ado between my Lord of Hertford and Lord Beauchamp about the Assurance of Land to Mr William Seymour. But my Sister Beauchamp grew great with Lord Hertford and so got the upper hand.

*　Edward Marsh, Lady Anne's secretary, who was subsequently knighted.

†　That is, the diary entries for that year, now sadly lost.

Upon the 22nd, Baskett went up with the great Horses to my Lord because my Lord intended to ride a Day's Journey with the Prince. Legge came down & brought me word that the King would make a Composition & take a Course to put me from my Right to the Lands, so as if I did not consider it speedily it would be too late, & how bitter the King stood against me.

My sister Compton sent to borrow 77 pound so I sent her 10 twenty shilling pieces.

Upon the 27th I spent my time in working & hearing Mr Rose read the Bible, & walking abroad. My Lord writ me word that the King had referred the drawing & perfecting the Business to the Sollicitor. My Soul was much troubled & afflicted to see how things go, but my Trust is still in God & compare things past with things present, & read over the Chronicles.

MARCH[36]

Upon the 1st after Supper my Mother Dorset* came hither to see me & the Child. Upon the 3rd Petley & Tom went to Buckhurst with my lord's Horses and Hounds to meet my Lord there, by whom I wrote a letter to my Lord to beseech him that he would take Knole on his way as he goes to London.

Upon the 5th, Couch puppied in the morning. The 8th I made an end of reading Exodus with Mr Ran. After Supper I play'd at Glecko with the Steward & as I often do after Dinner and Supper.

Upon the 9th Mr Ran said service in the Chapel, but made no Sermon. In the afternoon I went abroad in the garden & said my Prayers in the Standing. I was not well at night, so I ate a Posset & went to Bed.

The 11th we perceived the Child had two great teeth come out so that in all she had now 18. I went in the afternoon & said my Prayers in the Standing in the garden & spent my time in reading & working as I used to do. The time grew tedious so as I used to go to bed about 8 o'clock & did lie abed till 8 the next morning.

Upon the 12th I wrote to my Lord, to Sir Walter Raleigh, Marsh etc.

36   About this time the curtain in the Child's room was let up in the light which had been close shut for 3 weeks or a month before.

About this time the King and my Lord Chancellor delivered the Seals of Sir Francis Bacon and he was lord keeper.

*   Anne, Richard Sackville's stepmother, the fifth daughter of Sir John Spencer of Althorpe and second wife of Robert Sackville, 2nd Earl of Dorset.

The Knole Diary, 1603–1619

The 13th I made an end of Leviticus with Mr Ran. I sent by Willoughby a little Jewel of Opal to Lady Trenchard's girl.

The 14th I made an end of my Irish Stitch Cushion. This afternoon Baskett came from London & told me that my Lord and my Uncle were agreed & the Writings sealed.

The King set forward this day on his Journey to Scotland, the Queen & Prince going with him to Thibalds [Theobalds].[37]

Upon the 15th my Lord came down to Buckhurst & was ill by the way, that was fain to alight once or twice & go into a House. All the Household were sent down from London to Knole. The 16th my Lord sent for John Cook to make Broths for him, & Josiah to wait in his Chamber, by whom I wrote a Letter to entreat him that if he were not well I might come down to Buckhurst to him. This day I spent walking in the Park with Judith, carrying my Bible with me, thinking on my present Fortunes & what troubles I have passed through.[38]

Upon the 19th Willoughby brought me very kind messages from my Sister Compton, my Sister Beauchamp & the rest of the Ladies I sent her to. The 20th I spent most of my time in walking and playing at Cards with the Steward and Baskett, & had such ill luck that I resolved not to play in 3 months.

After Supper I wrote a Letter to my Lord to entreat him that he would come & see me & the Child as soon as he could. The 21st, Ned the Footman came from Buckhurst & told me that my Lord was reasonable well & had missed his Fit which did much comfort me.

The 22nd my Cook Hortitius came down from London by Dr Layfield, & the Steward came from Buckhurst & told me my Lord had not been well, so as his going to London had him put off till the next week, & that he had lent out his House to my Lord Keeper for two Terms till the Lady Derby was gone out of York House, & my Brother Sackville had written to my Lord to lend him the Litter to bring up my Sister Sackville to

---

37 The 14th being Friday, my Uncle Cumberland and my Coz. Clifford came up to Dorset House where my Lord and they signed and sealed the Writings and made a final conclusion of my Business, and did what they could to cut me off from my right, but I referred my Cause to God.

Upon this Friday or Saturday died my Lord Chancellor Egerton, Lady Derby's Husband.
38 This day I put on my Mourning Grogram Gown and intended to wear it till my mourning time was out, because I was found fault with for wearing such ill clothes. Upon the 17th the Woman made an end of the sheet of Lady Sussex's work that is for the Pallet which was begun in April, presently after I came out of the North from my Mother. About this time my Lord Hay was sworn a Privy Counsellor. About this time my Lord took Adam, a new barber, to wait on him in his Chamber.

Town, who was 13 weeks gone with Child. This day I began a new Irish Stitch Cushion, not one of those for Lady Rich, but finer Canvas. The 24th we made Rosemary Cakes.

The 26th, my Lord came here with Thomas Glenham from Buckhurst. He was troubled with a Cough & was fain to lie in the Leicester Chamber.

The 27th my Lord told me he had ackowledged no Statutes & that the matter was not so fully finished, but there was a place left for me to come in. My Lord found me reading with Mr Ran & told me it would hinder his Study, so as I must leave off reading the Old Testament till I can get somebody to read it with me. This day I made an end of reading Deuteronomy.

The 28th I walked abroad with my Lord in the Park & the Garden, where he spake to me much of this Business with my Uncle. I wrought much within doors & strived to set as merry a face as I could upon a discontented Heart, for I might easily perceive that Matthew and Lindsay had got a great Hand of my Lord & were both against me. Yet by this means they put Lord William clean out of all grace & trust with my Lord, which I hope may be the better hereafter for me & my Child, knowing that God often brings things to pass by contrary means.

Upon the 29th my Lord went to London, I bringing him down to his Coach. I found this time that he was nothing as much discontented with this agreement as I thought he would have been.

Ye 30th I spent in walking & sitting in the Park having my mind more contented than it was before my Lord came from Buckhurst.

APRIL

The 2nd my Lord came down from London with Tom Glenham with him. My Lord told me how the King was gone with so few Company as he had but one Lord with him through Northamptonshire.[39]

The 4th my Lord told me he had as yet passed no Fines & recoveries of my land, but that my Uncle Cumberland had acknowledged Statutes for the payment of the Money. And that all the writings were left with my Lord Keeper & Lord Hobart till 21st next Term, at which time they were

---

39 About this time the Marquis Damse was slain in France, which bred much altercation here. About this time Lady Robert Rich was brought to bed of a 3rd son called Henry, which was her 5th Child.

fully to be concluded on. This was strange news to me for I thought all matters had been finish'd.

This day we began to leave the little room and dine & sup in the Great Chamber.

The 5th, my Lord went up to my closet & said how little money I had left contrary to all they had told him. Sometimes I had fair words from him & sometimes foul, but I took all patiently, & did strive to give him as much content & assurance of my love as I could possibly, yet I told him that I would never part with Westmoreland upon any condition whatever.

Upon the 6th after Supper, because my Lord was sullen & not willing to go into the Nursery, I made Mary bring the Child to him into my Chamber, which was the first time she stirred abroad since she was sick.

Upon the 7th my Lord lay in my Chamber. Upon the 8th I sat by my Lord & my Brother Sackville in the Drawing Chamber & heard much talk about my Businesses & did perceive that he was entered into a Business between my Lady of Exeter & my Lord Roos of which he will not easily quit himself.[40]

Upon the 11th my Lord was very ill this day & could not sleep, so that I lay on a pallet. The 12th, Mrs Watson came here with whom I had much talk of my Lord's being made a Knight of the Garter. This night I went into Judith's Chamber where I mean to continue till my Lord is better.

The 13th my Lord sat where the Gentlemen used to sit. He dined abroad in the Great Chamber & supped privately with me in the Drawing Chamber & had much discourse of the manners of the Folks at Court.

The 14th I was so ill with lying in Judith's Chamber that I had a plain fit of a Fever.

The 15th I was so sick & my face so swelled that my Lord & Tom Glenham were fain to keep the Table in the Drawing Chamber & I sat within. Marsh came in the afternoon to whom I gave directions to go to Mr Davis & Mr Walter about the drawing of Letters to the Tenants in Westmorland because I intend sending him thither.

This night I left Judith's Chamber & came to lie in the Chamber where I lay when my Lord was in France, in the Green Cloth of Gold Bed where the Child was born.

---

40 Capt. Mainwaring and these Folk told me for certain that the match with Spain to our Prince would go forward. The King of Spain was grown so gracious to English Folk that he had written a letter on behalf of Lord Willoughby's brother to get him out of the Inquisition.

The 16th my Lord & I had much talk about these Businesses, he urging me still to go to London to sign & seal, but I told him that my promise was so far passed to my Mother & to all the world that I would never do it, whatever became of me and mine.

Upon ye 17th in the Morning my Lord told me he was resolved never to move me more in these Businesses, because he saw how fully I was bent.

The 18th, being Good Friday I spent most of the day in hearing Kate Buchin read the Bible & a Book of the preparation to the Sacrament.

The 19th I signed 33 Letters with my own Hand which I sent by him to the Tenants in Westmoreland. The same night my Lord & I had much talk and persuaded me to these Businesses, but I would not, & yet I told him I was in perfect charity with all the World. All this Lent I ate flesh & observed no day but Good Friday.

The 20th being Easter day my Lord & I and Tom Glenham and most of the Folk received Communion from Mr Ran, yet in the afternoon my Lord & I had a great falling out, Matthew continuing still to do me all the ill offices he could with my Lord. All this time I wore my white Satin Gown and my white Waistcoat.

The 22nd he came to dine abroad in the Great Chamber ; this night we played at Burley Break upon the Bowling Green.*

The 23rd, Lord Clanricarde came hither. After they were gone my Lord & I and Tom Glenham went to Mr Lune's House to see the fine Flowers that is in the Garden. This night my Lord should have lain with me but he & I fell out about matters.

The 24th my Lord went to Sen'oak again. After Supper we played at Burley Break upon the Green. This night my Lord came to lie in my Chamber.

The 25th being Friday I came to keep my Fish Days which I intend to keep all the year long. After Dinner I had a great deal of talk with Richard Dawson that served my Lady. He telling me all the names, how the possession of Brougham Castle was delivered to my Uncle of Cumberland's folks, and how Mr Worleigh and all my people are gone from Home except John Ruvy, who kept all the stuff in the Baron's Chamber, the Plate being already sent to Lord William Howard's.

The 26th I spent the evening in working and going down to my Lord's Closet where I sat and read much in the Turkish History† and Chaucer.

---

* 'Burley Breaks' was a seventeenth-century outdoor game, similar to the more modern 'Prisoner's Base'. A minimum of three couples took part, the object being for one couple to try and catch another before they could claim a 'base'.

† *The Generall Historie of the Turks* by Richard Knolles was published in 1610.

The 28th was the first time the Child put on a pair of Whalebone Bodice.

My Lord went a hunting the Fox and the Hare. I sent William Punn to Greenwich to see my Lady Roxburrow and remember my service to Mr Q. About this time my Lord made the Steward alter most of the rooms in the House, and dress them up as fine as he could, and determined to make all his old clothes in purple stuff for the gallery & Drawing Chamber.

MAY

Upon the 1st I cut the Child's strings off from her Coats and made her use tags alone, so as she had 2 or 3 falls at first but had no hurt with them.

The 2nd, the Child put on her first coat that was laced with Lace, being of Red Bays.

The 3rd my Lord went from Buckhurst to London, and rid it in four hours, he riding very hard, a Hunting all the while he was at Buckhurst, & had his Health exceeding well.

The 7th my Lord Keeper rode from Dorset House to Westminster in great Pomp & State, most of the Lords going with him, amongst which my Lord was one.

The 8th I spent this day in working, the time being very tedious unto me as having neither comfort nor company, only the Child. The 12th I began to dress my head with a Rowle without a wire.

I wrote not to my Lord because he wrote not to me since he went away. After Supper I went with the Child who rode the Pyebald Nag that came out of Westmoreland to Mrs —— [blank in manuscript]. The 14th the Child came to lie with me, which was the first time that ever she lay all night in a Bed with me since she was born.

The 15th the Child put on her white Coate and left off many Things from her Head, the weather growing extreme hot.

Mrs Ryder came here and told me Lord Sheffield's wife was lately dead since the King went from York.

The 17th, the Steward came from London and told me my Lord was much discontented with me for not doing this Business, because he must be fain to buy Land for the payment of the money which will much encumber his Estate.

Upon the 18th Mr Wolrich came hither to serve me. He bringing me news that all in Westmoreland was surrender'd to my Uncle Cumberland.

The 19th came my Coz. Sir Edward George who brought me a token from my Lady Somerset.

The 24th we set up a great many of the Books that came out of the North in my Closet, this being a sad day with me thinking of the troubles I have passed. I used to spend much time with Mr Wolrich in talking of my dear Mother & other Businesses in the North. This time my Lord's Mother did first of all sue out her Thirds which was an increase of Trouble and Discontent to my Lord.

The 25th my Lord St John's Taylor came to me hither to take measure of me and to make me a new Gown. In the afternoon my Coz. Russell wrote me a Letter to let me know how my Lord had cancelled my Jointure he made upon me last June when I went into the North, & by these proceedings I may see how much my Lord is offended with me, & that my enemies have the upper hand of me. I am resolved to take all patiently, casting all my care upon God. His Footman told me that my Coz. Russell & my Lady Bedford were agreed, & my Lord Herbert and his lady, and that the next week they were to seal the writings & the agreement, which I little expected.

The 27th I wrote a Letter to my Lord to let him know how ill I took his cancelling my Jointure, but yet told him I was content to bear it with Patience whatsoever he thought fit.

The 29th I wrote a Letter to my Sister Beauchamp and sent her a lock of the Child's Hair. I wrote a letter to my Sister Compton & my Aunt Glenham,* I being desirous to win the love of my Lord's kindred by all the fair means I could.

The 31st Mr Hodgson told me my Coz. Clifford went in at Brougham Castle and saw the House but did not lie there, & that all the Tenants were very well affected towards me and very ill towards them.

JUNE

The 3rd Mr Heardson came hither in the morning and told me that many did condemn me for standing out so in this Business, so on the other

---

* Anne Compton was the second wife of Richard Sackville's father, the 2nd Earl of Dorset; Anne Glenham, wife of Sir Henry Glenham, was his paternal aunt, being the eldest daughter of the 1st Earl of Dorset.

side many did command me in regard that I have done that which is both just & honourable. This night I went into a Bath.

The 6th after Supper we went in the Coach to Goodwife Syslies & ate so much cheese there that it made me sick.

The 8th, being Whit Sunday we all went to Church, but my eyes were so blubbered with weeping that I could scarce look up, & in the afternoon we again fell out about Matthew. After Supper we play'd at Burley Brake upon the Bowling Green.

The 9th I wrote a letter to the Bishop of London against Matthew. The same day Mr Hodgson came home, who had been with my Coz. Russell at Chiswick, and told me what a deal of care he had of me, and my Coz. Russell & my Coz. George sent me word that all my Businesses would go on well but they could not find that the Business or Agreement was fully concluded, in regard there was nothing had passed the Great Seal.

The 13th I [es]sayed on my Sea water Green Satin Gown and my Damask embroidered with Gold, both which Gowns the Taylor which was sent from London made fit for me to wear with open Ruffs after the French Fashion.[41]

The 16th. Mr Wolrich came home & brought me a very favourable message from the Court.

The 19th. I wrote a Letter to the Queen of Thankfulness for the Favours she had done me and enclosed it to Lady Ruthven, desiring her to deliver it.

The 20th I read a Letter from my Coz. George which advertized me of many proceedings and shewed me the care of my Coz. Russell had of all my Business, and within it a letter from the Lady Somerset. I returned a present answer to both these letters and sent my Coz. George half a Buck which my Lord had sent me half an hour before with an indifferent kind letter.

The 21st I spent the time as I did many wearisome days besides, in working and walking. After Supper I walked in the garden and gathered Cherries and talked with Josiah who told me he thought all men in the House loved me exceedingly, except Matthew and 2 or 3 of his Consorts.

The 22nd my Lord sent Adam to trim the Child's Hair, and sent me the Dewsetts of two Deer & wrote me a letter between kindness & unkindness.

The 25th my Lord went up to London to christen Sir Thomas Howard's Child with the Prince, my Lord being exceeding great with all

41 Ever since the King going to Scotland the Queen lay at Greenwich, the Prince being often with her till she removed to Oatlands.

KNOLE HOUSE, Kent, where Lady Anne lived during her first marriage (1609–24), engraved by Letitia Burn from a drawing by P. Amsinck (1809)

[of] them, & so with my Brother Sackville – he hoping by their means to do me and my Child a great deal of Hurt.

The 30th still working and being extremely melancholy & sad to see things go so ill with me, & fearing my Lord would give all his land away from the Child.

JULY

The 1st. Still working & sad.

The 2nd received a Letter from Sir George Rivers who sent me word that my Lord was setting his Land upon his Brother, & that the value of the Fines I released to my Lord was very great, which did much perplex me.

The 3rd I rode on Horseback to Withyham to see my Lord Treasurer's Tomb and we went down into the Vault and came home again, I weeping the most part of the day seeing my enemies had the upper hand of me. My Lady Rich sent a man hither with a letter of kindness, by whom I sent a Letter to my Lord desiring him to come hither because I found myself very ill.

The 7th and 8th still I kept complaining of my side which I took to be the Spleen.

The 9th, Marsh brought me the King's Award. The 10th and 11th I spent in perusing that and other Writings, the Award being as ill for me as possible.[42]

The 12th, Mr Davis came hither to whom I shewed the Award, desiring him to make an abstract of it to send down to the Tenants.

Presently my lord came down hither, he being something kinder to me than he was out of Pity in regard he saw me so much troubled.

The 15th, at night, Mrs Arundell's men brought me a Dapple Grey horse which she has long promised me.

The 16th, Lady Wootton came here on Horseback, she and my Lord having lain that night at Sir Percival Hart's, and so hunted Deer as far as Otford. She stayed not above an hour in regard she saw I was so resolutely bent not to part with Westmoreland.[43]

---

42   About this time there was a great stir about my Lady Hatton's Daughter – my Brother Sackville undertaking to carry her away with men & horses. And he had another squabble about a man that was arrested in Fleet Street. After this he went to the Spa and left my Sister Sackville to keep my Sister Beauchamp company.

43   About this time Lord Keeper and all his Co. left Dorset House.

The 20th I wrote Letters into Westmoreland and sent a bow'd Angel to Hugh Hartley's Wife, & to Lady Lo[w]ther a pair of Willoughby's Gloves. The same night Dr Donne came hither.*

The 27th I went to Church, (being Sunday), forenoon & afternoon, Dr Donne Preaching, and he & other strangers dining with me in the Great Chamber.

The 31st I sat still thinking the time to be very tedious.

AUGUST

The 1st I rode on Horseback, Moll Neville, Kate Burton & as many Horses as I could get, alighted at Sir Percival Hart's, and afterwards went to Lady Worth, whither my Lady Rich came from London to meet me.[44]

The 2nd, my Brother Compton came hither before Supper, my Lord came from London this time of his being here he lying in my Chamber.

The 3rd, in the afternoon we had much falling out about the House which my Lord would have me undertake, which I refused in regard things went so ill with me. This night the Child lay all night with my Lord & me, this being the first night she did so.

The 4th. In the morning my Lord went to Penshurst but would not suffer me to go with him although My Lord & Lady Lisle sent a man on purpose to desire me to come.[†] He hunted, & lay there all night, there being my Lord of Montgomery, my Lord Hay, my Lady Lucy & a great deal of other Company, yet my Lord & I parted reasonable good friends, he leaving me his Grandmother's Ring. The 8th. I kept my Chamber all day & at night Mr Ran came & persuaded me to be friends with Matthew, but I told him that I had received so many injuries from him I could hardly forget them.

---

44   About this time my Lord Roos went over beyond the sea, there being great discontent between him and his wife.

*   John Donne (1572–1631), the poet and churchman, who became Dean of St Paul's in 1621, was a friend of Edward Sackville, Richard's brother. He was made rector of Sevenoaks (where Lady Anne heard him preach) on 7 July 1616. He once said of Lady Anne that she could 'Discourse of all things, from Predestination to Slea Silk'. Donne's sermons and poems are represented among her books in the background of *The Great Picture.*

†   Robert Sidney, 1ˢᵗ Baron Sidney of Penshurst, Kent, was created Viscount Lisle in 1605 and Earl of Leicester in 1618. His wife, Dorothy Sidney, was a daughter of the 9ᵗʰ Earl of Northumberland.

The 10th (Sunday) I kept my Chamber, being very troubled & sad in mind.

The 11th my Lord went from Buckhurst, beginning his progress into Sussex. My Uncle Neville,[*] my Brother Compton, Tom Glenham, Coventry & about 30 Horsemen, they being very gallant, brave and merry. Mr Ran brought me a message from Matthew how willing he should be to have my favour, whereto I desired Mr Ran to tell him as I was a Christian I would forgive him, & so had some hours speech with Mr Ran. The 12th and 13th I spent most of the time in playing Glecko & hearing Moll Neville reading the *Arcadia*.[†]

The 19th my Lord wrote me a very kind Letter from Lewes to which I wrote an answer presently. In the afternoon I went to Penshurst on Horseback to my Lord Lisle where I found Lady Dorothy Sidney, my Lady Manners, with whom I had much talk, & my Lord Norris, she & I being very kind.

There was Lady Worth who told me a great deal of news from beyond the sea, so we came home at night, my Coz. Barbara Sidney bringing me a good part of the way.

The 28th Marsh came hither; he told me a rumour of my Brother Sackville's Fighting[‡] & many other Businesses of my Lord Essex & my Lord Paget.

The 29th, Mr Castor came hither & told me that my Brother was slain.

SEPTEMBER

The 1st. Sir Thomas Worth and his Wife came and sat with me most part of the afternoon, they telling me a great deal of news of Lady Carey. The Widow Duck came from London and told me there was no such thing as my Brother Sackville's Fighting with Sir John Wentworth.

Upon the 15th we rid on Horseback to my Lady Selby's, all this week I

---

[*] Sir Henry Neville, husband of Mary Sackville, another of Richard Sackville's aunts, being the third daughter of the 1st Earl of Dorset.

[†] Sir Philip Sidney's (1554–86) prose romance, *Arcadia*, published in 1590, was for the most part written at Wilton House for the entertainment of Sidney's sister, Mary (1560–1621), third wife of Henry Herbert, 2nd Earl of Pembroke, and patron of an influential literary circle (which, incidentally, included Samuel Daniel, Lady Anne's tutor); Lady Anne was to marry her second son and heir, Philip Herbert, in 1630.

[‡] A duel.

being at home and was sad to see how ill Things went with me. My Lord being in the midst of his merry progress far out of Sussex, where he had hunted in many Gentlemen's Parks. Then he went to Woodstock to meet the King, & he stay'd up & down at many Gentlemen's Houses a good while.

From thence he went to Bath where he stay'd not above two days, but yet returned to London till about Michaelmas.

The 29th my Lord came here to Knole from his long journey. At this Michaelmas did my Lord receive 4 thousand pounds of my Uncle the Earl of Cumberland and which was the first penny that I received of my portion.

OCTOBER

Upon the 4th came Sir Percival Hart & Sir Edward to dine, and after Dinner my Lord shewed them his stables and all his great Horses.

The 25th, being Saturday, my Lady Lisle, my Lady —— [blank in manuscript], my Coz. Barbara Sidney & I walked with them all the Wildernesse over & had much talk of my Coz. Clifford & other matters. They saw the Child and much commended her. I gave them some marmalade of Quince for about this time I had much of it.

The 28th I strung my Chains and Bracelets with Willoughby.[45]

The 30th fell the Child to be something ill and out of Temper like a grudging of an Ague, which continued with him [sic] about a month or 6 weeks after.

The 31st my Brother Sackville spent the day with playing Cards with my Coz. Howard.

NOVEMBER

My Brother Sackville and my Coz. Charles Howard went up to London, my Lord stayed behind, but went upon Monday to Buckhurst, so stay'd

---

45 These three days were the last that I ever was in my Mother's Chamber in St Austin Friars, which was the Chamber I was married in to Richard, Lord Buckhurst who was Earl of Dorset 3 days after I married him.

MARGARET SACKVILLE, (1614–76), Lady Anne's first daughter, 'the Child',
at the age of four, by Van Somer (1618)

there and at Lewes till I came hither again. I left Moll Neville and Kate Burton here to keep the Child company.

The 2nd being Sunday I went to Church with my Sister Sackville to St Bride's & afterwards my Coz. George & I went and dined with my Lady Ruthven, where I met my Lady Shrewsbury. In the afternoon I saw her Lord there. All the time I was at Court I wore my Green Damask Gown embroidered without a Farthingale. The same day I sent the Queen by Lady Ruthven the skirts of a White Satin Gown all pearl and embroidered with colours which cost me fourscore pounds without the Satin.

The 3rd I went to see my Lady St John, from there I went to Austin Friars where I wept extremely to remember my dear and Blessed Mother. I was in the Chamber where I was married & went into most of the rooms in the House, but found little or nothing of the Stuffs & Pictures remaining there. From thence I went to my House & so to Whitehall, where my Lady Ruthven and my Lady Arundel told me that the next day I should speak to the King, for my Lady Arundel was exceedingly kind to me all this time.

The 4th. I carried Lady Rich to dine with me to Mrs Watson's, where we met my Coz. Russell & my Coz. George and had an extreme good Feast. From thence I went to the Court where the Queen sent for me into her own Bedchamber and here I spake to the King.[46] He used me very graciously and bid me go to his Attorney who would inform him more of my desires. All the time of my being in London I used to sup privately and to send to Mr Davis to confer privately about my said Business.

The 5th, I carried Mr Davis to Gray's Inn to the Attorney, when I told him his Majesty's pleasure. From thence I went to Mr Walton's lodgings to entreat his advice and help in this Business so as I came down this night to Knole. The next day my Lord Hay was married to Lady Lucy Percy.[*]

The 17th. In the morning my Lord brought my Coz. Clifford (though much against his will) into my Bedchamber where we talked of ordinary matters some quarter of an hour and so he went away.

The 19th came Sir John Tayler with whom I had some 2 hours talk of ancient times of my Father and the North.

The 20th. I came down to Knole leaving my Lord behind me.

The 30th. I do not remember whether my Lord went to Church.

---

46 The 4th day King James kissed me when I was with him, and that was the first time that ever I was so near King James as to touch him.

* Sister to Lady Dorothy Sidney.

DECEMBER[47]

The 8th I was not very well, and Mr Thomas Cornwallis the Groom Porter came hither.

The 9th I spent in talking with him of Queen Elizabeth and such old matters at Court.

The 10th. My Lord went to Buckhurst where all Country Gentlemen met him with their Grayhounds. All the Officers of the House went to Buckhurst where my Lord kept great Feastings till the 13th, at which time all the Gentlemen went away. Sir Thomas Parker was there; my Brother Sackville & he had much squabbling. From this day to the 20th my Lord lived privately at Buckhurst having no company with him but Matthew.

The 15th, came Sir H. Nevill's Lady. I carried her up to my Closet and shewed her all my things and gave her a pair of Spanish leather gloves.[48]

The 22nd my Lord and all the Household removed to London, the Child going before in a Litter.

The 25th. Christmas Day. Mr —— [blank in manuscript] preached in the Chappel and my Lord & I dined below, there being great House-keeping all this Xmas at Dorset House.

The 28th I went to Church in my rich Night Gown & Petticoat, both my women waiting upon me in their liveries, but my Lord stayed at home. There came to dine Mrs Linsey & a great company of neighbours to eat Venison.

Now I had a great desire to have all my Father's sea voyages written, so I did set Jones to enquire about these matters.[49*]

---

47   The 2nd the Child grew ill with a cough and a pain in her head, so as we feared the Small-Pox, but it proved nothing for within 8 days she recovered.

48   About this time Lady Rich was brought to Bed of a Son, her 6th child. [She] should have christened it but it died in 3 or 4 days.

49   About this time Lady Rich was brought to bed of her 1st son at Baynard's Castle and in a little while after fell ill of the Small-Pox.

About this time died Jem Robin's man, but he left his Master no remembrance, for they were fallen out.

*   The record of the 3rd Earl of Cumberland's voyages which was subsequently made is now preserved in Cumbria Record Office, Kendal.

1619

JANUARY

The 1st of this month I began to have the Curtain drawn in my Chamber & to see Light. This day the Child did put on her crimson velvet Coat laced with silver Lace, which was the 1st velvet Coat she ever had. I sent the Queen a New Year's Gift, a cloth of silver Cushion embroidered richly with the King of Denmark's Arms, & all one with stripes of Tent Stitch.

The 2nd, 3rd, 4th, 5th I sat up and had many Ladies come to see me, & much other Company, and so I passed the time.

My Lord went often to the Court and abroad and on Twelfth Eve lost 400 pieces playing with the King.

The 6th. The Prince had The Mask at Night in the Banqueting House. The King was there but the Queen was so ill she could not remove from Hampton Court all this Xmas, and it was generally thought she would have died.[50]

The 11th my Lord went to Knole.

The 12th. The Banqueting House at Whitehall was burnt to the ground & the writings in the Signet Office were all burnt. The 16th came my Lord of Arundel & his Lady. The same day I sent my Coz. Hall of Gletford a Letter and my Picture with it which Larkin drew this summer at Knole.[51]

The 18th. My Lady Wootton came to see me and stayed most part of the afternoon with me, with whom I had much conference of old matters and of the Matthew business.

The 19th. My Lady Verulam came, my Lord & Lady Cavendish his Lady, my Lord Bruce, his sister [and] much other Company, my Lady

---

50 About this time died my Lord Cobham, he being lately come out of the Tower. He being the last of the three that was condemned for the first conspiracy against the King at his first coming to England.

51 I brought down with me my Lady's great Trunk of Papers to pass away the time, which Trunk was full of writings of Craven and Westmoreland and other affairs, with certain letters of her Friends and many Papers of Philosophie.

Herbert, my old Lady Donne, my young Lady Donne, with whom I had much talk about Religion.

The 20th, came my Lord Russell, Sir Edward Gage, my Sisters Beauchamp, Compton & Sackville and dined with me, and in the afternoon came my Lady Bridgewater & much other Company, & my Lady Warwick who told me a great deal of news.

The 22nd here supped with me my Sisters Sackville & Beauchamp, Bess Neville, Tom Glenham and my brother Compton & his Wife. I brought them to sup here on purpose hoping to make them friends.[52]

The 23rd I came from London to Knole in a Litter, the Child riding all the way in her Coach. I went through the City and over the Bridge, but she crossed the Water. We found my Lord at Knole, who had stayed there all this time since his coming from London.

The 24th, Sunday. Here dined Sir William and Lady Selby & Sir Ralph Boswell. All this week I kept to my Chamber, because I found myself ill and weak.

The 29th in the morning died my Sister Beauchamp's daughter Miss Anne Seymour in the same House her Father died in 2 months before. The child was opened, it having a Corrupt Body, so it was put in Lead [i.e. a lead-lined coffin] and the day following Legge brought it to Knole, which day was my Birthday, I being now 29 years old.

The 31st. My Coz. Russell's Wife was brought to bed of a Son (it being the 7th child) at Chiswick, which was christened in the Church privately and was named Francis.

FEBRUARY[53]

The 1st. Carried Lord Beauchamp's Child from Knole, where it had stood in his Chamber, to Withyham, where it was buried in the Vault; so now there was an end of the issue of that marriage which was concluded soon after mine.

---

52 My Lord came into my room and told me the news of my Sister Beauchamp's Child's death. About this time my Sister Compton was reconciled to her Husband, and went to his House in Finch Lane where they stay'd 10 or 12 days, and then he brought her into the country to Brambletye [near East Grinstead in Sussex].

53 About this time Ld Willoughby caused my Coz. Clifford to come before the Lords of the Council about Northern Business, so as the spleen increased between them more & more, and bred factions in Westmoreland, in which I held to be a very good matter for me.

The 2nd. My Lord went to Buckhurst meaning to lie there private a Fortnight or thereabouts. The 8th. Lady Wootton sent Mr Page to see me, and that day I made Pancakes with my women in the Great Chamber.

The 10th. Wat Coniston began to read St Austin [Augustine] *Of the City of God* to me, & I received a Letter from Mr Davis with another enclosed in it of Ralph Coniston, whereby I perceived things went in Westmoreland as I would have them.[54]

The 15th, Sir Thomas Lake, his Lady & Lady Ross were sent to the Tower. There was nothing heard all this Term, but the matter between the Countess of Exeter & them at which the King sat – 5 several days. It was censured on my Lady Exeter's side against them, who were fined great Fines both to the King and her. There was spoken extraordinary foul matters of my Lady Ross & reports went that amongst others she lay with her own Brother, so as these foul matters did double the miseries of my Lady Lettice Lake in her unfortunate Marriage.

Sarah Swarton was fined and censured to be whip't, which censure was not executed by reason she confessed all that she knew.

In Sir Thomas Lake's place Sir George Calvert was sworn Secretary.*

---

54 My Lady Suffolk at Northampton House about this time had the Small-Pox which spoiled that good face of hers, which had brought others such misery and to herself greatness which ended in much unhappiness.

* The eldest daughter of Sir Thomas Lake, one of King James I's secretaries of state, married William Cecil, Lord Roos, grandson of the Earl of Exeter, in 1616. The marriage was not a success, however, and they soon separated. In the subsequent dispute over Lady Roos' allotment, Sir Thomas Lake demanded that lands at Walthamstow which Roos had already mortgaged to him should be transferred to his daughter as a settlement. The Earl of Exeter refused to agree to this, and matters got out of hand when Lady Roos' brother, Sir Arthur Lake, assaulted Roos, while Lady Roos accused her former husband of having had an incestuous affair with the Earl of Exeter's very young wife. Lord Roos fled to Italy, and Lady Roos now produced forged letters seeking to prove that the Countess of Exeter had also plotted to poison both Lady Roos and her mother. Towards the end of 1618 Lady Exeter brought a case of defamation of character to the Star Chamber. The case was heard in February 1619 and many witnesses were called, among whom was Sarah Swarton, who was condemned to be whipped for being so bold as to give evidence, but was later released due to 'her honesty'. Lady Exeter's counsel, meanwhile, was able to show that Sir Thomas Lake had aided and abetted his daughter's libellous actions, and as a result King James pronounced judgement against the defendants and they were sent to the Tower of London. Sir Thomas and his wife were each fined £5,000, with an additional £1,000 damages to Lady Exeter, while Lady Roos was fined 10,000 marks and Sir Arthur, her brother, a further £300. All this was later commuted to a total of £10,200 plus damages. Lady Roos confessed her guilt in June 1619 and was released. Sir Thomas was released a year later, but his wife remained a prisoner until 1621. Sir Thomas, who had had to resign

My Lord should have gone to London the 24th of this month but I entreated him to stay here the 25th, because on that Day 10 years ago I was married, which I kept as a Day of Jubilee to me; so my Lord went not till the 27th, at which time he rid on Horseback by reason of the great snow, & was so ill after his Journey that whereas he intended to have returned 2 or 3 days, he stay'd 9 or 10.[55]

The 28th, Sunday. The Judges came to Sevenoaks. I did often receive Letters from Mr Davis and Mr Marsh by which I perceived my motion to Sir John Suckling on his behalf took good effect, and that business went well to my liking in Westmoreland, by reason of difference between Lord William and my Coz. Clifford.

MARCH

The 2nd. The Queen died at Hampton Court between 2 and 3 in the morning. The King was then at Newmarket. Legge brought me the news of her death about two in the afternoon, I being in the Bedchamber at Knole where I had the first news of my Mother's Death about the same hour. Legge told me my Lord was about to take some physic of Mr Smith and as he could not come from London these four or five days yet. She died in the same Room that Queen Jane, Harry 8th's wife died in, though Rina was there when the pangs of death came upon her, but went into another Chamber some half an hour before she died.[56]

The 4th. My Lord Sheffield was married at Westminster in St Margaret's Church to one Anne Erwin, Daughter of Sir William Erwin a Scottish man, which was held a very mean match, and undiscreet on the part of him.

---

55 About the 20th the King fell into an extreme fit of the [gall]Stone at Newmarket, so as many doubted his recovery, and the Prince rid down post to see him. The next day the King came to Royston and there voided a Stone and so grew reasonably well.

56 Most of the great Ladies about the Town put themselves in mourning and did watch the Queen's Corps at Denmark House which lay there with much state.

The Queen Dowager of Denmark was alive when her Daughter Queen Anne of England died.

---

from his government post, went into retirement, although he served as MP for Wells, Somerset, and Wooton Bassett, Wiltshire, in 1625 and 1626 respectively. He died in 1630. (A suggestion of Edward Sackville's involvement in the affair is hinted at by Lady Anne in her diary entry for 7 April 1617.)

The 5th. About 9 o'clock the Queen's Bowels all saving her Heart were buried privately in the Abbey at Westminster in the place where the King's Mother's Tomb is. There was none came with it but 3 or 4 of her servants and Gentlemen Ushers which carried it, and a Herald before it. The Dean of Westminster and about ten others were by.[57]

The 9th. My Lord came down from Knole and continued taking physick and diet.[58]

The 17th my Lord went to Buckhurst to search for Armour and Provision which should be laid up by the Papists. This day I made an end of my Lady's Book, *In Praise of a Solitary Life*.

The 18th. I compared the two Books of the Cliffords that Mr Keniston sent me down.

The 20th. My Lord of Warwick died at Arlington House leaving a great Estate to Lord Rich and my good friend his Lady, and leaving his wife which was my Lady Lampwell a Widow the 2nd time. This day Wat Coniston made an end of reading Mr Saragol's Book, *Of the Supplication of the Saints*, which my Lord gave me.

The 26th, Good Friday. After Supper I fell in a great passion of weeping in my Chamber, & when my Lord came in I told him I found my mind so troubled as I held not myself fit to receive the Communion this Easter, which all this Lent I intended to have done.

The 27th in the morning I sent for Mr Rand and told him I found myself not fit to receive the Communion. The next day when my Lord heard I had told Mr Ran so much he sent for him & told him the Communion should be put off both for him and his Household, except any of them should receive at the Church.

The 28th. Easter Day. Mr Rand preached in the Chapel but there was no Communion in the House but at the Church. In the afternoon I began to repent that I had caused the Communion to be put off till Whit Sunday, my Lord protesting to me that he would be a very good Husband to me and that I should receive no prejudice by releasing my Thirds.

The 29th. My Lord went to Buckhurst & so to Lewes, to see the

---

57   The 9th. The Queen's Corps was brought from Hampton Court to Denmark House by water in the night in a Barge with many Lords & Ladies attending it.

58   When my Lord was at London my brother Sackville fell sick of a fever and was dangerously ill. At length it turned to an ague which continued most of the month, so that it was generally reported he was dead. I began keeping Lent very strictly, not eating Butter or Eggs till 18th February. Moll Neville kept it with me but my Lord persuaded me and Mr Smith wrote unto me so as I was content to break it, besides I looked very pale and ill and was very weak and sickly.

Muster which the County prepared in so much better Fashion by reason of their affection to him, which was as much as my Lord hath in any County or can have.

APRIL

The 1st day in the morning I wrote in the Chronicles. The 4th, there was a general Thanksgiving at Paul's Cross for the King's recovery, at which was most of the Privy Council, & the Bishop of London preached.

The 5th. Lord Hume died in Channel Row, who married Mrs Mary Dudley my old Companion, & left her as well as he could possibly.

The 6th. My Lord came from Buckhurst to Knowle. At his being at Lewes there was great play between my Lord of Hunsden, my Lady of Effingham & my Lord who lost them £200, & the Town entertained him with Fireworks.

The 6th. There came a Letter to my Lord to advise him to come to Royston to the King because most of the Lords had been with him at the time of his Sickness.

The 9th. My Lord went from Knowle to London. The next day he went to Royston to the King, with whom he watched that night. My Lord of Warwick & my Lord North watched with him. The King used him very well, so that my Lord came not back till the 13th to London. There he stayed till I came up.

The 17th I came to London, Moll Nevill, the Gentlewomen & most of the Household came with me so that I left none to wait on the Child but Mary Hutchins.

Sunday the 18th I went to Warwick House to see my young Lady of Warwick where I met my Lord of Warwick, Mr Charles Rich, Mr Nathaniel Rich & Lady Harriett Rich. After all the Company were gone to Sermon my Lord came thither. This day I put on my black Mourning Attire & went to my Sister Beauchamp where I spake with Mrs Bathurst & told her I did both forget & forgive anything she had done against me & that I had spoken to Lady Warwick in her behalf.

Monday the 19th. I went to Somerset House & sat a good while there by the Queen's Corps, & then went into the Privy Galleries & shewed my Coz. Mary those fine delicate things there.

From thence I went to Bedford House & stayed with my Lady of Bedford a little while, & she and I went to Channel Row to see my Lady Hume the Widow.

This day my Lord, my Lord Hundson & my sister Sackville christened Hammon's Child at St Dunstan's Church.

The 20th I went to Parson's Green to my Lady St John's, where I met the Spanish Friar that is the Agent here.

This day and the next my Lord had Cocking at the Cock Pit where there met him an infinite Company.

The 20th, the King was brought in a Litter from Royston to Ware, & the next day to Tibbalds, being carried most part of the Way by the Guard, for that he was so ill he could not endure the Litter. Thursday the 22nd I went in the morning to see my Sister Compton & found my Brother Compton there. I was in the room where my Lord's Mother-in-Law died, the Countess of Dorset, & went up & down the Rooms. Afterwards my Sisters Beauchamp and Sackville came to see me.

Friday the 23rd I went to Black Friars to see my Lady Cavendish & my Lady Kinloss in that House where my Lady Somerset was brought to Bed in her great Troubles. Then I went to Denmark House & heard Prayers there, & this night I watched all night by the Queen's Corps. There watched with me my Lord Carew's Lady, my Lady Elizabeth Grye, & various other Ladies & Gentlemen. Besides there sat up my Brother Compton, my Coz. George, my Coz. Thatcher, Mrs Reynolds. The beginning of the night there came thither my Lord & my Lady Warwick, Sir H. Rich, Charles Rich, my Lord Carew & Sir Thomas Edmondes, but all these went away before 12 o'clock. I came not away till 5 o'clock in the morning.

Saturday 24th, my Lord went to Tibbalds to see the King who used him very graciously. This night my Coz. Clifford came out of the North where matters went more to my Content & less to his than were expected. Either this night or next morning Sir Arthur Lake's Lady was brought to Bed of a Son.

Sunday 25th after Dinner, I & my Lady Warwick went to Denmark House & went to Sermon in the Great Hall. After Sermon my Lord came thither to fetch me, so we went to Hyde Park & took the air. After my Lord came home he went to see my brother Sackville who still continueth to look ill & is very sick and out of temper in his Body.

Monday the 26th. My Lord's Cocks fought at Whitehall when my Lord won five or six Battles. I went in the afternoon to see my Lady Windsor,[*] my Lady Rawleigh in her House which is hard by Austin

---

[*] Daughter of the Earl of Worcester and wife of Thomas, Lord Windsor.

Friars. Then went to Clerkenwell to the House that Sir Thomas Challum built.

Tuesday the 27th I put on my new Black Mourning Night Gown & those White Things that Nan Horn made for me. This day Mr Orfuir brought me two of the Tenants of Westmoreland who craved my assistance against my Uncle Cumberland.

The 28th, my Lord & I, my Coz. Sackville and Lady Windsor went to the Tower to see my Lady Somerset, where we saw her little Child. My Lord went to see the Earl of Northumberland* & I and Lady Windsor went to see Lady Shrewsbury, & after Supper my Lord and I went by water to Channel Row to see my Lord of Hertford & his Lady, where we found my Lady Beauchamp, my Lord Essex's Sister; then I went to Arundel House & talked with her about Lords being made Knights of the Garter.

The 30th, my Lord Southampton was sworn a Privy Councillor at Tibbalds.

MAY

The 1st. After Supper Mr Davis came & did read to my Lord & me the Bill my Uncle Cumberland & my Coz. Clifford put in the Chancery against the Tenants of King's Meabourne.

The 2nd. When I returned home I found Mr Hammers & his Wife there. I told her that for my part she had made so many scorns and jests of me she was nothing welcome to me.[59]

The 3rd. About 2 or 3 o'clock in the morning Sir Arthur Lake's Wife died, having been grievously tormented a long time with pains & sores which broke out in Blotches so that it was reported she died of the French Disease [syphilis].

This day Williams, a Lawyer, was arraigned & condemned at the King's Bench of Treason & adjudged to be hanged, drawn & quartered for a certain Book he had made & entitled *Balaam's Ass*. For which Book, one Cotton was committed to the Tower and a long time kept Prisoner there upon suspicion of it, but of late got out on bayle and was now well

---

59   The 3rd. Barnwelt was Beheaded at the Hague, which is like to breed altercation for the best, for this man hath long been a secret friend to the Spaniards and an Enemy of the English.

*   Henry Percy (1564–1632), the ninth earl, imprisoned since being arrested on suspicion of complicity in the Gunpowder Plot of 1605.

quitted, but Williams was carried to Newgate, & on the 5th hanged, drawn & quartered at Charing Cross.

The 5th. My Lord of Kent's daughter Lady Susanna Longueville and her Husband came & dined with me. The 6th, my Lord sat up playing at Cards & did not come home till 12 o'clock at night.

The 7th. Presently after Dinner my Coz. Clifford came & sat in the Gallery ½ an hour, & so he and my Lord went abroad.

The 8th. John & Richard Dent were before the Chancellor, my Coz. Clifford and John Taylor being present, where the Chancellor told them that from Tenants' rights he meant utterly to break them, willing them to be good Tenants to my Uncle Cumberland, whereat the poor men were much perplexed & troubled but I gave them the best Comfort & Encouragement I could.

Sunday the 9th. My Lord & I went not to Church in the Morning because Skinnie was married that day to Sara. In the afternoon I was not well, so neither my Lord nor I went to Church.

My Sister Beauchamp came & sat here & my Brother Compton whom I made promise me & he gave his Hand upon it, that he would keep his House in Finch Lane until Lady Day next because my Sister Compton might sometimes come up to London. After I was gone to Bed I had them into the Chamber. Sir John was very forward to do me all the pleasure he could, & Mr Sherborne promised to speak to the Chancellor in behalf of the Tenants.

The 10th. Sir John North came & told me much news from beyond the Sea.[60]

The 11th. In the morning Lord William Howard came up to me in Lady Margaret's Chamber & conferred with me about an Hour, promising to do all the good he could in the Northern Business. This day my Lord went to Salisbury House to see my Coz. Clifford, there being ordinary passages of kindness between them, so that he useth to keep my Lord company at running at the Ring & going to Hyde Park & those places.

The 13th I was one of the Mourners at the Queen's Funeral.[61] I attended the Corps from Somerset House to the Abbey at Westminster. My Lord was also one of the Earls that mourned. I went all the way hand in hand with my Lady Lincoln after the Sermon, &, all the Ceremonies

60 About this time my Lord of Doncaster went to his Embassage into Germany being sent by the King both to the Emperor and the Pope to mediate between them.
61 The 13th. It is past 13 yrs and a month since my father's Funeral was solemnised in the Church at Skipton, as Queen Anne's Body was this night buried in the Abbey Church at Westminster.

ended, my Lord, myself & the Earl of Warwick & his Lady came home by barges. Being come home I went to my Sister Beauchamp to shew her my Morning Attire. At the Funeral I met with my old Lady Pembroke & divers others of my Acquaintance with whom I had much talk. My Coz. Clifford was also a Mourner & bore the Banner after the Lords. When all the Company was gone & the Church Door shut up, the Dean of Westminster, the Prebends, Sir Edward Zouch, who was Knight Marshal, came up a private way & buried the Corps at the east end of Henry the 7th Chapel about 7 o'clock at night. There was 180 poor Women Mourners.

I went to see Lord Hertford (which was the last time I ever saw him) in Channel Row & spake very earnestly on Wood's behalf, but I could not prevail & his answer was that he would not pay any of his Grandchildren's Debts after his Death.

This night my Lord made a great Supper to two or three of the Frenchmen that came over with the Embassador. After Supper there was a Play & then a Banquet at which my Lady Penniston and a great many of Lords and Ladies were there.

The 15th. I went by Water to the Savoy to my Lord Carew, & spoke to him very earnestly in behalf of Peter Coolinge & his Son for a Gunner's place in Carlisle, & received a reasonable good answer from him. After the Shower was past, my Lady Dudley which was my Mother's old friend came to see me & brought her Daughter Margaret with her.

My Lord & I intended to have gone home into the Country & had sent the Coach and Horses but about then there was a Great Shower which stayed our going.

My Lord brought me to Westminster Abbey where I stay'd to see the Tombs and the place where the Queen was buried in an Angle in Henry 7th's Chapel.

The 17th. My Lord & I & all the Household came down to Knowle. I took my leave also of the two Tenants and gave them Gold & Silver.[62]

The 24, 25, 26, and 27th I went abroad with my Brother Sackville, sometimes early in the morning & sometimes after Supper, he and I being kind & having better correspondence than we have had. The 31st I stay'd at Home & was sad & melancholy.[63]

---

62 After I came out of Town my Lord Chancellor had the Tenants before him and willed them to yield to my Uncle Cumberland, at which time he gave Mr Davis bad words.
63 The 27th my Lord and my Bro. Sackville and I, Moll Neville and Mr Longworth rid abroad on Horseback in Whitby Wood and did not sup till 8 or 9 o'clock. After Supper my

JUNE[64]

The 2nd. I rose about 4 o'clock in the Morning & rid abroad on Horseback & my Coz. Mary with me. I was sad & melancholy all night. I brake a Piece of my Tooth off right before.

The 4th, I and Moll Neville rid about 3 or 4 o'clock in the morning & up to the Beacon, & went up to my Lady Selby's for some Bread & Butter. This night was the first that Lady Margaret lay alone, Maria having a Bed made hard by.

The 6th, Sunday, I heard neither Sermon or Prayers because I had no Coach to go to Church. All this week I spent at my Work & sometimes riding abroad. My Coz. Maria read Ovid's *Metamorphoses* to me.

The 18th. My Lord came down from London after Supper from the Term.

The 20th my Lord & I went to Church at Sevenoaks.

The 23rd my Lord went up to London to take up certain Bonds which he did discharge with part of my Portion.

The 24th my Lord received the last payment of my portion which was £6,000, so as he hath received in all £17,000. John Taylor required of my Lord an acquittance which he refused to give in regard he had delivered in the Statutes which were a sufficient discharge.

The 25th. The King dined at Sir Thomas Watson's & returned to Greenwich at night.

The 28th, my Lady Walton borrowed my Lord's Coach & went to

Lord and I walked before the Gate where I told him how good he was to everybody else and how unkind to me. In conclusion he promised me in a Manner that he would make me a Jointure of Four Thousand Pounds a Year, whereof part should be of that Land he has assured to my Uncle Cumberland.

This Term there was great expectation that my Lord and Lady Suffolk and that Faction would be proceeded against in the Star Chamber, but at their suit it was put off till Michaelmas Term. This Term Lord William Howard put a Bill into the Star Chamber against Sir William Hatton and other's of my Coz. Clifford's faction. This Term my Lord kept an exceeding great table at Dinner and had much Company. He had often Cocking and sometimes with the King at Greenwich and won a great deal of money.

The 19th. Lady Rosse's submission was read in the Star Chamber but Sir Thomas & Lady Lake refused to submit, for which their contempt they were committed close Prisoners in the Tower.

The 21st, Sir Thomas Glenham married Sir Peter Vavasour's Daughter with whom he had a great portion. This marriage was at her father's House and very Private.

About this time my Coz. Mary made an end of reading Parson's resolutions to me.

64 The 1st [June] my Sister Beauchamp took her journey to Glenham where she intends to sojourn two or three years so as her household is dispersed. Only some necessary attendants remain and Mrs Batten came into Kent.

FRANCIS RUSSELL (d. 1641), 4th Earl of Bedford, Lady Anne's maternal cousin, engraved by J. Cochran from a painting by Sir Anthony Van Dyck

London, for altogether, as I think for Jemima, she came not to avoid the King's importunity for the passing of Purbeck whereof her son-in-law was made Viscount.

The 30th, my Brother Compton came here & all his Mother's Place was delivered to him so after Dinner he returned to Brambletye where his wife lives with him, but with many discontents.

JULY

The 2nd. My Lord and Sir Henry Vane played at Bowls. This night my Lady Margaret was 5 years old so my Lord caused her Health to be drank throughout the House.

The 4th. Mr Chantrell preached at Sevenoaks, my Lord having sent for him purposely for that end.

The 19th. Lady Devonshire came back from the Wells & dined at Sevenoaks, & came not hither but sent her Woman to see me.

22nd. My Lady Margaret began to sit to Mr Vansommer for her Picture.[*]

The 27th. About this time my Lady Bedford had the Small-pox and had them in that extremity that she lost one of her Eyes. About this time my Coz. Clifford's wife was brought to Bed at Lanesboro' of a Son, which lived not seven hours & was christened Francis & was buried there. The same day Lord Rutland & Lady Kath. Manners came and dined here from the Wells and in the evening went to London.[65]

AUGUST

The 14th. My Cousin Mary & I had a bitter falling out.

The 15th, being Sunday I went not to Church at all. I fell out with Kate Burton & swore I would not keep her & caused her to send to her Father.

---

65 This Sunday my Coz. Oldworth was true and shewed me those remembrances which are to be set up at Cheyneys for my Great Grand Father of Bedford and my Grandfather of Bedford and my Aunt Warwick. About this time my Lady Law was married to Secretary Maubton. All this Summer Lady Penniston was at the Wells near Tunbridge drinking the Waters. This coming hither of Lady Peniston's was much talked of abroad and my Lord was condemned for it.

[*] A portrait of Margaret Sackville dated 1618 and attributed to Van Somer is reproduced on p. 63

The 18th, Sir Edward Burton came hither & I told him I was determined I would not keep his Daughter.

The 24th. After Dinner came Sir Thomas Penniston and his Lady,[*] Sir Maximilian and Lady Dallison. The 25th they stay'd here all day, there being great Entertainment & much stir about them.

The 26th they all went away.

The 27th, my Lord rid about betimes in the Morning & came not in till night. This night the 2 Green Beds in my Chamber were removed.[66]

The 30th, My Lord sat much to have his Picture drawn by Vansomer, & one picture was drawn for me.

SEPTEMBER[67]

The 21st. All this week I spent with my Sister Compton & my Sister Sackville, being sad about an unkind letter from my Lord.

OCTOBER

The 1st, came Lord Dacres, his new wife, my Lady Wildgoose, Mr Pembroke Lennard to see me & sat 2 or 3 hours with me in the afternoon.

The 2nd. Kate Burton went away from serving me to her Father's house in Sussex.[68]

The 6th. Lady Selby was my Deputy in christening Sir Henry Vane's Child. Mr Walter Stuart & Sir Robert Yeaksley were Godfathers. The Child was named Walter.[69]

The 10th. Mary was brought to bed of a Boy. The same night I began to be ill.

---

66 About this time my Lord intended to keep a more sparing House; put away Thomas Work and Gifford and took one in their place, which was Sir John Suckling's man.

67 The 11th, I paid Mr Beat 10 pieces upon his return from Jerusalem, who told me much news from Rome, Naples etc.

68 Upon the 2nd I began to think I was quick with Child, so as I told it to my Lord, my Sister Sackville and my Sister Compton.

69 The 7th. Bess of the Laundry went away and one Nell came in her room. About this time I kept in my Chamber and stirred not out of it till the latter end of March, so as most of my friends thought I should not have escaped it.

* Lady Pennistone was for some time a mistress of Richard Sackville.

The 14th came Sir Francis Slingsby & brought his Daughter Mary to serve me who came that night & lay in Judith's Chamber, so that I mean to keep her continually about me.

Upon the 18th at night the Fire Dog play'd with Fire,[*] so as I took cold with standing at the Window.

The 24th. My Lady Margaret christened Mary's Child with Sir William Selby & my Coz. Sackville, & called him Richard. But neither my Lord nor I was at Church.[70]

The 25th came down hither to see me my Lord Russell & my Coz. Sir Edward George. My Lord made very much of them and shewed them the House and the Chambers and my Closet, but I did not stir forth from my Chamber.

The 26th, I kept James Wray a day or two who told me of many old matters & the certain Day of Death of my Brother Robert.[71]

The 29th came little Sir Harry Neville and dined here & went back to Penshurst. This night the Drawing Chamber Chimney was on Fire so that I supped in the new Drawing Chamber with my Lord. After this I never stirr'd out of my own Bed Chamber till the 23rd of March.[72]

NOVEMBER

Upon the 2nd I had such ill luck with playing at Glecko with Legge & Basket that I said I would not play again in six months.

Upon the 8th, shortly after Supper when I came into my Chamber I was so ill that I fell into a Swoon which was the first time I ever swooned.

---

70   About this time the Gallery was hung with all my Lord's Caparisons which Edwards the Upholsterer made up.

71   The 28th. The Palsgrave was crowned King of Bohemia at Prague and the 25th the Lady Elizabeth was crowned Queen.

About the end of this month my sister Beauchamp came from Glenham to live with my Sister Sackville at the end of Dorset House, which end my Brother Sackville and my Lord did lately repair and make fine.

72   All this term there was much sitting in the Star Chamber by all the Heads of the Council about my Lord Suffolk's Business. In the end the answer was given that he should pay Six Thousand Pounds to the King, and that he and his Lady should remain Prisoners in the Tower during His Majesty's Pleasure.

The 16th at night Willoughby came to lie in the Child's Chamber, and Pennis to do all the work in the Nursery.

[*]   A rare weather condition producing a fiery sky similar to an aurora borealis.

The 20th. My Lord & Lady Suffolk were sent to the Tower.[*]

Upon the 24th Sir Francis Slingsby came hither to me & read to me in the Sea Papers about my Father's Voyages.

The 28th. Though I kept my Chamber altogether yet methinks the time is not so tedious to me as when I used to be abroad.

About this time I received Letters from Mr Davis by which I perceived how ill things were likely to go in Westmoreland, especially with Mr Hilton & Michael Brunstall.[73]

The 29th, all the Ladies hereabouts being very kind to me all the time of my not being well. This day I received a Letter and a box of Sweetmeats from my Coz. Hall which was brought to me by one of his Tenants, to whom I gave a good reward & returned [with] her a letter of many thanks.[74]

DECEMBER

The 2nd. Wat Coniston made an end to reading a Book called *Leicester's Common Wealth*,[†] in which there's many things concerning the reignment & Death [of] the Queen of Scots, which was all read to me.

The 7th I gave Sir Robert Taxley my Sable Muff.

Sunday. My Lord neither went to Church nor heard the Sermon here, because Mr Rann was at Oxford. Sir Ralph Boswell dined here & played & sung to me in the afternoon.

The 13th. My Lord gave me 3 Shirts to make Clouts of.

The 14th, Wat Conniston began to read the Book of Josephus.

---

73 About this time of my Lord's being in London he kept a Great Table having a great Company of Lords and Gentlemen that used to dine with him.

All this Winter my Lady Margaret's speech was very ill so as strangers cannot understand her. Besides she is so apt to take a cold, and so out of temper that it grieved me to think of it. I verily believe all these conveniences proceed from some Distemper in her Head.

74 The 29th November was the last time my Lord came to my Lady Penniston at her Mother's Lodgings in the Strand. The 30th my Lord and Lady Suffolk came out of the Tower.

* Thomas Howard (1561–1626), 11th Earl of Suffolk, was Lord High Treasurer from 1614 till his dismissal for embezzlement in July 1618; on 13 November 1619 he and his wife were fined £30,000 (subsequently reduced to £7,000) and were imprisoned in the Tower of London for a month.

† A tract ascribed to Robert, 2nd Earl of Leicester, but, according to G.C. Williamson, more probably written by a Jesuit priest.

The 15th. My Lord & I by Mr Amherst's directions set our hands to a Letter of Attorney for Ralph Conniston to receive those Debts which were due to my Lady of the Tenants, & this day he went on his Journey to the North.

After Supper my Lord & I had a great falling out, he saying that if ever my land came to me I should assure it as he would have me.

The 18th. My Lord came & supped with me in my Chamber, which he had not done since his coming from London, for I determined to keep to my Chamber & did not so much as go over the Threshold of the Door.

The 26th there dined below with the Gentlewomen Mrs Care, Goody Davis & Goody Crawley. I writ a letter to my Lord to thank him for the Pedigree of the Sackvilles which he sent me.

The 27th. Judith & Bromedish aired the Furs which came down from London, & I spent the time as before in looking at the Chronicles.

The 30th and 31st I spent in hearing of reading & playing at Tables with the Steward. About this time my Lord of Doncaster came home from his long embassage into Germany.[*]

FINIS

---

[*] James Hay (1580–1636), Viscount Doncaster (later 1st Earl of Carlisle), was a diplomat at King James' court. In February 1619 he was sent to Bohemia to assess the political situation following the crowning of a new king, the Elector Frederick.

THE YEARS
BETWEEN
1620–1649

'Preserve your Loyalties, Defend your Rights.'

Lady Anne's motto

No notes of Lady Anne's have survived covering the years 1620, 1621 and 1622, so other sources will have to be relied upon to continue the story.

We find that she first of all became very depressed at the successive deaths of her three little boys; not only for the obvious maternal reasons, but also because it became painfully clear to her that her brother-in-law, Sir Edward Sackville, who she heartily disliked, still remained her husband's heir.

Her fifth child, Isabella, was born in 1622, and both she and her sister Margaret, referred to as 'The Child' in the 'Knole Diary', grew up, married well, and were a constant source of pride to their mother. The Earl of Dorset, however, although only thirty-four, was in declining health, worn out by extravagant living. His reckless expenditure had also left him in heavy debt. He was forced to sell or lease most of the Sackville properties, and even tried to sell off Knole House itself. Edward Hyde, Earl of Clarendon (1609–74) tells us that, 'his excess of expenditure in all the ways to which money could be applied was such, that he so entirely consumed almost the whole of the great fortune descended to him, that when he was forced to leave the title to his younger brother, he left, in a manner, nothing to support him'.

It would appear likely that when Dorset fell seriously ill for the last time, both his little girl, Margaret, and her mother were also ill, for another reference culled from Henry Fisher's transcription of 1727 (British Library, Harleian MS. 6177) tells us:

On 10th July in 1623 my Lord, in Great Dorset House, he being then very sickly, did make over to me my jointure of those lands in Sussex, part whereof I now enjoy, and part thereof I have assigned and made over to my two daughters.

My first Lord dyed at Great Dorset House the 28th March in 1624, being Easter Sunday, about 12 o'clock at noon . . . but I was not with him when he dyed, being then very sick and ill myself at Knowle.

In May – a little after my first lord's death – I had the small-pox so extreamly and violently that I was at death's door, which infection I took of my eldest child, who had it there [Knowle] in great extremity some twelve days after her father was buryed.

My first lord, Richard Sackville, Earl of Dorset, was, in his own nature, of a just mind, of a sweet disposition and very valiant in his own person; he had a great advantage in his breeding, by the wisdom and devotion of his grandfather, Thomas Sackville, who was then held one of the wisest men of that time.

ISABELLA SACKVILLE (1622–61), Lady Anne's second daughter by her first
marriage, by an unknown artist (c. 1630)

The Years Between, 1620–1649

Tho' I was happy in many respects being his wife, yet was I most unhappy in having the malicious hatred of his brother, then Sir Edward Sackville, toward me, who afterwards came to be Earl of Dorset without heirs male; and by the cunningness of his wit he was a great practison against me from the time I married his brother till his own death in 1652. For he out-lived his brother 28 years and almost 4 months, and I then lay in Skipton castle in Craven, at the time of his death, but I, whose destiny was guided by a Mercifull and Divine Providence escaped the subtlety of all his practises & ye evils he plotted against me.

Pss. 35, 37 & 140; Ps. 3.10.

Anne Clifford, Countess of Dorset, after thirteen years of what could hardly be called blissful marriage, thus found herself a widow – with of course her daughters: Margaret hardly ten, and little Isabella a mere two years of age.

It is interesting that Lady Anne has left some most revealing recollections of this time, her first period of widowhood:

I lived Widdow to this Noble Richard Sackville, Earle of Dorsett about six yeares two monthes and fower or five daies over. Most part of which time I lived with my two Daughters either in Cheynie Howse in Buckinghamshire, the chiefe seat of my Mother's father and grandfather, or in Bollbroke Howse in Sussex, my chiefe Joynture Howse, or at London in severall hyred howses there, as in Tuttle [Tothill] Street Howse in Westminster, and in St Bartholomewes in a Howse there, which was auntientlie part of the Pryorie, and besides for a while I and my eldest Daughter lay together in Woburn Howse in Bedfordshire, the August after her father's death, in which Howse died my grandmother of Bedford.

And just a yeare after the Deathe of my first Lord, dyed King James, I then lyeing in Cheynie Howse in Buckinghamshire with both my Daughters, from whence I and my two children removed to Bollbroke Howse in Sussex to live there a good while. Where I must not reckon it amongst the least of God's goodness and deliverances to mee that on the sixt day of May in one Thowsand six hundred and twentie sixe, after I had newly received my Ladie Daie Rents, and had some money in the Howse before, I 'scaped myraculouslie by God's Providence an attempt by my Enemyes to have robbed mee. Besides the extreme fright it would have putt mee to, had it not bene timely recovered and prevented by one who accidentallie saw them enter in at the window. And it is thought to have bene plotted by a gret man, then mine extreame Enemy. But God delivered mee.

Pss. 64, 124.

It is clear from this last statement that Anne had held strong suspicions that her brother-in-law, the fourth earl, was behind this break in. Nothing, however, has been found to support this fear, and it may be that she over-reacted to what must have been a very harrowing experience. Her recollections continue:

In August One Thowsand six hundred twentie eight were the first claimes made by waie of Law and Advise of Counsell after the Awardes before mentioned, to mayntaine my right in the Landes of my inheritance, in Craven and Westmerland; I then lying with both my Daughters in Cheynie Howse in Buckinghamshire. Which claims are entered in this my Booke of Recordes of my time.

The one and twentieth of Aprill in one thowsand six hundred and twentie nyne, in the Church of St Bartholomew had I the happiness to see my oldest Daughter marryed to John, Lord Tufton. There being present at the said Marriage myself and my youngest Daughter, and ye sayd Ld Tufton's Father and Mother, and my worthie Cozen german Francis Russell, after Earle of Bedford – who gave her in marriage – and manie others. This John Lord Tufton came to bee earle of Thanett about two yeares and two monthes and some fowrtene daies after his marriage with my daughter, by the death of his father Nicholas, Earle of Thanett. Which Daughter of myne hath now by her sayd Lord tenne children all living, six sonnes and fower daughters. So as God made her a fruitful Mother according to the prayers of my Blessed Mother.

These few lines are all that have survived to tell us in Anne's own words of her life between 1624 and 1630, the year in which she embarked on a second and even more disastrous marriage.

If we remember the trials that Lady Anne had had to endure in her first marriage – the constant bickerings between the couple, together with the ever nagging anxiety that Dorset might well succeed in his endeavours to secure her inheritance for himself – it does seem curious that she should have contemplated a second husband. Particularly such a man as Philip Herbert, Earl of Pembroke and Montgomery.

Herbert was a violent and contemptible man, and utterly unlike Sackville, who, for all his failings, did at least attempt to love Anne.

Indeed Herbert had hardly anything to commend himself, save perhaps his good looks.

Anne herself, still not forty, was an attractive proposition. Although without the still uncertain prospect of her inheritance, she still possessed a reasonable jointure from Dorset as well as a certain amount of wealth in her own right. She claims that the smallpox attack had 'martered my face', but the many portraits that were to appear of her at this time and later, flattering though they may have been, give no hint of any real disfigurement.

It may be that she was carried away by Herbert's personal charm, although, apparently, he showed little of it directly to her. His honesty, to the point of bluntness, may have impressed her. Whatever the cause of her change in mind and decision to marry again, no one has been able to make out a convincing case for her reasons. Even her friends and relatives appeared amazed and incredulous when they heard the news. Perhaps it was just for the sake of her children.

If Anne's motives are mysterious, may we also not wonder at her bridegroom's choice of someone whose temperament was so clearly contrary to his own? Anne was studious and fond of reading; Herbert hardly ever touched a book. She was intensely devout, he was by all accounts an agnostic. She was stately and solemn; he was nothing more than a flippant fop, caring little for anything or anybody other than dogs and horses.

Like the Earl of Dorset, Philip was well known and indeed well respected by some at court. His first marriage had been to Lady Susan de Vere in 1604, a daughter of the 17th Earl of Oxford. Within a year of this event he was created Earl of Montgomery, having already been made a Knight of the Bath. His first wife bore him seven sons and three daughters, of which two sons and a daughter died in their infancy. Susan died in February 1629, and on 3 June 1630, Philip Herbert married Anne, Countess of Dorset. Shortly before the marriage he had inherited the Earldom of Pembroke on the death of his elder brother William. He was also by this time well in favour with King Charles I and had been created a privy counsellor and Lord Chamberlain of the Royal Household. Anne takes up the story once more:

On the 3rd Daie of June, after I have continewed a Widdow 6 yeares 2 monthes and 5 or 6 daies over, was I marryed in Chenies Church in Buckinghamshire to my 2nd Husband Philip Herbert, Earl of Pembroke and Montgomery, Ld Chamberlain of the King's Howshold and Knight of the Garter; he being then one of the greatest subjects in

PHILIP HERBERT (d. 1650), 4th Earl of Pembroke and Montgomery, Lady Anne's second husband, whom she married in 1630, engraved by W. Hall from the Pembroke family portrait by Van Dyck in Wilton House (1832)

the Kingdom. My youngest daughter was present at this my 2nd marriage, but not my eldest.

This 2nd marriage of myne was wonderfullie brought to pass by ye Providence of God for the Crossing and disappoynting, the envie, malice and sinister practices of my Enemyes.

Job 5, 11, 12, 13, 14.

Here in this last phrase lies perhaps the real reason why Anne chose to marry a second time. She felt the need of a protector, for herself and for her children. Anne goes on, her love of coincidence once again to the fore:

And methinks it is remarkable I should be this 2nd time marryed in ye church of Chenys, in the vault whereof lye interred my Great Grandfather and Grandfather of Bedford and their wives – Auncestors to my Blessed Mother – as also her son, ye Ld Robert Clifford, and her eldest sister Anne, Countess Dowager of Warwick, and their neice, Lady Frances Bourchier daughter of the Earl of Bath.

The first few years of this second marriage seem to have been idyllic in Anne's eyes. Philip Herbert took his new wife down to the Pembroke seat at Wilton in Wiltshire, and within a short time she became immersed in the restoration programme being undertaken there by Inigo Jones. She had two more children, both sadly premature, neither of whom survived. Once these formalities were concluded, however, Herbert hardly lived with Anne again as man and wife.

Through surviving letters we learn that Anne retired to her books once more. At Wilton she also befriended a distant kinsman, the poet, vicar and hymn-writer, George Herbert, but even this lasted less than three years, due to Herbert's tragically early death of consumption in 1633 at the age of thirty-nine. Shortly afterwards, in 1634, Philip Herbert, preferring the life at court, left Anne at Wilton; they hardly ever lived together again for the remaining sixteen years of their marriage. Herbert died in 1650, being the first subject of the 'Kendal Diary'; by that time, of course, Anne had at long last secured her inheritance and was living in her northern estates. She recalls the struggles involved:

I had by this Ld of myne 2 sonnes that were borne both before their tyme, while I lived at Whitehall in which Court at London I continewed to live with him for some 4 yeares and six monthes after I was marryed to him. And being still mindful to vindicate my right and interest in the Landes of my Inheritance in Westmerland and Craven, in August & September 1632, by Commission under my 2nd Lds & my hand & Seal, procured legal claims to be made, as were formerly executed in the time of my widdowhood; which claims are also entered in ye records of ye time, when I was Countess of Pembroke.

Also in August 1637 the 2nd claimes while I was Co. of Pembroke in the lifetime of my 2nd Lord were made in like manner to all ye Landes of mine Inheritance . . . which are also extant in my Recordes, and they were the last claimes made thereunto, for the Civil Warres broke out in ye Northern Partes, so that no more claims could be made there, during my Uncle Cumberland & his sonnes lifetime.

Ps. 1.23.

The 18th December 1634, by reason of some Discontent, I went from living at ye Court at Whitehall to live at Baynards castle in London, where & at his houses at Wilton & Ramsbury I continued to live for ye most part during ye time of his life after; in which houses of his lived then his sister-in-law Mary Talbot, Countess Dowager of Pembroke & most of her children, for ye Widowed Countess outlived him about a month.

From the foregoing it can be seen that Anne was still battling in the courts. She had hoped that her second husband would support her in this; but as with Richard Sackville she had to continue the fight alone. Her notes continue:

I must not forget God's Goodness & Mercy to me in sending my eldest Daughter, ye Countess of Thanett her first born child, being a son, whereof she was delivered in Bollbroke Howse in Sussex ye 7th August 1631. And after she had many more children, both Sonnes & Daughters, to my great comfort, so as now she hath 10 children alive.

Gen. 19.1.

The 5th of June 1635 did my 2nd Lord in Baynards castle, make over to mee my Joynture of those landes of his in the Isle of Sheppey in Kent, which he had formerly made in Joynture to his first wife the Lady Susan Vere, Countess of Montgomery. And at the time of making the Joynture he released his right to all my landes in Westmerland & £5,000 out of ye landes in Craven, for a part of my younger Daughter's portion, if ever these landes should fall to mee in his life, as afterwards they did. And this agreement was chiefly made between us by my worthy Coz. German Francis, Earl of Bedford.

WILTON HOUSE, Wiltshire, the family seat of the Earls of Pembroke and Montgomery, engraved by an unknown artist
(c. 1885)

This last entry refers to a serious disagreement between Anne and her husband over the question of a suitor for her younger daughter Isabella. Herbert was keen that she should marry one of his own sons – quite a reasonable idea, and not without merit. All the Herbert boys were quite presentable young men, and Anne, during the time she had known them, had grown quite fond of them and they had got on well together. However, Isabella was by now a young woman, a little older than her sister when Margaret was married, and Anne in her wisdom had decided that Isabella was entitled, as was becoming usual with younger children, to choose whom she wished for a husband. As has been seen, though, Isabella's £5,000 was the real prize that Herbert was after. Lady Anne once more stood her ground: the money should not go to any son of Herbert's, and, more importantly, Lady Isabella should have the right to choose her own marriage partner. After this episode (which only went to sour their relationship still further) Lady Anne reflects, not for the last time:

. . . the marble pillars of Knole and Wilton were to mee oftentimes but the gay Arbours of Anguish, insomuch as a Wiseman that knew the inside of my fortune [her cousin Francis] would often say that I lived in those my Lordes great familyes as the River Rhone runnes through the lake of Geneva, without mingling anie part of its streams with that Lake, for I gave myself wholly to Retyredness as much as I could, in both those great families, and made good bookes and vertuous thoughts my companions.

To resume Anne's reminiscences, we move on now to 1641:

The 21st daie of January 1641 dyed my Uncle Francis Earl of Cumberland when he was neare 80 & 2 yeares, in Skipton Castle in Craven. His onlie child Henry, Lord Clifford who succeeded him in ye earldom lived but 2 yeares & some 20 daies after him.

She adds a quotation from the book of Job, not, perhaps, without a quiet smile:

Is there not an appointed time to man on earth ? Are not his days also like the days of a hireling?

Then follows a sad entry:

The 9th daie of May in 1641 died my worthy Coz. German Francis Russell at his Howse called Bedford Howse in the Strand, to my great grief and sorrow, for he was a most worthy man.

Lady Anne continues:

And when the Civill Warres between the King & Parliament began to grow hotter and hotter in England, my 2nd Ld & I came together from Wilton ye 12th October in 1642, with my younger Daughter the Lady Isabella Sackville. And the next day we came to London where my 2nd Lord went to lye in his lodgings in ye Cockpitt in St James Park over against Whitehall to be near the Parliament. But I and my Daughter went to lye at Baynards, which was then a houseful of Riches & was ye more secured by my lying there; where I continued to lye in my own Chamber without removing 6 yeares & 9 monthes, which was ye longest time I continued to lye in all my life, the Civill Warres being then very hott in England. So I may say that it was a place of refuge for mee to hide myself in till these troubles were over-passed.

Isa. 43.2.

About ye beginning of ye yeare of 1643 my eldest Daughter, ye Countesse of Thanett, went over to France to her Lord and their eldest sonne, where she stayed some 17 or 18 monthes about Paris and Roan [Rouen] and those places, and in April & May 1644 she returned with her Lord to England to me & four of their younger children, leaving their eldest son behind them. Where she was delivered ye 30th August of her 7th child, Mr Thomas Tufton, at her husband's house in Aldersgate Street in London; for she was great with child with him when she came back into England. And she & her Lord & their eldest son were in France when my Coz. Henry Earl of Cumberland dyed.

As we have just seen, Henry Clifford, the fifth earl, died at York without a male heir. He was Anne's last adversary and so the inheritance that had been denied her for so long was now indisputably hers. The male line of the northern Cliffords was now extinct, and the Shepherd Lord's prophecy was complete.

Since the Civil War was by now getting more serious and more divisive in its loyalties, particularly in the north, Lady Anne had to wait a further seven years before it was deemed safe for her to travel. She had always remained a staunch royalist and therefore stood the very real risk of impeachment. It is therefore something of an irony that she spent these years in London under the protection of the very man who had so dispassionately deserted her – her husband, Philip Herbert.

That she was able to do such a thing came about quite simply. The Earl of Pembroke had been a friend and confidante of King Charles, and had gained high office in consequence. But when war broke out in earnest between crown and parliament, Herbert, deciding that parliament would win, changed sides. So, provided that she kept a low profile and avoided any controversy, Anne was comparatively safe in one of his houses; and with his own comfort, as ever, his primary concern, he settled her at Baynards Castle, a veritable treasure-house of his family wealth – as little more than a housekeeper.

The next entry, the only one for the year 1645, indicates the tensions in the marriage:

> The 16th of May in 1645 dyed Mary Curzon, Countess of Dorsett, a virtuous & good woman, in Whitehall – she that was my dear & good friend, though her husband my brother-in-law was ever my bitter enemy & persecutor.
>
> About this time, and also some yeares before, happened a great cause of Anger & falling out between my Lord & mee because he desired to have one of his younger sonnes marryed with my daughter Isabella, which I could in no way remedie, my daughter being herself extremly averse to ye match, though he believed it was in my power to have brought it to pass, being so persuaded by some of my Friendes. But at length it pleased God that on the 5th day of July, being Monday, in 1647, this youngest daughter of myne was marryed to James Compton Earl of Northampton, in the Church in Clerkenwell. But I was not present at ye marriage for many reasons. In which church my Mother & I had been parishioners for some 7 yeares together in my childhood.

During the time that Lady Anne was forced to live in London, apparently almost as a fugitive, she did manage to accomplish a remarkable task. This was the commissioning of a giant family picture, executed in triptych form; in fact, two copies are known to have been made. One was destined to be hung in the castle at Appleby, the other at Skipton. The Skipton version sadly deteriorated with time, and when the then Lord Hothfield, a direct descendant of the Tuftons, moved south to his house at Hothfield in Kent, it is said that only the centre portion went with him, and this was lost in a subsequent fire. Luckily, the Appleby painting enjoyed far better treatment. Until a few years ago it was in the care of the County Record Office in Carlisle, and, after a change of policy, it has now been restored to the great hall of Appleby Castle for all to see.

This triptych (reproduced overleaf) is believed to be the work of Jan van Belcamp, a pupil of Vanderdort. The picture is over eight feet high, and each of the end panels is four feet wide. The left-hand panel shows Lady Anne aged fifteen, at the time of her father's death, when she should have inherited the Clifford estates. On the wall behind her hang portraits of the two main influences on her childhood: Samuel Daniel, her tutor, and Mrs Anne Taylour, her governess. The central figures depicted on the main panel are her parents, together with her young brothers, Robert and Francis. The earl wears under his coat of velvet the special suit of armour that he commissioned on his appointment as Queen's Champion. Behind this group are four more portraits, representing Anne's aunts – Lady Warwick, Lady Bath, Lady Wharton and the Countess of Derby. All these ladies are frequently mentioned in the diaries. Bordering the central panel are nearly forty coats of arms – those borne by Anne's ancestors since the earliest times.

In the right-hand panel Anne is shown as she was in 1646 when the painting was commissioned – the only likeness that could have been painted from life. She is now approaching sixty years of age, and stands aloof and secure. Each portrait in the triptych has its own description and identity, and each of the many shields bears its own notes relating to its bearer. One can only summarize the whole work as a magnificent, but wholly allowable, show of glorification. It is indeed strange that Lady Anne has left us no mention of this painting anywhere in her journals.

It was not until June 1649, some six months after King Charles' execution, that it was deemed safe enough for Lady Anne to move north and claim her estates. When she arrived she found her castles in varying states of disrepair and neglect, and the churches at Brougham, Kirkby Thore, Mallerstang and Appleby damaged and desecrated by the parliamentarians. Her castle at Skipton had withstood a famous siege for over four years, and was in fact the last royalist stronghold in the north to surrender. When in 1646 the garrison could hold out no more, they were granted the rare honour of being allowed to march away, armed and with colours flying, in recognition of their bravery and stamina.

The major part of the 'Kendal Diary' begins when she moved there in 1649, but as there are only a few entries for that year, and they are not in sequence, it seems appropriate to include them now. The first description is of Anne's parting from Philip Herbert:

THE GREAT PICTURE, depicting Lady Anne at the ages of fifteen and fifty-six (left- and
and Lady Margaret Russell (central panel),

ght-hand panels) and her brothers, Robert and Francis, and parents, George Clifford
tributed to Jan van Belcamp (1646)

The 3rd of June in 1649, I took my last leave of my second husband ye Earle of Pembroke in his lodgings in the Cockpit near Whitehall, which was ye last time he & I ever saw one another, it being then Sunday; and ye same day I went from thence to my daughter Northampton's Howse at Islington, which was ye first time I was ever in any of her Lord's Howses, nor have I been in any of them since. And methinks ye destinie is remarkable she should be settled in Islington so near Clerkenwell where my Mother & I lived long in my childhood.

And her Lord's Chiefe Howse at Ashby [Castle Ashby, near Northampton, then the seat of the Earls of Northampton] should be so near Lillford in Northamptonshire, where both my Mother and myself in our younger years had our breeding, as also my elder Daughter of Thanett should be settled at Hothfield in Kent, not far from Sutton [Valence] where my Blessed Mother & I lived a good while whilst I was a Maid.

And ye 11th day of July 1649, having a little afore in ye Baynards Castle taken leave of my 2 Daughters and their Lords, and my Grandchildren, did I go out of London onwards on my journey towards Skypton.

So I went not far from North Hall, where I had formerly lived, and by easy journeys on ye road I came to Skypton ye 18th day of ye month into my Castle there, it being ye first time of my coming into it after ye pulling down of most of ye old castle, which was done some 6 monthes before, by Order of Parliament because it had been a garrison in ye late Civil Warre. And I was never till now in any part of ye castle since I was 9 or 10 weeks old.

About ye 28th of ye month I went into ye decayed Tower at Barden, it being ye 1st time I was ever in ye Tower; and so I continued to lye in Skypton till ye 7th of ye month following, which was August, and ye 7th of that month I removed from Skypton Castle to Appleby Castle, and lay on the way at Kirby Lonsdale. So the 8th day of August in 1649 I came into Appleby Castle ye most auncient seat of myne inheritance, and lay in my own chamber there. And I continued to lye till about ye 13th of February following.

So various are ye pilgrimages of this human life.

Eccles. 3.5.

And from the death of my Coz. german Henry, Earl of Cumberland, till this my first coming into Appleby Castle was just 5 yeares 8 months wanting three days.

Ps. 121.1.

And ye 18th of August I went through Whinfield & into Brougham Castle for a while, in which castle & park I had not been since 9th December 1616, when I was Countess of Dorset, till this day.

Almost immediately after her arrival in the north, Anne set about repairing and restoring her ancient heritage. In this she ran the very real risk of incurring Cromwell's wrath, which could well result in her properties suffering yet again. Her friends tried to dissuade her in her intentions, counselling that her plans ought to be delayed until the political climate stabilized – after all, it was less than a year since the king's execution and anti-royalist feelings, even though the main war was at an end, were still high.

But Anne was not to be browbeaten by such warnings, and her response was typical of her nature and temperament at this time:

Let him [Cromwell] destroy my Castles if he will, as often as he levels them I will rebuild them, so long as he leaves me a shilling in my pocket.

Incredibly, she was left alone, and over the next few years she spent thousands of pounds of her own money on a complete refurbishment programme, not only of the castles, which were successively her homes, but also of local churches, bridges and schools.

Then, in her role as hereditary Sheriffess of Westmorland, there were courts to convene to hear complaints and punish offenders, boundaries to be ridden, and a general putting to rights to be organized of an area covering nearly all the historic county of Westmorland, and the Craven district of North Yorkshire as well. Thirty years of neglect and deprivation had to be rectified, and Anne was a woman of sixty when she took on this Herculean task.

All five of her castles, as well as Barden Tower and some seven churches, were restored to something like their former glory, and on each a plaque was placed recording this and including a favourite text from Isaiah: 'And they that shall be of thee shall build the old waste places; thou shalt raise up the foundations of many generations, and thou shalt be called the repairer of the breach, the restorer of paths to dwell therein' (Isa. 58.12). Beneath this the words *Laus Deo* were inscribed on each plaque.

In addition to all these restorations, Anne undertook to build St Anne's Almshouses in Appleby and to erect a new bridge over the River Eden there. She also endowed with land at Temple Sowerby a trust to repair the village bridge, the church and a new grammar school.

The countess found her manorial rights from long abeyance all but lost, and she was obliged to institute a series of law suits before her affairs could be put on to a proper basis.

An amusing incident was the disputed payment of 'the boon hen', an extra item claimed by the landlord in addition to the usual annual rents. This was a custom dating back to medieval times. Her opponent, one Murgatroyd, lately retired to Appleby from Halifax, refused to pay this additional fee of a hen to the countess, his landlord. He seriously underestimated her, for she took him to court on the matter. Anne, who had defied the judiciary, the king and two husbands, was unlikely to be moved by this man's plea! Lady Anne duly won the case, and then, in a manner typical of this remarkable person, invited Mr Murgatroyd to dinner, where the main course proved to be the very subject of the dispute.

Anne never visited London again; indeed she tells us that she would not wish to do so. The profligacy of the court of Charles II disgusted her as much as had the period under Cromwell. She makes passing reference to the Great Fire of 1666, and a visit or two by some foreign dignitary. Of her distant cousin, Thomas Clifford, who was created 1st Lord Clifford of Chudleigh during her lifetime, there is no mention. Perhaps this omission reflected her abhorrence of Roman Catholicism, the faith to which he became converted.

Instead her diary continues on a purely domestic level. The visits of her children and grandchildren are recorded in minute detail. So too are her journeys to and from her various castles, sometimes in horrendous weather conditions – even today, in a heated car, we might hesitate before crossing those bleak fells. Her usual method of transport was by a coach drawn by six horses, or a simple horsedrawn litter.

Anne writes from the north: 'I doe more and more fall in love with the contentments and innocent pleasures of a Country Life.' And she wishes with all her heart that these same pleasures might be conferred on to her posterity. 'But', she adds, 'this must be left to a Succeeding Providence, for none can know what shall come after them. . . . But to invite them to itt that saying in the 16th Psalme, vv 5, 6, 7 and 8, may bee fittingly applyed: "The Lott is fallen unto mee in a pleasant place. I have a fair Heritage."'

THE KENDAL
DIARY
1650–1675

'Now clean, now hideous, mellow now, now gruff,
She swept, she hiss'd, she ripen'd and grew rough,
At Brougham, Pendragon, Appleby and Brough.'

*Attributed to Thomas Gray when he visited the tombs of
Lady Anne Clifford and her mother in St Lawrence's
Church, Appleby, in 1767. It is in fact a parody of an
inscription on the Countess of Cumberland's tomb, and
first published in 1884.*

In the Yeare of
Ower Lorde God 1650

And the three and twentieth of Januarie following dyed my second Lord, Phillipp Herbert, Earl of Pembroke and Montgomerie in his Lodgeings at the Cockpitt nere Whitehall in London. He being then sixtie five yeares three monthes and thirteen daies old. And the news of his death was brought mee downe post from London to Apleby Castle the twentie seventh daie of that monthe (being Sundaie), for he dyed upon a Wednesdaie and his dead bodie was Buryed in the greate Church at Salisburie the nynth of Februarie following by his Brother and their Father and Mother.

Job 7.1.

And his eldre Brothers widdow, Marie Talbott, eldest Daughter and Co-Heir to Gilbert Talbott Earl of Shrewsbury dyed the 25th day of the month following after his death, at Ramsbury House in Wiltshire, and was buryed a while after by her Husband Wm. Herbert Earl of Pembrooke in the Cathedral Church at Salisbury.

This second Lord of myne was born a second sonne the tenth of October in one Thousand five hundred and eighty fower in his Father, Henry Herbert, Earl of Pembrookes Howse at Wilton in Wiltshire, which was once a Nunnery. His Mother was Mary Sydney and daughter to Sir Henery Sydney, and only sister to the Renowned Sir Phillip Sydney.[*] He was no scholler at all to speak of for hee was not past three or fower monthes at the Universitie of Oxford, being taken awaie from thence by his friends presently after his Father's death in Queen Elizabeths time, at the latter end of her Reigne to follow the Courte (as adjudgeing him fittest for that kind of life) when hee was not passing fiftene or sixtene yeares old. Yet he was of a verie quick apprehension, a sharp understanding, verie craftie withall, and of a discerning spiritt, but extremely chollerick by nature which was increased the more by the

[*] Poet and novelist (1554–86); see note to p. 61.

Office of Lord Chamberlain to the King, which he held many yeares.

He was never out of England but some two months, when he went into France with other Lordes in the yeare one thowsand six hundred twentie five to attend Queen Mary at her first coming over into England to be marryed to King Charles her Husband.

Hee was one of the greatest men of his time in England in all respects, and was generallie throughout the Realme very well beloved. Hee spent most of his time at Court, and was made Earle of Mont-gomerie by King James the fourth of Maie in one thowsand six hundred and five, and Knight of the Garter a little after. The yeare after he was marryed to his first wife. But she dyed before hee came to be Earle of Pembroke, for his elder Brother Earle William dyed but the tenth of Aprill in one thowsand six hundred and thirtie, a little before I was marryed to him.

This second husband of myne dyed the three and twentieth of Januarie one thowsand six hundred and fiftie (as the Yeare begins on Newyeares daie) and was buryed the ninth of Februarie following in the great church at Salisburie. I was lying then at my castle at Aplebie in Westmorland.

Job 8.

A little after my second Lords death, viz: on the thirteenth of Februarie following, I removed from Aplebie Castle in Westmorland to my Castle of Skipton in Craven, lyeing one night by the waie at Kirkby Lonsdale, and so the fowerteenth I came hither and continewed to ly in my said Castle for a whole yeare together. And that was the first time I came to Skipton where I was borne; when I was the second time a Widdow (I being then Countesse Dowager of Pembroke and Mont-gomerie) as well as Countesse Dowager of Dorset, and I did not returne from thence till the eighteenth of Februarie some twelve monthe after; and this was the first time that I lay for a twelve monthe together in anie of my owne Howses, and there I found by experience and Retyred Life that saying to be true: Eccles. 7.13. Pss. 104.13, 24; 16.6.

And this time of my stayeing there I enjoyed my selfe in Building and Reparacons at Skipton and Barden Tower, and in Causeing the Bounda-ries to be ridden, and my Howses kept in my severall Manners in Craven, and in those kind of Countrie Affaires about my estate. Which I found in extreme Disorder by reason it had bene so long kept from mee, from the death of my Father till this time, and by occasion of the late Civill Warres in England, and in this time the suites and differences in Law began to grow hott between my Tennants in Westmorland and some of my Tennants in Craven and mee. Which suites with my

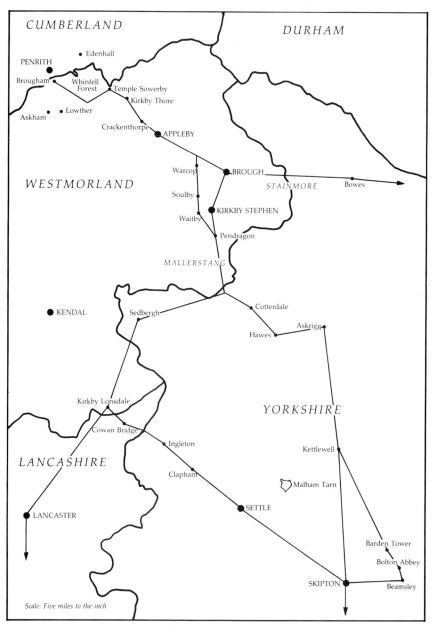

Location of sites in Westmorland and Yorkshire mentioned in the diaries, showing also the routes taken by Lady Anne

Westmorland Tennants are still depending and God knows how long they may last.

But the difference with my Tennants in Craven were for the most part by Compromise and Agreement reconciled and taken upp.

And while I now aboad there, was my eldest Daughter the Countesse of Thanet delivered of her Sonne George Tufton at Hothfield House in Kent, I accounting it a great Blessing to have a Grandchilde of myne to bear my noble fathers name.

Gen. 26.22.

And about the begining of this September did my Cozen Elizabeth Clifford, Countess of Corck with her two Sonnes and fower daughters come to lye att her Howse in Bolton in Craven nere to mee at Skipton for a monthe. Shee that was Daughter and Heire to my Cozen Henerie late Earle of Cumberland. During which tyme there passed many Curtisees betwixt her and mee, I dyneing sometymes at Bolton with her, and she sometimes at Skipton with mee.

Notwithstanding that by reason shee was Heire to her father Henerie Earle of Cumberland and to my Father George Earle of Cumberland, there were divers Differences then on foot betwixt us. Butt we passe them by as Prov. 19.1.

And the tenth of that Moneth was the first time I saw her or anie of her Children in the Northerne Partes, when I dyned at Bolton with them.

And the twenty sixt of that Moneth was the last tyme I saw the Countesse of Corck my Cozen at my Castle of Skipton, for then she took her leave of mee there and went a little while after to Lonsborough and so upp to London, where shee and her children remayned till about the begining of September one thowsand sexe hundred fiftie two, and went with her Lord and some children out of England into Ireland to his greate estate there. But in this yeare one thowsand six hundred and fiftie, her Husband the Earle of Corck continewed to lie at Bolton for some two or three monthes and often saw mee and my first Grandchild at Skipton.

For the eighteenth daie of December, did my said first Grandchild Nicholas, Lord Tufton, come thither to mee and stayed there till the twentieth day of the Monthe following, then he returned upp to London and from thence went beyond Sea to travell into Italie to Rome and to other places abroad; and this was the first tyme that I saw him or anie of my Grandchildren at Skipton, or in anie part of the Landes of myne Inheritance.

Ps. 45.16.

And about August this Summer did Francis Thorpe, one of the Barons of the Exchequer, and Mr Justice Harborton the two Judges of Assize for the Northerne Circuit, come to Applebie Castle to keep the Assizes there, where they now lay in the Castle of Applebie some three or fower nights.

In the Yeare of Lorde God 1651

The next yeare, one thousand sixe hundred fiftie and one, about the eighteenth and nineteenth of Februarie (as the yeare begins on New yeares daie) I returned back to Aplebie Castle in Westmerland, lyeing one night by the waie at Kirkby Lonsdale. In which Castle of myne I continewed to lye for a whole yeare with[out] removing anie whither, and spent much in repayring of my Castles of Apleby and Brougham to make them as habitable as I could, though Brougham was verie ruinous and much out of repaire. And in this yeare the one and twentieth of Aprill I helped to lay the foundacion stone of the mill wall in the great Tower of Apleby Castle in Westmerland called Caesar's Tower to the end it may be repaired againe and made habitable (if it please God) after it had stood without a roofe or covering or one Chamber habitable in it ever since about one thousand five hundred sixtie nyne, a little before the death of my Grandfather of Cumberland, when the roof was pulled down in the great Rebellion time in that March;[*] which Tower was wholy finished and covered with lead in July in 1653.

And the three and twentieth daie of the said Aprill, five daies after, I was present at the laying of the first foundacion stone of my Almshouse or Hospitall here in Apleby Towne; for where I purchased Landes in the mannour of Brougham the fourth daie of Februarie following, and the Land called St Nicholas nere Aplebie the twenty nynth daie of December in one thousand sixe hundred fiftie and two; and it was finished in Jan and March 1653.

And about this Aprill and May in one thousand sixe hundred fiftie and one were the Bounderyes ridden for mee in my Landes here in Westmerland. Which (as I have been informed) had not bene done since my Mother had the same in Joynture till this time.

Prov. 22.28.

---

[*] Aske's Rebellion and the Pilgrimage of Grace.

APPLEBY CASTLE, Westmorland, engraved by an unknown artist (c. 1780); Caesar's Tower is on the right

And this Summer Major Generall Thomas Harrison came hither with his forces, for then the Warres was hott in Scotland.[*] So as then manie places of Westmerland and especially my Castle of Aplebie was full of soldiers what laye here a great part of the Summer. But I thank God I received no harme or Damage by them, nor by the King and his Armie who that August came into England and within six or seven myles of Aplebie Castle.

And that Christmas I kept here in Aplebie Castle (as I had done the Christmas before at Skipton). But by reason of the Warre and troubles in the North this Summer, no Assizes were this yeare kept either in Aplebie or anie where in these Northerne partes.

And in this settled aboad of mine in theis three ancient Houses of mine Inheritance, Apleby Castle and Brougham Castle in Westmerland, and Skipton castle or House in Craven, I doe more and more fall in love with the contentments and innocent pleasures of a Country Life. Which humour of mine I do [wish] with all my hearrt (if it bee the Will of Almightie God) may be conferred on my Posteritie that are to succeed mee in these places, for a Wife and Lady oneself, to make their owne houses the place of Selfe fruition and bee comfortably parte of this Life.

But this must be left to a Succeeding Providence, for none can know what shall come after them. Eccles. 3.22. But to invite them to itt that saying in the 16th Psalme, vv 5, 6, 7, and 8, may bee fittingly applyed: 'The Lott is fallen unto mee in a pleasant place. I have a fair Heritage.' And I may truly say that here:

From many Noble Progenitors I hold
Transmitted Lands, Castles and Honours, which they sway'd of old.

All which Benefitts have been bestowen upon mee for the heavenly goodness of my Deare Mother, whose fervent prayers were offered upp with greater zeale to Almighty God for mee and mine, and had such return of Blessings followed them, as that though I mett with some bitter and Wicked Enemies and many greate oppositions in this world, yet were my Deliverance so greate, as would not befall to any who were not visibly susteyned by a Divine favour from above.

Ps. 41.

---

[*]   Major-General Thomas Harrison had travelled north with a large cavalry force to assist Cromwell, who had been campaigning in the Scottish Lowlands since July 1650, by defending the northern English counties from invasion by Scottish royalists.

And in this Countrey Life of mine I find also that saying of the Psalmist true: 'The Earth is full of the Goodness of the Lord.'

Pss. 33.5; 104.24; 119.64.

The 29th of December in this yeare did I signe and Seale a Pattent to Mr Thomas Gabetis to be my Deputy Sheriff for ye County of Westmerland for the execution of which Office he had ye Counsell of States order for his approbacon bearing date 21st November before.

In the yeare of ower Lorde God 1652

The fower and twentieth of Februarie in one thowsand six hundred fiftie two did I remove from this Apleby Castle lyeing one night by the waie at Kirkby Lonsdale, and the next daie being the twentie fift I came to Skipton Castle after I had now layen in the Castle in Westmerland a yeare and fower dayes over.

And when I now returned to Skipton I continewed to ly in my owne Chamber there till the twenty ninth of November following when I returned to Apleby again. So as I stayed this time at Skipton nyne months and odd days.

The nynteenth of this May did my Grandchild Mr John Tufton, second sonne to my eldest Daughter and her Lord the Earle of Thanett come down hither to mee, which was the first time I saw him at Skipton and here in Craven and Westmerland. He continewed to ly till the twentie eight day of March in one thowsand six hundred fiftie three, on which date hee went from Apleby Castle into the South to see his Father and Mother, and go to Eaton College there to studdy for some time, and to live as a Scholler.

The seventeenth of this July (being Satturdaie) dyed Edward Sackville Earle of Dorset in Great Dorsett House in London. And hee was buryed within a while after in the Vault in Withiam Church in Sussex by his wife and his eldest brother, my first Lord, and manie of their Auncestors. Of whose death Mr Christopher Marsh brought mee word to Skipton the fower and twentieth daie of that Month when he came to ly there in my famillie till the thirtieth daie of September following. Which Edward Earle of Dorsett was the most bitter and earnest Enemye to mee that I ever had. But Allmightie God delivereth mee most miraculouselie from all his Crafty Devises, as Deut. 23.5, for without the merciful power of God it had bene impossible for mee to have escaped them. As Pss. 18.4, 43, 47, 48; 116.8; 124. Isa. 13.11 & Job 28.3.

And now on this 24th of July did Mr George Sedgwicke come hither from London to mee as my Secretary and one of my Cheefe Officers.

The Kendal Diary, 1650–1675

On the second daie of August this yeare was borne The Lady Mary Tufton my Grandchilde, at her Father the Earle of Thanetts House of Hothfield in Kent. (She being the eleventh child of her Mother.) So as I account myselfe happie to have a Grandchilde of myne of that Blessed name.

Luke 1.48.

And about the eight daie of September did my Cozen the Countesse of Corcke* with her six children goe from Bristol over sea into Ireland to Leismore and Corck and those places in Munster to her Husband Richard [Boyle], Earle of Corck, who went thither a few monthes after her.

And in the monthe of August in this yeare did Judge Rilyston and Serjeant Parker come to Apleby Castle to keep the Assize there in their Northerne Circuite, where they now lay some 4 or 5 nights together at my charge, myself and my family then lyeing in my Castle of Skipton in Craven.

The sixte of November was my Cause in Chauncerie betwene mee and my Tennants in Westmerland dismissed out of that Court and I was left to my Remedie at Common Law, to which Business God send some good Conclusion for it hath bene both chargeable and troublesome unto mee.

And the nyne and Twentieth of this monthe, I with my Grandchilde Mr John Tufton and my family came from Skipton, lyeing one night by the waie at Kirkby Lonsdale, and so the next day wee came into Appleby Castle where this Grandchilde of myne and I kept our Christmas this yeare; and this was the first tyme that anie of my Grandchildren were with mee in Westmerland.

The numerousness of my posteritye and all other Benefits what-soever, I believe were bestowed upon mee for the Heavenly Goodness of my Deere Mother whose fervent prayers were offered upp with zeal to Allmighty God for mee and myne, and had such a Returne of Blessings following them as that time I mett with some bitter and wicked enemyes, and numerous great oppositions in this Worke, yett was my deliverances as great as could not befall to any that were not visibly sustayned by a Divyne favoure from above.

Ps. 7.1.

And in this Country life of myne, I mynde that saying of the psalmist true –'The Earth is full of the goodnesse of the Lorde.'

Pss. 33.5; 104.24; 119.64.

---

* Elizabeth Clifford, daughter of the 5th Earl of Cumberland, from whom she inherited the Bolton Abbey estates, including Barden Tower (see pedigree on pp. 272–3.)

In the yeare of
ower Lorde God 1653

In the begining of this yeare, one thousand six hundred fiftie three (as the yeare begins on New yeares daie) did I cause severall Courtes to be kept in my name in divers of my mannors within the Countie of Westm'land. But the Tennants being obstinate and no fractor, i.e. though they appeared, would not answere as they were called. And also many causes of Enactment did I cause to be sealed in this Countie, in order to a Tryall with my Tennants at Common Law. (God save them good signs.)

And the thirtieth daie of this January, being my Birth daie, did I pass my Clymacterial yeare of sixtie three. The yeare amongst phisitians accounted so remarkable.

The twentie eight of this March my Grandchilde Mr John Tufton went from Aplebie Castle to Yorke, from thence to London, and so to Hothfield howse in Kent to see his Father and Mother, Brothers and sisters, and within a while after to Eaton Colledge, there to studdy where he now remayned from the 25th of Aprill for 3 months more till ye fifte of July in the yeare following. Then he went from thence to Skipton and so to Oxford by the 2nd August following, to be a student there.

And in the begining of this yeare was my Almeshowse here at Aplebie quite finished, which has bene almost five yeares in building. So as I now putt into itt twelve goode women (eleven of them being widdows, and the twelfth an injured maid) and a Mother, a Deceased Minister's widdow; some of whome I putt into the said House in December, and the rest in Januarie and the begining of March following.

The twentie seaventh of this May was my youngest Daughter the Countesse of Northampton delivered of her second Childe (which was

CASTLE ASHBY, Northamptonshire, engraved by M.S. Barenger from a drawing by J.P. Neale

also a Sonne) in her Lord's Howse called Can[on]bury by Islington neare London; who was Christened there the next day after by the name of William, I lyeing then in my Castle here at Appleby in Westmerland.

The Birth of which Child I account as an extraordinary great Blessinge and seale of Gods mercies to mee and mine. But hee dyed to my great griefe and sorrow on the 18th day of September 1661, in his father's House at Castle Ashby in Northamptonshire.

The fifteenth of June followinge did her Husband, James Compton Earle of Northampton, come from his Journy from London over Staynmoore to my castle of Appleby to mee. Where he now lay in the Baron's Chamber for the most part [until] the nine and twentieth of the same Monthe (excepting two nights that he went to Carlisle and Naworth Castle and those parts).

And the fifteenthe of this monthe was the first time that I saw him or any Sonne in Lawe of mine here in Westmerland, or in anie parts of mine Inheritance . And this twentie ninth Day of this Monthe when he went from hence, he went into my decayed Tower of Barden, and into my Howse of Sillesden, and the most remarkable places of my Inheritance in Craven.

And the second Day of March following, hee went away from heere towards his House att Islington by London, and came thither to his Wife about ten dayes after.

The five and twentieth day of this June died att ye House of Raynham in Kent, Frances Cecill Countess Dowager of Thanett, daughter of Thomas, Earle of Exeter, who was Mother to my Sonne in Law ye Earle of Thanett. And she was buryed a little after in Raynham church in Kent by her Husband Nicholas, Earle of Thanett and her Grandchilde and mine, ye Lady Anne Tufton.

The eightennth of July was my Grandechild the lady Margaret Tufton married in her father's House in Aldersgate streete in London to Mr George Coventry, eldest Sonne to Thomas, Lord Coventry, whose father Thomas Lord Coventry was Lord Keeper of the Greate Seale of England.

And she went from thence about tenne daies after ye marriage with her Husband and his father down into ye Country to their House att Croome in Worcestershire to live there with them. Which marriage I accounted a great Blessing of God Almightie to mee and mine.

Ps. 116.12, 13, 14.

About ye latter end of this July was the Greate Tower att Appleby called Caesar's Tower covered with Lead, which had layne open and uncovered as a Ruinous Place ever since the yeare of our Lord One thowsand five hundred sixtie and nyne (being the yeare before my Grandfather of Cumberland dyed) till this time. The Middle Wall of which Tower and Repayring of itt, I began in Aprill in the yeare One Thowsand Six hundred fiftie and one, and finished now.

And in this yeare about ye beginninge of March was my Newe Stables begunne to be built without the Castle, and adjoyning to the Barn, built there about two yeares since by my directions, where there never was any Buildings before.

The Seventeenth day of August did Judge Puleston and Judge Parker come hither and lay in Appleby Castle for five nights, and kept ye Assizes here in the Moote Hall. So as on the twentieth day, the case betwene mee and my Westmerland Tennants came before Judge Parker but was dismissed by reason of a generall exception taken against most of the Jurie.

And the two and twentieth day those Judges went away from hence towards Lancaster. And this was the first time that I lay in Appleby Castle when there was an Assize held here.

And about the time of the keepinge of these Assizes, did my Cozen Philip, Lord Wharton with his now second wife and his eldest Daughter by his first wife, and his Brother Sir Thomas Wharton and his wife and their mother the Lady Philadelphia Wharton, the Widowe, come to lye for a fewe nights in Wharton Hall in Westmerland. Soe as I went to them to Wharton, and they came hither to mee at Appleby . And this was the first time I sawe any of them here in Westmerland.

The first day of September following did my Sonne in Lawe ye Earle of Thanett and my Daughter his wife, with their eldest Sonne Nicholas, Lord Tufton, come from London over Stain-moore hither to Appleby Castle to mee, wherre they continewed to lye eleven nights together; my Daughter and her Lord in ye Chamber under the Drawinge Roome, and my Lord Tufton in the Baron's Chamber. This beinge the first tyme that this first Childe of mine or her Lord or any of my owne Children came to me into Westmerland, or into any part of ye Lands of mine Auncestors (excepting her second Sonne John Tufton, who had bin with mee in Westmerland before the last yeare).

And the seaventhe day of this September my daughter of Thanett and her Lord and their eldest Sonne went away from mee out of Appleby Castle in Westmerland into Worcestershire, passing through Lancashire and those parts, and soe through the Cittie of Worcester unto their daughter att ye Lord Coventries House att Croome in that Countie. Soe as they came hither the seaventeenth day of this Month, and lay there nine nights, as being more on their Journey towards London, and their

House of Hothfield in Kent. This being the first tyme that any Child of mine came into Worcestershire or soe near ye River of Severne.

The ninth day of November following, (being Wensday), came my Cause betweene me and my Westmerland Tennants to be heard att ye Common Pleas Barre in Westminster, before three of the Judges of that Court, viz: Pulestone, Atkins and Warburton, in the case of Skaife of Stayn-more. Which was given against mee by the Jury against Evidence and Direction of Court, and of the Judgement of all that heard the same debated.

The ninth day of December I removed from Appleby Castle into Brougham Castle in Westmerland, where I continued to lye in the Chamber where my Father was borne, and my Blessed Mother dyed, till the eleventh of Aprill following that I removed thence to Skipton. And I had not layne in this Brougham Castle in Thirty Seaven yeares till now. For ye month of December in One Thousand six hundred and sixtene (when I was married to Richard, Earle of Dorset) I went out of itt upp towards London to him, and never lay in itt till this night. In which long time I past through many strange and hard fortunes in the Sea of this World. Soe as I may well apply that Saying to myself: Ps. 107 & Ps. 109.27.

And for repayring of this Brougham Castle which had layne so itt were, ruinous and desolate ever since King James, his lying in itt in 1617, till I made itt lately habitable, caused me againe to apply that Saying to my selfe: Isa. 58.2–12, Ezek. 36.28, 33 & 36.

As also in my repaires of the Great Tower, called Caesar's Tower in Appleby. And in this yeare was built and finished att my owne charge, a water corn mill (which was begun to be erected there the yeare before) within my Manner of Sillesden in Craven in high Exulden, not farr from the place where the Wyndemill formerly stood, that was built there by my Auncestors.

In the yeare of Lord God 1654

The Eighteenth of March, in One Thousand sixe Hundred fiftie and foure (as the yeare begins on New yeares day) died, in one of the new built Houses in Queene Streete, Mary B[e]aumont, Countesse Dowager of Northampton, Mother to my Sonne in Lawe James Compton Earle of Northampton, and she was buryed a while after in Compton Church in Warwickshire.

And the eleventh of Aprill I removed from Brougham Castle in Westmerland, and lay by the way att Kirkby Lonsdale, and came the next day to Skipton, to lye there againe in it after I had layne in Westmerland without removing out of that Countie, for a yeare and four months. And soe I now continued to lye in the Round Roome whereof I used to lye, till the second day of August following that I came back againe into Westmerland.

The twentie sixte day of May did my Lord of Northampton with my daughter his Wife and their little Sonne, Lord William Compton, come hither to mee at Skipton where they now continued to lye in this House or Castle of mine. My Daughter and her Lord in the Round Chamber above myne, and the little Lord in the Chamber next to the old Castle. Soe this twenty sixte day was the first tyme that I ever saw my Daughter of Northampton or her Lord or their Child here att Skipton. And the first time that I ever saw this younger daughter of myne or any Childe of hers in any of the lands of myne Inheritance. Which gave me reason to apply to my selfe that saying of Israel unto Joseph: Gen. 48.11[*] – for I never saw any Child of hers till now.

And he wanted but a day of a yeare old when I first saw this Grandchild of myne. And his father's second brother, Sir Charles Compton, came hither nowe with them.

And the fifthe day of June following, I went with my daughter of Northampton and her Lord into my Mother's Almeshouses at Beamsley, and into my Lady of Corkes House att Bolton (though she her selfe was then in Ireland) and into my decayed Tower of Bardon, itt being the first time that ever I was in any of these places with any Childe of mine owne.

---

[*] 'I had not thought to see thy face; and lo, God hath shewed me also thy seed.'

And the eighth day of this month was my Grandchild, the little Lord Compton carried away from mee by his Nurse, that gave him birth (who was born in Scotland), to Ottley, where hee lay this one night, and which on the next day his Father and his Mother overtook him.

For the ninth day of this month, my younger Daughter and her Lord and his brother Sir Charles Compton went away from mee from Skipton Castle to Ottley, and soe took the Child away with them to Yorke, for they lay one night on their journie homeward, and they came well (I thank God) the Seventeenth day to their House att Castle Ashby in Northamptonshire.

The two and twentieth of this month was my Daughter of Thanett delivered of Lady Anne Tufton her fifth daughter and twelfth childe, and Second of that Name, at Hothfield House in Kent. And the fifth of July did her sonne, my grandchild John Tufton come from Eaton Colledge from studying there, to Skipton to me for a little while, from whence he went immediately up to Oxford and was settled there in Queens Colledge the second of August following.

The second day of this August, I and my family removed from my House and Castle of Skipton in Craven into Kirkby Lonsdale where I lay in the Inne there all night, and the next day (being the third) I came into Appleby Castle in Westmerland after I had layne there in Skipton Castle from the twelfth day of Aprill last till now. And I continued to lie in Appleby Castle till the five and twentieth of this month, that I removed to Brougham Castle.

And while I now lay in Appleby Castle did ye two Judges, Hugh Wyndham and Richard Newdigate come hither in their Circuits where they now lay five nights together. Judge Newdigate in ye Barons Chamber and Judge Wyndham in ye greate Tower called Caesar's Tower. This being the first time that any of ye Judges or other Persons of Note and Quality lay here, since I latley repaired itt to my exceeding great Cost and Charge.

And the twelfth day, while the Judges now lay here, was my Cause betwene me and my Westmerland Tennants heard in the Moote Hall in Appleby before Judge Newdigate, where itt was conceived I had a reasonable good Suit, having obtayned a speciall Edict against them; though my Tennants still persisted in being wilfull, refactory and Obstinacy against mee.

The twenty fifte day of this Monet beinge Friday, I removed from Appleby Castle with my familie into my Castle of Brougham in Westmerland, where I now continewed to lye till the eighth of January following, when I removed from thence back againe to Appleby Castle; I having the time now with this private life of mine att Brougham to contemplate the great mercies of God, in delivering mee from soe many Evills as I had passed over, and drowning mee in his Blessings in this my old age, to live happily and peacably in these ancient places of mine Inheritance.

And whilst I now lay here in Brougham Castle in my owne Chamber, where my father was borne, and my Mother died, I had the joyfull newes howe that on the second day of this September (being a Saturday) my Grandchilde ye Lady Margarett Coventry, wife of Mr George Coventry, was delivered of her first Childe, that was a Sonne, in her father-in-lawes, the Lord Coventrys House of Croome in Worcestershire. Which Childe was christened the seventeenth day following (being a Sunday) by the name of John. This being the first Child that made me a Great Grandmother, which I account a greate Blessing of God.

And my daughter of Thanett was there at ye Birth and Christening of this first grandchild of hers. Soe as he suckt the milk of her Breast many times, she having with her her nowe youngest child, the lady Anne Tufton, being about nyne weeeks old. But my grandchild, the Lady Margarett Coventry, after my daughter of Thanetts departure from Croome, gave this Child of hers Sucke herselfe, as her Mother had done most of her Children.

In the Yeare of owre Lord 1655

The eight day of January in One Thousand six hundred fiftie and five (as the yeare begins on New Yeares Day) I removed from Brougham Castle with my family to my Castle at Appleby in Westmerland againe, and lay in it till the eighteenth of September following, and then I removed to Skipton.

In which time, on the tenth day of August did the two Judges of Assize, the Lord Chief Barron Steele and Serjeant John Parker come hither to Applebie in their Circuite and lay here in Appleby Castle six nights together, and kept the Assizes in the Towne. Myself and my family then lying in the sayd Castle of Appleby also.

The eighteenth day of September following I removed againe with my family out of Applebie Castle in Westmerland towards Skipton Castle in Craven (lyeing all night by the Way at Kirkby Lonsdale) and came safe thither the nineteenth; I having not bin in this Castle of Skipton since the seconde day of August was a twelve month, till now. So I lay then in my said Castle of Skipton till the first day of August next following, which was about ten monthes and tenne daies over, at which time I removed the said 1st Aprill 1656 out of the said Castle of Skipton towards Brougham Castle in Westmerland to lye there in it for a while, lyeing all night by the Way at the Inne at Kirkby Lonsdale.

So as I continewed to live in my said Castle of Brougham till the second of October following at which time I, with my family removed to Appleby Castle in Westmerland.

About the tenthe of this month in this yeare 1655, as the yeare begines on New Yeares Day, whilst I lay in Appleby Castle did I cause a great parte of Applebie Church to be taken downe (it being very ruinous and in danger of falling of itselfe) and so I caused a Banke to be made in the North East Corner of the Church for myselfe to be burried in, (if it pleaseth God). And the repairinge of the said Church cost me about some six or seven hundred pounds, being finished the yeare following.

The Kendal Diary, 1650–1675

And about the twentieth of this month was my first Grandchilde the Lord Nicholas Tufton, sent as a Prisoner into the Tower of London by command of the Lord Protector and his Council upon suspition that he had a hand in the late Plotte, so as this Grandchilde of mine continewed to lye in it as a Prisoner nine months and fower dayes. The twentie fourth of December following he was inlarged out of his imprisonment in ye said Tower of London and went home to his father and Mother againe – this being the first time of his imprisonment in that Tower. Notwithstanding he was committed againe to the same Tower as a Prisoner in the eleventh or twelfth of September in the yeare following.

The fyftenth day of this Aprill was my Grandchilde the Ladie Frances Tufton sente from her father and Mother from their House in Aldersgate Streete in London over sea into Utrecht in Holland to be cured of the Ricketts, which she had in great extremitie; soe she remained in that Citty of Utrecht till about the 9th of March 1657, at which time she came over in a Dutchman of Warre to Gravesend, and soe to London with her Brother Mr John Tufton and his Company to their father's House in Aldersgate Streete in London.

And the fourteenth of this July when I now lay in this Appleby Castle, was my daughter of Northampton deliver'd of her third Childe, the lady Anne Compton (who was her first Daughter) in her Lord's House att Islington by London. Which Lady Anne Compton died the 15th day of December in 1660 in her father's House at Lincolne Inne feilds att London. I then also lyinge in Appleby Castle in Westmerland.

And this summer by my appointment, was the wall of the little parke att Appleby made new and higher rounde about save only towards the water side.

This summer also (though I lay in Appleby Castle in Westmerland) yet by my appointment and at my Charge was the steeple of Skipton Church on the East and North parte of it (which had bin pulled down in the time of the late civill warre) built up againe, repaired and leaded all over, and some parte of the Church it selfe be also repaired with a Tombe to be erected and sett up in it in memory of my Noble Father.

And about the fifth of this October in 1655 when I lay now in my House here at Skipton, did I begin to make the Rubbidge to be carried out of the old Castle at Skipton, which had layn in it since it was throwne downe and demolished in December 1648 and the January following.

In the Yeare of our Lorde 1656

In this yeare one Thousand sixe hundred fifty sixe, as the yeare begins on New Yeares daie, about the third of January did my Grandchilde John Tufton, after he had continewed about a month with mee att my House or Castle of Skipton in Craven, go away from thence back to Queens Colledge at Oxford to lye in that Universitie as a Student till the sixt of May following. Att which time hee went quite awaie from living as a Student there, upp towards London to his father and Mother and most of their Children. Whither he came well to them the next daye, into their House att Aldersgate Streete there. And from thence, about the fourteenth of June following he went out of England into the Low Countries with George Sedgwick whom I had appointed to be his Governor. Soe as they stayed now in Holland and those Provinces till the beginning of May following, in one Thousand sixe hundred and fifty seven. (Having spent most of their time in the Citty of Utrecht.) And came over safe into England and arrived at London the ninth of May in 1657. From whence hee came to mee to Skipton Castle the twelfth of June following, and with him George Sedgwick his Governor and Alexander Whitcher my Grandchilde's man, to live there with mee as they had done formerly.

The first daie in Aprill, I with my family removed out of my Howse or Castle of Skipton in Craven into the Inne at Kirkby Lonsdale in Westmerland, from whence the next daie I continewed my Journey to my Castle of Brougham in the said Countie, where, by the way I went into Mr Dalston's howse in Melkinthorpe, and stayed there a while; which was the first and last tyme that ever I was in thatt Howse. And so thatt evening from thence I came into my said Castle of Brougham, where I lay in the Chamber which my Noble father was borne in and in which my Blessed Mother dyed, for some six monthes, viz: Aprill, May, June, July, August and September, which was the first tyme thatt I lay those few monthes altogether in thatt Castle, though I have formerly layen in itt in September and the rest of the monthes; and the second of October following I removed with my family out of thatt Brougham Castle into my Castle of Appleby in Westmerland.

And the sixteenth daie of Maye was the Cause betwene mee and my Westmerland Tennants hearde at the Common Pleas Barre in West-minster hall, before fower of the Cheife Judges there, to witt – my Cozen Oliver St John, Lord Cheife Justice of the Common Pleas, Judge Atkins, Judge Hugh Windcham and Judge Matthew Hailes. Where a Jury approval being sworne, and my Cause was openly pleaded by Serjeant Maynard, S'jeant Newdigate and S'jeant Furnivall who were of Counsell for mee. And S'jeant Earle and S'jeant Evers who were of Counsell for my said Tennants. Att which tyme they putt mee upon all manners of proofs, being plaintiffs in the Cause. Though they were made forth by my Witnesses very full to the satisfaction of the Courte. So thatt the Jury gave in a verdict for mee against my said Tennants. And the next daie being the seventeenth of that Moneth, another Jury appeared for the second Tryall, but the same went by Defaulte of the Tennants who onely appeared, but would not appeall att all. So that the Jury did not go from the barre butt immediately gave in another Verdict on my behalf, and the Court thereupon awarded mee Costes in both the said Causes, Vallew of two hundred and fifty poundes, and both Verdicts exempli-fyed under the Sealle of the Courte.

The second daie of this July dyed betimes in the morning in Baynards castle, to my great griefe, my cheif Officer for my Estate in Sussex, and Deare friend Mr Christopher Marsh, who was burried the same night in the Church there called St Bennet by Paules Wharfe, (my Daughter Thanett and her eldest Sonne the Lord Nicholas Tufton being att his Buriall).

And the day after (being the third of this monthe) did my Daughter of Thanett with her fower youngest Children, namely Cecilly, George, Mary and Anne begin their Journey in the Coache out of London Towne toward the North, who came safe and well to mee with her Children, (for which I thank God), to Brougham Castle in Westmerland the eleventh of thatt month.

And Richard Clapham came along with them, who first of all tould mee the sad Newes of the said Mr Marshes death. And this was the first time I saw three of my said Grandchildren, to witt George, Mary and Anne Tufton; as also the first time I saw my Grandchilde the Lady Cicelly in the North, though I have seene her before att London in Baynards Castle and in her father's House in Aldersgate Streete.

So they continewed with mee in my said Castle for seventeen nights together, during which tyme my Daughter with my Grandchilde the Lady Cicilly and her brother George went for a while in their Coache to Eden Hall in Cumberland and to Lowther Hall in Westmerland. And whyle they were with mee did Charles Stanley Earle of Derby come to Brougham Castle to visit mee , and lay there some three or fower nights, being the first time thatt he was ever in that Castle, where his Great Grand Mother, my father's sister by the halfe blood was borne.

And the eight and twentieth of this July did my Daughter of Thannett with fower of her Children, Cicelly, George , Mary and Anne go out of my Castle of Brougham from mee, where I took my leave of them in the open Ayre in the Courtyard.

And so through Whinfield Parke to my Castle of Appleby in the said Countye, where they lay in it one nighte; and they went the next Daye after from thence out of Westmerland over Stainmoore onwards on there journy towards London, whither they came safe and well the fifth day of the month following, into their House in Aldersgate Streete, where they continewed to lye for some eight nightes together. And when they were past, on the Nineteenth of the same month they wente from thence into the Inne at Rochester in Kent, where they lay that night, and the nexte day they went into Hothfield House in the said Countye to my Lord of Thannett and three of his Soñnes, my Grand-children Richard, Thomas and Sackvill, for which safecomeing home of theirs from mee out of these Northerne partes, I praise God with my hearte.

And I had not seene my Daughter of Thannet since the twelfth of September in 1653, when she went there from Appleby Castle from mee, till this eleventh Daie of July that she came to mee in Brougham Castle.

And the one and twentieth of August in 1656, when I lay in Brougham Castle did the two Judges of the Northerne Circuite, John Parker Esquire, Serjeant att Lawe and then one of the Barrons of the Exchequer who lives near Rochester in Kent, and Erasmus Earke Esquire, Serjeant att lawe who lives in Norfolke, come into Appleby Castle in Westmer-land to keep the Assizes in the said Towne for the said Countie, where in the Castle they continewed to lye for five nights together at my Charge. Parker in the Barrons' Chamber, and Earle in Caesar's Tower. And the third Day of the Monthe following they went away from thence to Kendall and soe forward on their Circuite.

And dureing the time they kept the Assizes in Appleby did my Cozen Philip, Lord Wharton lye for some three or four nights together in the Chamber of the said Castle where I used to lye myself; he having some

MARGARET SACKVILLE as Countess of Thanet, after Peter Oliver (c. 1639)

businesse att the Assizes. And the same third Day did my said Cozen the Lord Wharton come to Brougham Castle to mee for a while, it being the first time that ever he was with me in the said Castle where-in his Uncle George Wharton was borne, though I had seene him before in Appleby Castle in 1653.

And the eleventh daie of this September by the commaund of my Lord Protector and his Councell, was my first Grandchilde the Lord Nicholas Tufton the second time putt up as a Prisoner in the Tower of London, where he lay under restrainte till the 25th day of June 1658, that he was released of his said imprisonment.

The 28th of July was my Grandchild the Lady Margaret Coventry delivered of her second Child Miss Anne Coventry, who dyed ye next day.

And the second day of October did I and my family remove out of Brougham Castle to my Castle of Appleby in the same Countye of Westmerland, where I then continewed to ly for about 6 months. Viz: till the fourteenth day of Aprill following. I then removed from thence in two dayes into my Castle of Skipton in Craven.

And about Middsommer this yeare did my Cozen Elizabeth Clifford, Countess of Corck come from her husband, Richard Earle of Corck, out of Ireland with their two Sonnes and their daughter Elizabeth for a while into England. Where neither shee or anie of her children had bene since about September in 1652 till now.

And now, about the begining of this October, shee and her daughter Elizabeth went away againe out of England over Sea into Ireland, to her husband the Earle of Corcke. Butt this Countess now left behynde her in England her two Sonnes, Charles, Lord Dungarvan, and his brother Richard Boyle, att the Universitie of Oxeford, to ly there as a Student in the Queenes Colledge for a time.

And on November the twelfth was the Case betweene mee and my Westmerland Tennants heard in Westminster Hall before the fower Judges of the Common Pleas, Oliver Lord St John, Cheife Justice, Judge Adams, Judge Windham and Judge Hailes. In which Cause James Straker was Defendant against mee on the Tennants behalfe. The Jurie all appearinge being sworne and unpannelled and the Case called. The Defendant appeared not, nor any for him. So as hee was non seated, one hundred pounds costs were against him, and the land decyded to bee myne and not the Tennants. And since I leased out to another for one and twenty yeares.

And the sixteenth day of this November whilst I lay in Appleby Castle, was my Daughter of Northampton deliver'd of a second

Daughter and fourth Chylde, the Ladie Isabella Compton in her Lordes Howse att Castle Ashby in Northamptonshire; which Lady Isabella dyed the third day of March in 1657 in the late Countess Dowager Rivers' house in Queens Streete in London, wherefore her father and mother then lay, shee being about a yeare and almost three monthes old, and was buryed in the vault of Compton Church in Warwickshire. I then lying in Appleby Castle.

In the yeare of our Lorde God 1657

The third day of February in this yeare 1657, did Mr Thomas Gabetis my Deputy Sheriff in the County of Westmerland, and Mr John Turner, Mr Thomas Johnson, John Darby and Thomas Carlston Heade Bailiff for the Westward, enter James Walker's house in Nether Brough commonly called Kirke Brough in the said County, where they fairely and gently Dispossessed the said James Walker's Wife and famillie of the said Howse and the Landes thereto belonging. The said Sherrif by vertue of a Writt issued out of the Common Place at Westminster Delivering over the same to the said John Darby my servante, who was the Lessee upon the ejectment for my use.

And within a whyle after I did lease over the said James Walkers Howse and Tenement to John Salkeld of Brough for one and twenty yeares at a yearly Back Rent. The same being held before at a fynalle rent as other the Landes and Tenements in the County of Westmerland are held of mee.

And by that meanes I altered the tenure of this Lande which was the principall thing I was at in my suites in Law with my Westmerland Tennents, as being a great Benefitt and advantage to mee and my Posterity, and not only to mee but to all the Landlords and Tennants in that County.

About the 30th daie of this Januarie in her House called Chiswick neare London, died that Countess Dowager of Bedford who was wife to my Cozen german Francis, Earle of Bedford, and who was married to him two daies after I was married to my first Lord; and her dead Bodie was buried in the Church at Chenyes in Buckinghamshire. I then lying at Appleby Castle in Westmerland.

And the 14th daie of Aprill did I remove with my family out of my Castle of Appleby in Westmerland towards Skipton in Craven, whither I came safe and well the next daie being the fifteenth daie, haveing layne by the way all night at Kirkby Lonsdale in the Inne there, as I usually doe in my journy betwene Westmerland and Craven. And I continewed to ly in my said Castle of Skipton till the seaventeenth daie of October following, that I removed from thence towards Appleby Castle on Westmorland again.

About the 25th or 26th of Aprill aforesaid, did Gabriell Vincent, now Steward of my Howse and Gentleman of my Hors (by my directions) sett the Masons and Carpenters on work in the further repayring of Skipton Castle, which hee reformed soe thatt the Michaelmass following – (or but a few dayes after) – there were thirteen Roomes finished; seven whereof were upper Roomes. Also a little Closett built on the North Wall, the Coyneing House now repayred and slated and the Conduit Court cleaned of all the Rubbish that was throwne in att the Demolissine of the Castle. Which Roomes were all covered with Slate about Michaelmass also, with Gutters of Leade about the Roomes thatt are covered with Slate, for I was not permitted to cover it with Lead.

And this Aprill, about the three and twentieth daie, was another Tryall betwene mee and my Westmerland Tennants at the Common Pleas Barre in Westminster Hall before my Cozen Oliver St John, Lord Chiefe Justice, Judge Atkins, Judge Windham and Judge Hales, where the Verdict was for mee, and was so recorded in Court. This being the fowrth verdict I have had against my said Tennants att the said Common Pleas Barre in Westminster.

And this Summer whyle I lay in my House or Castle of Skipton in Craven, about this tyme was the Tombe finished which I caused to be erected and sett upp for myselfe in the Northeast Corner of Appleby Church here in Westmerland over the Vaulte there, which, by my directions had bene made in one thousand six hundred fifty five, when I then repayred the said Church. In which Vault I intend to be buryed myself.

And about the ninth daie of May following, did my Grandchilde Mr John Tufton and his Governor Geo. Sedgwick, and my Grandchild's mann Alexander Whitcher, come over Sea in a Dutch mann of Warre, out of the Low Countryes with my Grandchild the La. Frances Tufton, his Sister, and her womman and others in their Companie, and arrived the said Nynth daie safe att London, from whence my said Grandchilde Mr John Tufton, George Sedgwick and my Grandchylde's mann Alexr Whitcher came downe to mee to Skipton ye 14th June following.

And the Nyneteenth daie of June did my Daughter of Northampton and the Earle her husband with their oldest Sonne William, Lord Compton and his Uncle Mr Henry Compton, the said Earle's youngest Brother, come to me and my Grandchylde Mr John Tufton from their

HOTHFIELD HOUSE, Kent, the country seat of the Earls of Thanet, engraved from a drawing by J. Loch (1804)

House att Castle Ashby in Northamptonshire, to my House or Castle of Skipton in Craven where they lay now for eleven nights. This being the first time thatt young Mr Henry Compton was ever there; but my Lo. of Northampton, my Daughter his wife and their Sonne William Lo. Compton had bin once there with mee about three yeares before. And this Nyneteenth daie saw the first tyme thatt my said Daughter, her Lord or any of their Children ever saw anie of her sister, my Daughter of Thannett's Children in any part of my Inheritance in the North.

The fourth daie of the next month, my Daughter of Northampton and her Lord and their eldest Sonne the Lord Compton and Mr Henry Compton, my Lord of Northampton's Brother came safe to their House att Castle Ashby in Northamptonshire, to my two Grandchildren Lady Anne and La. Isabell Compton their two Daughters, to ly there with them agen in the said Castle.

And this August Barron Parker and Anton Crook Serjt at Law came to Appleby to keepe the Assize there, where they now lay in the Castle five nights together. I then lying with my family in my Castle of Skipton in Craven.

The fourteenth daie of September was my Grandchilde the Lady Margrett Coventry deliver'd of a Daughter in her father, the Earle of Thannett's House att Hothfield in Kent, which was christened the daie after by the name of Magarett, (it being her second Daughter but third chyld; for her second Sonne and eldest Daughter are both dead). And this was the first time shee was delivered of anie of her Children in the said House wherein her selfe was borne, and wherein her Father and Mother and their younger children and her owne eldest Sonne John Coventry now lay. I lying now in my Howse or Castle of Skipton in Craven.

The first of October did Mr John Turner with his wife Elizabeth Turner (who was a Miss Rolls, and had served mee from her childehood till now, viz: since the latter end of May 1629) and their daughter Elizabeth, goe quite away from my Howse or Castle of Skipton and from serving mee, onwards on their Journy towards London. Whither they came safe and well the fifteenth daie following, to Baynards Castle (haveing layne some three or four nights by the way in their Howse in Oxfordshire). But notwithstanding, her Husband is to continew my Officer for the Receivinge of my Jointure Rents in the Isle of Sheppey in Kent as long as he shall please.

The seventh daie of the said October did I and my family with my Grandchylde John Tufton, remove from my Howse or Castle of Skipton in Craven towards Appleby Castle in Westmerland, whither I came safe and well the daie following, being the eight daie (having layen one night as I usually did att Kirkby Lonsdale by the way in the Inne there). And so I now lay in this Appleby Castle till the three and twentieth day of Aprill following, that I removed from thence with my family to Brougham Castle in Westmorland. But whylst I now lay in Appleby Castle I had newes of the sad losse and death of ye Lady Isabella Compton, second daughter to my Daughter of Northampton and her Lord. Which Lady Isabella dyed ye third day of March in the late Countess Dowager of River's house in Queene Streete, London, where her father and Mother now lay, she being a yeare and about eight monthes old at her death, and was buryed in the Vault of Compton Church in Warwickshire.

In the yeare of ower Lorde God 1658

And the three and twentieth day of Aprill after I had layen in Apleby Castle from the eight of October last till now, did I remove with my Grandchilde Mr John Tufton and my family into my Castle of Brougham in Westmorland. And thee 17th day of February, whilst I lay at Appleby Castle before my now coming to Brougham, did I send my Grandchilde Mr John Tufton with his two men to Croome House in Worcestershire to see his sister Coventry and her husband and children and her father-in-law the Lord Coventry, where he lay for a few nights with them, and returned to mee back againe to Appleby Castle the 29th daie of March following. Soe hee went thither by Lancaster, Preston, Manchester, Chester, Flint Castle, Denbigh and other partes of North Wales, and came back againe by Warwick, Coventry and Littlefeilde and those parts. This being the first time he was ever in those places in Wales.

The 16th daie of June this Summer did my grandchilde Mr John Tufton goe for one night to Corby Castle in Cumberland, my Cozen Sir Francis Howard's House, where he lay that one night and returned back againe to mee the next day to Brougham Castle.

The 25th daie of this June was my first Grandchilde Nicholas, Lord Tufton, released of his Restrainte and Imprisonment in the Tower of London where he had layne the second time as a Prisoner ever since the eleventh day of September in 1656.

And the same 25th daie of June after I had taken my leave of him the night before, did my Grandchilde Mr John Tufton go away from mee from Brougham Castle towards London to his Father and Mother, whither he came well to them to their House in Aldersgate Streete the first daie of the month following, and lay there till the tenth of August, that he went over sea into the Low Countryes with his Sister the Lady Frances Tufton, where they remayned about some two Monthes, and returned againe together into England the 7th of October following.

And this Summer did I cause great repaires to bee made on the oulde

Walles of Skipton Castle in Craven, and also at Barden Tower. My Steward, Gabriell Vincent, lying in both of these places a great part of the Summer to take order about the finishing of the said Repaires.

And the beginning of this Spring I did cause Bongate Church nere Apleby to bee pulld downe and new built upp against att my owne charge.

This Summer also I caused the Chappell att Brougham to bee pulled downe and new built upp againe larger and stronger than it was before, at my owne charge.

This Summer on the Nynteenth, Twentieth and one and twentieth dayes of August was the Assizes kept at Appleby. John Parker one of the Barons of the Exchequer and Richard Nudigate one of the Judges of the Upper Bench, where they now lay three nights in Appleby Castle. Judge Parker in the Baron's Chamber, and Judge Nudigate in the Great Tower. And by the way thither, as they came from Carlisle, they both of them came to see mee at Brougham Castle and dyned there with mee.

And at this Assize my Cozen Philip, Lord Wharton, and his brother Sir Thomas Wharton lay both at Appleby Castle, where my Lord Wharton had some Tryalls.

And after, both hee and his Brother came two or three tymes to Brougham Castle (where I then lay) to see mee. This being the first tyme I saw my said Cozen the Lord Wharton after the death of his second Wife. And hee and his Brother went both of them out of Westmerland a while after.

And the Twentyeight of this August, did my Daughter the Countess of Thanett come hither to mee to Brougham Castle from London , with three of her younger Sonnes, Richard, Thomas and Sackvile. This being the first time I ever saw these three Sonnes of hers here in Westmerland, or in any other parte of the Landes of myne Inheritance, and the third tyme of her coming into this County to mee. And I saw her not since the twenty eight of July 1656 till this Twentyeight of this month that she now came hither to mee, where shee and her three Sonnes now lay for nyne nights together. Soe as I have now seen Nyne of my said Daughter's Children here in Westmerland which I account a great and singular Blessinge and Goodnesse of God towards mee.

And they went away from hence from mee the sixt day of September following, through Whinfield to Appleby Castle where they lay that night, and the next day went over Staynemoore towards London. Whither they gott well to their House in Aldersgate Streete the fourteenth daie of the same Month. And the seventeenth day they went downe to their House at Raynham in Kent and there lay all night, from whence they gott well to Hothfield the next day to my Lord of Thannett, my Sonne in Law and to his eldest Sonne my Lord Tufton, with fower other of his youngest Children, who are all of them his Wyfe's, my eldest Daughter's children, for which God be praised.

This Summer, by some few mischievous people, secretly in the night was there broken off and taken downe from thatt Tree nere the Paile of Whinfield Parke (which for that cause was called the Hartshorne Tree) one of those ould Hartes hornes which (as mentioned in the Summary of my Auncester Robert, Lord Clifford's life)[*] were sett up in the yeare 1333 att a general hunting, when Edward Balioll the King of Scotts came into England by permission of King Edward the third, and lay for a while in the said Robert Lord Clifford's Castle in Westmerland. Where the said King hunted a great Stagg which was killed nere the said Oake Tree. In memory whereof the Hornes were nayled upp in it, groweing as it were naturally in the Tree, and have remayned there ever since till thatt in the year 1648 one of these Hornes was broken downe by some of the Army, and the other was broken downe as aforesaid this yeare. So as now there is no parte thereof remayning and the Tree itself being now so decayed, and the Partes of it so peeled off that it cannot last long.

Whereby wee may see that Tyme brings to forgettfullness any memorable thing in this world, bee they never soe carefully preserved, for the Tree with the Hartes horne upon it was a Thing of much note in these partes.

And whilst I now lay in Brougham Castle, did my Grandchilde Mr John Tufton and the Lady Frances Tufton his sister, come home from the City of Utrecht in the Low Countryes and took shipping at the Brill in Holland the seventh day of October, landed the eight daie at Deale in Kent, and so came safe with their Company on the nynth daie following to their Father's House at Hothfield.

Eccles. 8.6.

The 30th day of this October did I and my family remove from my Castle of Brougham to Appleby Castle againe, after I had layen in this Brougham Castle from the 23rd day of Aprill untill now. And I continewed to lye in this Appleby Castle till the 5th day of May in 1569, at which time I removed from thence with my family to my Castle of Skipton in Craven.

---

[*] See the second volume of the Books of Record.

In the yeare of
our Lorde God 1659

And while I now lay in Appleby Castle in Westmerland, upon Thursday the 14th day of Aprill was my younger Daughter, Isabella, Countesse of Northampton brought to bed of her third Sonne and her fifth child, in a hyred house where she and her Lord and their familie now lay in Lincolns Inne fields att London, who was christened the day after by the name of James, this being the first time that she had two Sonnes alive at one time. But this Grandchild of myne dyed in Canonbury House by Islington the first day of August 1662, a good while after his Mother's death.

And the 5th day of this May being Thursday, did I remove with my family from Appleby towards Skipton in Craven, whither I came well the next day having layd one night by the way in the Inne at Kirkby Lonsdale.

And I had not layne in this Skipton Castle nor bin at itt since the 7th day of October in 1657, when I removed from thence with my familie to Appleby Castle in Westmerland, being about a yeare and 6 monthes. And now I did continue to lye in this Skipton Castle in the Round Chamber (where I had layne at such times as I have lived there ever since I first came to lye there in 1649), till the 9th December following, at which time I removed from thence to Barden Tower to lye there in itt for a time, this being the first time since I was borne that I came to lye in this Barden Tower.

And the 23rd Day of this May my Grandchild Mr John Tufton and his Sister the Ladie Frances Tufton, with Mrs Sibilla Baker her Gentle-woman, that had bin abroad with her in the Low Countryes, and Henrie Hatfield that now served my Grandchilde John Tufton in Alexander Whitcher's place, lately deceased, did come hither to me into my House or Castle of Skipton in Craven from their Journy from Yorke and from London. And this was the first time I saw this Grandchilde of mine, the Ladie Frances Tufton either in Craven or in any of the Landes of mine

Inheritance. And I had not seen her Brother John since Midsummer last that he went from mee from Brougham Castle towards London, till now.

Soe these two Grandchildren of mine lay here at Skipton Castle untill the 4th of Julie, that they went from hence to the Wells at Knaresborough where they lay for 17 daies to take the Watters, and the 28th of the same month they returned back to mee at Skipton againe, and stay'd there till the 10th of September following, when they went away from hence with their two servants in my Coach and six horses to Yorke, lying there all day on Sundaie, and the next day being the 12th of that month they went away in an Hired Coach towards London, whither they came well to their Mother to her Lodging in Aldersgate Streete, the 17th day of this month. And three daies after, Ladie Frances went downe to her Sister, Ladie Margaret Coventrie to Croome in Worcestershire, whither she came well the 24th day of the sayd September.

And the beginning of this Summer, a little before my comeing out of Westmorland, did I cause the Church of Nine Kirke to be pull'd down and new built up againe in the same place, larger and bigger than it was before, which was finished the latter end of the Summer – (Though my selfe and my familie were then at my Castle of Skipton in Craven) – And this Church of Nine Kirke would in all likelyhood have fallen downe it was soe ruinous, if it had not bin repayred by mee.

And this Aprill after I had first bin there my selfe to direct the Building of it, did I cause my old decayed Castle of Brough to be repaired, and also the old Tower called the Roman Tower in the sayd Castle, and a Courthouse for keeping of my Courtes in some 12 or 14 Roomes to be built in it upon the old foundacion.

The 21st day of August this Summer by reason of the troubles now a foot in these Northerne Partes, though it was Sundaie, yet did the two Judges of Assize for the Northerne Circuit, Francis Thorpe and John Parker come that night from Carlisle to my Castle of Appleby in Westmerland, where they continued to lye till Fryday morning following, from whence they then went to Kendall that night and the next day to Lancaster to keepe the Assizes there alsoe. And notwithstanding these Judges now lay here, yet was there then a Garrison of Soldiers in the Castle.

And the 27th of this August being Saturday was my grandchilde the Ladie Margaret Coventrie delivered of a Sonne which was her 5th Childe, and is now her second Sonne, in her father in law the Lord Coventrie's House at Croome in Worcestershire. I then lying at Skipton Castle in Craven as also did her Brother, Mr John Tufton and her Sister Ladie Frances Tufton, this being the first time that my said Grandchilde

Lady Margaret Coventrie had the blessing and happinesse to have two sonnes alive together at one time. Which sonne Thomas dyed at Croome where he was borne the 17th June 1660.

And about the 4th day of this August was my Sonne in Law the Earle of Northampton committed close Prisoner to the Tower of London upon some suspicion that he was ingaged in the late Insurrection in England,* my Daughter his Wife being also there in his Lodgings, where he continued Prisoner till the second Day of November following, that he was released of his sayd Imprisonment in the Tower and went to live with my Daughter his wife in the House in Lincoln's Inne Fields in London where they lived before.

And this Summer my first Grandchilde Nicholas, Lord Tufton went from his father and mother and having layne for some time at the Wells at Epsome in Surrey, he went over secretly into France, from whence in the Winter following he came over againe to his father and Mother and his Brothers and Sisters.

And this Summer, though I found the Castle of Skipton for the most part well finished and better than I expected it could have bin, yet I could not lye in it partly by reason of the garrison of Foote soldiers which was put in there about the 4th of August under the command of Ensign Robert Fennett, for the securing thereof by reason of the troubles now in England.

And about the sayd 4th of August was there also a garrison of foote soldiers putt into Appleby Castle in Westmerland, into the great Tower there call'd Caesar's Tower, which I lately repayred, but after they had layne a while there, they went away and quitted it, and after they were gone others came in their Roome but stayed not long, as likewise into Brougham Castle for a while; both of which Castles these soldiers not long after quitted and went away.

And the 9th of this December after I had layne in this House or Castle of mine of Skipton ever since the 6th of May last, did I remove from thence with my familie to Barden Tower to lye in it for a time, which was the first time that I did ever lye in this Barden Tower, having lately repaired it to my great Costs and Charges, when it was then a most ruinous and decayed place. For my Mother had never layne in it since she was with Childe with mee, nor my Father in a good while before. Neither did my Uncle of Cumberland or my Cozen his Sonne ever lye in

---

* A Presbyterian rising led by Sir George Booth, which contributed to the political chaos ensuing upon Cromwell's death on 3 September 1658 and the resignation of his son, Richard, in May 1660.

it after they came to this Estate in Craven. And I lay now in this Barden Tower till the 8th day of October following, that I removed thence with my familie towards Appleby Castle in Westmerland.

Soe this yeare I had the Blessing to have two male children borne into the world of the generation of my Bodie; these are – James Compton, now youngest sonne of my Daughter of Northampton, and the other, Thomas Coventrie now youngest sonne to my Grandchilde the Ladie Margaret Coventrie. But this Thomas Coventrie dyed at Croome in Worcestershire, where he was borne, the 17th day of June in 1660. And this James, Lord Compton dyed at Canonbury neere Islington the 1st of August 1662, after the death of his Mother, so as they both dyed in infancy.

In the yeare of ower Lorde God 1660

The 25th Day of Aprill this Yeare a New Parliament began to sitt at Westminster wherein were chosen, most part by my means, Knights of the Shire of Westmerland, my two Cozens – Sir Thomas Wharton and Sir John Lowther of Lowther, Knight and Barronett; and for Burgesses of the Burrough of Appleby my Cozen Sir Henry Cholmely and Christopher Clapham Esq, which Parliament proved to be a happie Parliament by calling in our Rightful Prince King Charles the Second into England, wherein also Generall George Monck the Generall of the Armie in Scotland was a great and a Happie Instrument; his Majestie with his two Brothers the Dukes of Yorke and Glocester comeing out of the Low Countries by See into England about the 25th day of May, and landed at Dover in Kent, and so went by Land to Canterbury and Rochester, and the 29th day following (being his Majestie's Birth day) Hee made his triumphant entrie through the Cittie of London to Whitehall to ly there againe.* But this great joy was clouded with sorrow for the death of his younger Brother Henry, Duke of Glocester, who dide the 14th day of September following of the small Pox at Whitehall in the Princes Lodging there, and was buryed a while after in King Henery ye 7th's Chappell at the Abbey Church in Westminster among many of his Auncesters. And his eldest sister Mary, Princess of Orange dyed at Whitehall the 24th daie of December following, and was buryed by him in the said King Henery ye 7th's Chappel. She was Widdow to William, the last Prince of Orange.

---

* Cromwell's disaffected commander-in-chief of the army of occupation in Scotland, George Monck, invaded England on 1 January 1660 and occupied London on 3 February. The Long Parliament (which had assembled on 3 November 1640) was dissolved on 16 March, and the way was made clear for the restoration of the monarchy by the new parliament's acceptance of a declaration made by the exiled Charles II, which had been issued at Monck's prompting.

BROUGH CASTLE, Westmorland, drawn and engraved by Samuel and Nathaniel Buck (1739)

And in Aprill and May this yeare did the Masons begin to build up againe and repaire my Castle of Brough in Westmerland, a good part whereof had bin repaired the last Summer, and the Remainder thereof now this Summer, being taken in hand after it had layne Ruinous ever since the year 1524, that it was burnt downe in Henrie Lord Clifford's time, about two yeares and a little more before his death, he dying in the 15th yeare of King Henerie the 8th. And this Brough Castle and the Roman Tower in it was soe well repaired by mee that the 16th of September in the next yeare I lay there for three nights together, which none of my Auncestors had done in 140 yeares till now.

And in June this Yeare by my directions was also my decayed Castle of Pendraggon in Mallerstang in the said Countie of Westmerland begun to be repaired, which had layne waste (as appears by manie Records in Skipton Castle before the late Civill Warres) ever since the time of King Edw. the 3rd, when the Scotts did then burne down the Timber of it, and demolish'd with their often Inroads and Incursions into England, there being in his time sharp and bitter warrs betweene the two Nations; and it was soe well repaired by mee that on the 14th Octobre in the yeare following I lay there for 3 nights together, which none of my Auncestors had done since Idonea, ye younger sister to Isabella de Viteripont lay in it, who dyed the 8th yeare of Edward the third, without issue.

The 17th day of June being Trinitie Sunday, dyed little Thomas Coventrie second Sonne to my Grandchilde the Ladie Margrett Coventrie, in his Grandfather, the Lord Coventrie's House at Croome in Worcestershire, where this Child to whom I was great Grandmother, was borne into the world but the 27th of August before, and his dead Body was buryed in the Church there; whose death I esteemed as a Loss and Crosse to us all; and then did his little Sister Margaret and her father lye in the sayd Croome House in Worcestershire, but his Mother and his oldest brother lay then in Thanett House in Aldersgate Streete, London, with her father and Mother.

And the 10th day of March in this yeare dyed my vertuous and good Cozen german Margarett Wharton, then the widdow Lady Wharton in her House at Canterbury, formerly a part of the Pryory there. She that was borne in Skipton Castle in Craven in 1581. And she was burried a while after near to her Husband Edw. Lord Wharton in ye Church of Barton in Kent. And when she dyed did I lye in Barden Tower in Craven.

The 27th day of Julie in this yeare 1660 did my youngest Daughter Isabella, Countess of Northampton with her two eldest Children William, Lord Compton and Ladie Anne Compton come hither to mee into Barden Tower in Yorkshire from their journy from Edington in Wiltshire and Compton in Warwickshire, where they now lay in this Barden Tower with mee 10 nights together in the 4 roomes on the Westside of the Great Chamber, this being the first time that I ever saw Ladie Anne Compton or any of my said Daughter of Northampton's Daughters. And whilst they were here did my Daughter of Northampton with these two children of hers goe the 31st day of this month into Skipton Castle for a while to see it, this being the first time she ever saw it since I last repaired the decayed part of it. And the first time her Daughter Ladie Anne was ever in this Skipton Castle. Neither had my sayd Daughter or her eldest Sonne bin in it since the 30th day of June 1657 till now. And on the 6th day of August following my sayd Daughter of Northampton and her two eldest Children and servants went away from hence towards her Lord's House of Compton in Warwickshire whither they came safe and well about 5 or 6 daies after with their whole company, my Lord of Northampton himself meeting them there from London.

And this 6th day of August was the last time I ever saw these two Grandchildren of mine, William, Lord Compton and Ladie Anne Compton his sister, for she dyed the 14th of December following and he dyed the 18th September in 1661, just 9 months after his sister's death, to my unspeakable greife and sorrow. And it was likewise the last time I saw their Mother, my Daughter.

The 5th day of September being Wedensday did the King's two Judges of Assize for the Northerne Circuit, viz: Sir Thomas Twisden and Sir Robert Bernard come into my Castle of Appleby in Westmerland when they now lay 5 nights together. Judge Twisden in the Barron's Chambre and Judge Barnard in the cheife chambre in Caesar's Tower. And when they were past, the 10th of the same month they went away from thence forward in their Circuit. And this was the first time that this Sir Thomas Twisden was ever in Appleby Castle or any part of mine Inheritance, whose great Grandfather was that Sir Thomas Hennige that was Vice Chamberlain to Queene Elizabeth and in great favour with her the most part of her Reign. And my father and Mother loved that Vice Chamberlain extremely and he them.

Towards the latter end of this Summer I caused my Mill about a mile from Barden Towre in Yorkshire called Hough's Mill to be pulled downe and newbuilt up againe with stone and wood at my owne charge, for it was so ruinous as it was like to fall down, having not bin repair'd many yeares before till now.

The second Day of this Octobre in 1660 did Richard, Earle of Corke and his two Sonnes my Cozens, Charles, Lord Dungarvan and Mr Richard Boyle come hither into this Barden Tower and dined with mee, but went back againe the same day into their House at Bolton some two miles hence, whence they now lay for a little time; and I had sene none of them since about last Summer was 10 yeares when they then were at Skipton Castle with me sometimes, and I with them at Bolton till this day that they came hither to mee againe.

The 8th of Octobre in this yeare did I and my family remove out of my Towre of Barden in Craven towards Appleby Castle in Westmerland, and lay three nights by the Way, viz: the first night at Paitley Bridge, the second at Street House not far from Bidell and the third night at Bowz [Bowes], and so over Stainmoore to Appleby Castle and came safe and well thither the 11th day, after I had layen in that Tower of Barden ever since the 9th day of December in 1659, till now. And by the Way in this my journy from Barden to Appleby Castle I went hard by Snape, a House of the Earle of Exeters. And I had not bin at Bowz nor on Stainmoore nor in these Waies since the 9th of December 1616 when I then went up from Brougham Castle in Westmerland to London to my first Lord Richard Earle of Dorsett and the Ladie Margt Sackville, my then only child, till the 11th day of this October that I came to lye in this Appleby Castle againe, where I had not layn since about the 5th day of May in 1659 till nowe.

And I had not layne 3 nights together out of some of my Houses in Craven and Westmerland since the yeare 1649, when I came from London into the North, till this time that I lay out three nights as I was in my journy from Barden Tower to Appleby Castle; for heretofore I did but to lye out one night in my Removes between Craven and Westm'r-land since my sayd comeing downe and that was at Kirkby Lonsdale.

And when I now came to lye in Appleby Castle in Westmerland I continued to lye in it till the 29th of October in 1661, excepting 6 nights, 3 whereof I lay in Brough Castle and the other 3 in Pendraggon Castle in that Countie, and that 29th day of October in 1661 I removed with my familie from Appleby Castle into my Castle of Brougham in the same Countie.

And the 15th day of this December (being Satturday) while I then lay in this Appleby Castle in Westmerland, dyed my Grandchilde the Ladie Anne Compton eldest Daughter to my Daughter of Northampton and her Lord, in her Father's House in Lincolns Inne Fields at London, when she was 5 yeares and about five months, to my great greife and sorrow, for she was a child that promised much goodnesse. And the 6th day of August before she went away from mee from Barden Tower in Craven with her eldest Brother ye Lord Compton and their Mother towards Warwickshire, Northamptonshire and London; it being the last time I ever saw this Grandchilde of mine the Ladie Anne Compton. And she was burried in the vault of Compton Church in Warwickshire, by her father's Ancestors.

About the second of November this yeare did Queen Marie [Henrietta Maria], Queene Dowager of England, Daughter to King Henry the 4th of France, widdow to our late Kinge and Mother to our now King Charles the second, come over seas out of France into England with her youngest Daughter the Princess Henrietta, and she now lay at Whitehall in her owne Lodgeings there for about two months, for on the second of Januarie following she went away from thence with her sayd youngest Daughter to Portsmouth, and so over seas into France againe; and this Queene had not bin in England since July in 1644 till now.

And a little after their comeing againe into France was the sayed Princesse Henrietta married to her Cozen german the Duke of Orleans and Anjou. He that is second and only Brother to the now Kinge of France. And this 2nd of November was the first time that the sayd Queene Dowager came into England after her Sonne King Charles was restored to his Crowne, and though she went soone after into France, as above-said yet she came againe into England ye 28th of July 1662 and stay'd till 1665.

About the 7th day of December did three of my Daughter of Thanet's younger Sonnes, that is to say John, Richard and Thomas Tufton, goe from their Father and Mother and eldest Brother and their two youngest Brothers and their four younger sisters, out of Thanet House in Aldersgate Streete and out of London Towne. And soe, after a short stay at their Father's House at Hothfield in Kent they went to Dover and from thence in the Packett Boat to Calais in France. And from thence they went to Paris, to Orleans and from thence to Blois where they intend to live for a time. This being the first time that my Daughter of Thanett's said two sonnes Richard and Thomas were ever beyond the Seas, but their Brother John had bin twice before this beyond the Seas in the Low Countries though never in France; and they all three came over well into England againe to their Father and Mother and some of their Brothers and Sisters at Hothfield in Kent about the beginning of March in 1663 as ye yeare begins on New Yeares Day.

In the yeare of
ower Lorde God 1661

The 14th day of March in this yeare was my Daughter of Northampton delivered of her third Daughter and sixth Childe, the Ladie Alethea Compton – in her Lordes House in Lincolnes Inne feilds at London, which Childe was christened about two daies after. I then lying in Appleby Castle in Westmerland. And the 14th daie of October following dyed her Mother, my Daughter of Northampton in the said House in Lincolnes Inne feilds after she had but a while before come up thither to take phisick, from Castle Ashby in Northamptonshire, from her last seeing her eldest Sonne William Lord Compton whom she left there behind her, and from Woburne, ye Earle of Bedford's House in Bedfordshire.

And about the 21st day of May was the old decayed Mill at Brough pull'd downe and is to be newbuilt againe by my dictations. Which was done so well and in so good a manner that I was in al myselfe, and lyked it very well on the 16th of September following when I went to lye in Brough Castle.

The 23rd of Aprill in this yeare (I then lying in Appleby Castle in Westmerland) was our King Charles the second crown'd King of England in Abbey Church at Westminster with great solemnitie, for which God be praised.

And the 17th of May this yeare did Elizabeth the Widdow Queene of Bohemia,[*] come over seas out of the Low Countries into England to the Cittie of London, to her two nephews Charles the second our King of England, and James, Duke of Yorke, after she had bin now out of England 48 yeares and a month over. And she now continued to lye at London for the most parte in the Lord Craven's House in Denorie Lane till the 13th of Februarie following [when] she died in the newbuilt

[*] Daughter of James I and sister of Charles I, known as the 'Winter Queen'; she was married in 1613 to Frederick V, Elector Palatine in Germany.

House called Leicester House in the fields not farr from Charring Crosse, to which House she removed about a month before her death. And now none of her Children were with her when she dyed, but her Sonne Prince Rupert who was then in England and present at her death.

And the 9th day of August this yeare did my Daughter of Thanett come hither to mee over Stainmoore into this Appleby Castle in Westmerland from Her journy from London with her three youngest Daughters, Ladie Cecily, Ladie Marie and Lady Anne Tufton to my great joy and comfort, where she and her Daughter Ladie Cecily now lay together in the Baron's Chamber, and her two younger Daughters in the next Chamber to it for 11 nights together, in which time they went with mee the 11th daie of this month into Appleby Church, and the 18th of it into Bongate Church.

And on the 20th day they went away from mee from this Appleby Castle after I had taken leave of them in my owne Chamber, onwards on their journy towards London, over Stainmoore. And by the Way they went awhile into my Castle of Brough in Westmerland to see the new Buildings there, which was the first time that ever any of my posteritie came into that Castle since it was lately repaired by mee.

And I had not seene this eldest Daughter of mine since the 6th of September in 1658 when she went away with three of her younger Sonnes from my Castle of Brougham in Westmerland towards London, till now. And I had not seene these three youngest Daughters of hers since the 28th of Julie in 1656 till this time. And this is the fourth time my Daughter of Thanett hath come into Westmerland to mee.

And the 6th day of July was my Grandchilde the Lady Margaret Coventrie deliver'd of her third Sonne and fifth Childe, Mr William Coventrie who dyed the 14th of Julie 1662.

And the 24th of August this yeare (being Saturday) did Sir Christopher Turner one of the Barons of his Majesties Court of Exchequer, and Sir Robt. Bernard a Serjeant at Law, His majesties Justices of Assize for the Northerne Circuit, come from Carlisle hither to Appleby Castle where they now lay 5 nights together. Judge Turner in the Baron's Chamber and Judge Bernard in the best Roome in Caesar's Towre. And on Thursday following (the 29th day), about 9 a clock, they went away from hence towards Lancaster to keep the Assizes there also, lying at Kendall that night by the way. And I lay now here in this Appleby Castle while these Judges lay here, which I had not done since August 1653 till now.

The 10th day of September this yeare, I sent downe to my Almeshouse here at Appleby the King's Letters Patents under the great Seale of England for making the said Almeshouses a Corporation, being a perpetuitie granted to me for the foundation thereof , dated at Westminster the 2nd day of the last month; which was now layed up in the Chest or trunk in the Mothers Chamber there under lock and key, to be kept amongst the rest of the writings and Evidences concerning the foundacion of the said Almeshouse, and the lands of St Nicholas neere Appleby, and the Manor of Brougham which I purchased for the maintenance thereof.

On Saturday the 18th day of this September about 2 a clocke in the afternoone (to my great greife) dyed my most deare Grandchilde William, Lord Compton in his father's House at Castle Ashbie in Northamptonshire, when he was eight yeares three monthes and about eighteen days old. He being a Childe of great hopes and perfection, both of Bodie and Mind. And his Brother and his Sister and their father lay there then with him. But his Mother was then at London under the Phisicians handes, and lay in her Lords House there at Lincolns Inne feilds. I then lying in Appleby Castle in Westmerland as I did also at his birth. And thither this sad newes was brought mee by a letter from his father the 27th day of the said September to Appleby Castle where I then lay.

And the 16th day of this month did I remove out of Appleby Castle into Brough Castle in Westmerland where I now lay for three nights together, the first night in that halfe round Tower call'd Clifford's Tower, and the other two nights in the second Roome of the great Tower call'd Roman Tower, both of which Towers and Castle were newly repaired by mee to my exceeding great Cost and Charges after they had layen desolate ever since the Timber thereof was casually burnt in the yeare 1521, some two yeares and a little more before the death of that Henrie Lord Clifford, my Auncestor who was father to Henrie Lord Clifford first Earle of Cumberland. Soe as none of my Auncestors have layed in it since about the 14th or 15th of Aprill in 1659 when it was then a repairing till this time that I now lay in it.

And the 14th of October in this yeare, about 8 a clocke in the morning, dyed my youngest Daughter Isabella, Countesse of Northampton, in her Lords House in Lincolns Inne feilds at London, when she was 39 yeares old and some 13 daies over; her two Children (that are now onlie left alive), viz: James, Lord Compton and Lady Alethea Compton and their father the Earle of Northampton lying then in that House; and then did I ly in my owne Chamber in Apleby Castle in Westmerland from whence I removed ye same day some two or three howres after, into Pendragon Castle in Westmerland to lye there for three nights. But I did

PENDRAGON CASTLE, Westmorland, drawn and engraved by Samuel and Nathaniel Buck (1739)

not have the sadd Newes of her Death till after I came from thence into Apleby Castle againe.

Also, the same 14th day of this October about 9 a clock in the morning, after she was dead (though I then knew it not) did I remove out of Appleby Castle in Westmerland into Pendraggon Castle in the same Countie, where I now lay in the second Storie that looks East and South, for three nights together; and when they were past I came from thence into this Appleby Castle againe to lye in it as before. This being the first time I lay in the said Pendraggon Castle since it was lately repaired and made habitable by mee to my great costs and charges after it had layen desolate ever since the 15th yeare of Edward the third in 1341, which is 320 yeares agoe, for then (as old Records and Chronicles it appears) the Scotts made an Inroad into the West of England totally destroying it and pulling downe all the timber and a greate parte of the Stone building of it. But before that it was the cheife and beloved habitation of Idonea the younger Daughter and Coheire of Robert de Viteriponte my Auncestor, she dying without issue (as appears by Inquisition) later after her death in the 8th yeare of Edward the third; and then all her Inheritance in Westmerland came to her eldest Sister Isabella's Grandchild Robert, Lord Clifford and his posteritie to whom I am heire by a lineal descent.

And after I came from Pendraggon Castle in Westmerland, I lay now in Appleby Castle some 12 nights, before I removed from thence to Brougham Castle in the sayd Countie, whither I and my familie came safe the 29th daie of this October, to lye there in it for a time in the same Chamber where my Noble Father was borne and my Blessed Mother dyed, after I had layne in Appleby Castle ever since the 11th of this October, was almost a month (excepting only six nights, 3 wherof I lay in Brough Castle and the others in Pendraggon Castle in Westmerland as is before mentioned).

And the 27th daie of this October whilst I lay in Appleby Castle in Westmorland dyed Thomas, Lord Coventrie in his House in Lincolns Inne fields, London, of the Gangreene that was in severall of his Toes; he whose eldest Sonne now George, Lord Coventrie, did about 8 yeares 3 months and some daies over marrie my Grandchild the Ladie Margaret Tufton, then and now the oldest Daughter to my Daughter of Thanet and her Lord.

And the 29th daie of this Octobre (as is before set downe) did I remove with my familie out of Appleby Castle in Westmorland to Brougham Castle in the same Countie to lye there for a time in the same Chamber wherein my Noble Father was borne and Blessed Mother dyed. After I had layen in Appleby Castle aforesaid ever since the 11th of Octobre was a twelvemonth. And I now continued to lye in the sayd Chamber in Brougham Castle for 9 months and 2 daies, viz: till the 1st of August following that I removed from thence into my sayd Castle of Appleby againe to lye in it for a little time. And during ye time of my lying in Brougham Castle I received the Sacrament there once at Christmas in the Chappell at Brougham Castle, once at Ninekirks on Easter Daie, and once at Brougham Chappell the 27th of July; which Chappell I had lately built, and this was the first time that I ever received the Sacrament in this Brougham Chappell.

In the yeare of
ower Lorde God 1662

On the 13th of Februarie this yeare dyed Elizabeth, Queen Dowager of Bohemia. She that was Aunt to oure King Charles the second and James, Duke of Yorke; and she dyed in Leicestre House in the fields neere Charring Cross at London, and was burried in Henry the Seventh's Chappell in the Abbey Church at Westminster neere to her Father and Mother and her nephew, Henry Duke of Gloucester and his sister Elizabeth, after she had now liv'd in England since about the 17th day of May last. And she dyed the Eve of that day was 49 yeares that she was married to Frederick, Prince Elector Palatine her Husband. I now lying in Brougham Castle in Westmorland when she dyed.

And the 22nd of March in this yeare I had a swounding fit hereby I was in great Danger of death, but it pleas'd God to restore mee to life and health againe in a very short space.

The 30th day of this March being Easter Sundaie, I received the Blessed Sacrament in the Church called Ninekirkes, this being the first time I came into it againe after I had repaired and newbuilt the sayd Church.

The 12th day of Aprill this yeare my Sonne in Law James, Earle of Northampton came hither to me from his journy from Castle Ashby in Northamptonshire and the Southerne partes, by Skipton – (where he had not bin since the latter end of June in 1657, when he was there with his Wife and his Sonne William, Lord Compton).

And he went into the Castle to see the Roomes in it, and in his journy from Skipton he lay at Ingleton by the Way, and the same 12th day came hither to me into this Brougham Castle in Westmerland with his Cozen Mr John Mordant, a younger brother to the last Earle of Peterborough, and they staied here with mee at Brougham Castle 7 nights together, his Lordship lying in the Barron's Chambre and his Cozen Mordant in Graystocks Chambre, and when those 7 nights were past they went away from hence to Carlisle, and so to Edenburgh in Scotland and other places there, where they lay a good while. They returned back by Carlisle hither the 11th day of May following, though it were Sundaie, and then they lay here againe in the same Chambers for 8 nights together. And this was the first time that my Lord of Northampton did ever lye in this Brougham Castle.

And he went the 13th day of Aprill being Sunday, in the afternoone into the Chappell at Brougham to hear the Sermon there, that being the first time he was ever in that Chappell. And the 18th of May following, he went to the Church at Nine Kirks in the forenoon to the Sermon there, that being also the first time he was ever in that Chappell.

And the 19th of May they went away from mee from Brougham Castle to Kirkby Lonsdale where they lay that night, and the next night they lay in Barden Tower in Craven, this being the first time that either my Lord of Northampton or his Cozen Mordant ever lay in that Barden Tower. From whence, the 21st day, they went onwards on their journie Southwards. And he came well to his House in Lincolns Inn fields at London to his two children James, Lord Compton, and the Ladie Alethea Compton his Sister.

Our younge Queene Katherine, the Infanta of Portugal Daughter of the late King and Sister to this King of Portugal, after she had taken leave of the Queen Dowager her Mother, the King of Portugall her brother, and her younger Sisters, aboard one of our Kings Great Shipps rideing neere Lisbon, took her voyage and landed safely about the 14th of May at Portsmouth in Hampshire, after she had layen upon the Seas in her journie from Lisbon ever since about the 23rd of Aprill till now; and our King Charles the second came to her to Portsmouth about the 20th day of this month, and married her there in a publick manner the next day, being the 21st of this May, and so from thence Hee and She went the 28th day to Winchester, and so by Farnham Castle to Hampton Courte whither they came to lye the 29th of this May. And thither my Daughter went to see this new Queene the 4th of June following, I then lying in Brougham Castle in Westmerland.

This Summer did I cause a New Brewhouse and Bakhouse to be built up in the Court within the Walles of Brougham Castle in Westmerland, whereof one side was built in the old wall towards the North and the other syde on the old Wall towards the West. And now did I also cause the old Brewhouse and Bakhouse to be taken downe and the ground levelled, which old Brewhouse and Bakehouse stood neere to the Tower of Leagan. And this removing of it made the Court larger and hansomer than it was before.

And this Summer did I cause a Kitching, a Stable, a Bakehouse and

Brewhouse to be built in the Court of my Castle of Brough in Westmerland, within the Walles that were lately built there by mee. The Kitchin, Bakehouse and Brewhouse to the North, and the Stable to the Southside thereof.

And this Summer did I cause a Wall of Lime and Stone to be built round about that piece of Ground which I had taken in about Pendraggon Castle, of about 10 quarters in height and 90 Roodes in compasse, and two gates to be made to lett in Horses and Coaches. And within the sayd Wall I caused to be built a Stable and Coachouse, a Brewhouse, Bakehouse and Washhouse, and a little Chamber over the Gate that is arched.

And on the first day of August this yeare, being Lammas Day, about noone I removed with my family out of Brougham Castle in Westmerland to my Castle of Appleby in the sayd Countie, after I had layen in Brougham Castle ever since the 29th of October last till this time, being 9 monthes and 2 daies over. And in this Remove of mine I went through Whinfeild Parke, where I had not bin during the time of my last laying in Brougham Castle till now. Soe I now lay in this Appleby Castle till the 15th day of September following that I removed from thence with my family to Brough Castle in the said Countie, and so to Pendraggon Castle, and so to Barden Tower in Yorkshire, whither I came the 26th of the same September to lye there in it.

And the same first day of August whilst I lay in this Brougham Castle, and some 4 or 5 howre before my remove from thence to Appleby Castle, about 7 a clock in the morning died my Deare Grandchild James, Lord Compton, in his fathers House at Canonburie by Islington neare London, he being the onlie surviving Sonne of his Mother, being but 3 yeares and three monthes old and 16 daies over at his Death; and he was burried ye 8th of this month at night in ye Church at Compton in Warwickshire, his dead Bodie being first open'd and his lungs found much annoyed with glandols sticking to his Ribbes. His Sister, ye Ladie Alethea Compton being also at Canonburry at his death. She being the now only surviving Childe of her Mother; but his father, my Lord of Northampton was then either in Northamptonshire or Warwickshire.

And the 14th day of the month before dyed that William Coventrie who was third Sonne to my Grandchilde ye Ladie Mary Coventry, in her husbands the Lord Coventries House at Croome in Worcestershire, being about a yeare old; and was burried the night after in the Church there at Croome. I then lying in Brougham Castle in Westmerland; and the newes of his death came first of all to mee to Appleby Castle in Westmerland the 5th of this month, by a letter from my Daughter of

The Kendal Diary, 1650–1675

Thanet the same day that I heard of my Lord Comptons death.

And the 16th day of this August did Sir Christopher Turner Kt one of the Barrons of his Majesties Exchequer and Judge of the Assizes for this Northerne Circuit, come hither to Appleby Castle from Carlisle, and he lay 6 nights together in the Barrons Chamber, and on Friday following being the 22nd day, about 10 a clock, hee went away from hence from mee and us here out of this Aplebie Castle to Kendall and so to Lancaster to keepe the Assizes there also. And I now lay here my selfe in this Applebie Castle whilst this Judge stayed here. And this Baron Turner was now the onlie Judge of Assize for this Northerne Circuite, though heretofore two Judges used alwaies to come the Circuite hither.

The 28th of Julie in this yeare, a little before I removed from Brougham Castle, did our Queen Marie the Frenchwoman, Mother to our now King Charles, land at Greenwich in Kent, being newly come from her journie from Calais in France, in a great Shipp over the Seas and so up the River of Thames thither, where she lay for a little while and afterwards continued her journey from thence up the sayd River of Thames in her Shipp to London to her two Sonnes, the King and the Duke of Yorke and their two Wifes. I then lying in Brougham Castle in Westmerland.

And this Queene had not bin in England since about latter end of Januarie 1661, when she took shipp at Portsmouth with her youngest Daughter the Princess Henrietta, and so went out of England over Sea into France, till this time. And she stayed in England from the sayd 28th day of July till the day in 1662 that she went over againe into France.

And on the 15th day of September following did I remove with my familie out of Appleby Castle in Westmerland into my Castle of Brough in the same Countie, where I lay 3 nights together, one night in the highest Roome in Cliffords Tower, and the other two nights in the great Tower call'd the Roman Tower, as I did ye last time I lay there before. And from thence out of that Brough Castle I removed the 18th day of the same month going through Kirkby Stephen and Wharton Parke nere Wharton hall, into Pendraggon Castle in Westmerland, where I lay for 6 nights in the Chamber within the Great Chamber, the windowes whereof looke toward the West and the South, though the 3 nights that I lay there before I lay in the Chambre that is now the great Chambre there.

And from this Pendraggon Castle I removed againe the 24th day of this month, and went through Ravenstonedale into Mr John Otwaie the Lawyers House, in Ingmer by Sedbergh in Yorkshire where I lay in it that one night. And I was not out of Westmerland since the 11th of

October 1660 till now. And the 25th day, from Mr Otwaies House I went neere Kirby Lonsdale within sight thereof, and so by Cowan Bridge, Ingleton and Clapham and those Waies I had formerly gone, into the Inne at Settle where I lay that night, and never lay there before. And the next day being the 26th day, I came over the Moore by Malham Tarne where I had not bin in for 10 yeares before, and so into my House called Barden Tower, and lay in the same Roome where I used to lye.

And continewed to lye in it till the 6th day of May following in 1663, when I removed from thence with my familie into Skipton Castle where I then began to lye in the Chamber wherein I was borne into the World, in that 1st of ye Castles which was repayred by me.

And I had not bene in this Skipton Castle since the 9th of December in 1659, that I removed from thence into Barden Tower, it being a strange and miraculous providence of God that I should at this great age of 73 yeares, come to ly in the same Chamber where I had not layen since I was a childe of eight weekes old, till now.

And some 4 or 6 weekes before my coming out of Westmerland did my Cozen Elizabeth Clifford, Countesse of Corke and her Husband Richard Boyle, Earle of Corke with their five younger children, viz: two Sonnes and three Daughters, goe from their House in Whitefryers at London wherein Elizabeth, Countess of Kent formerly dyed, onwards on there journie towards Bristoll and those parts and so into Wales, where at Milford Haven in Pembrookshire they all went in a Shipp on the Seas wherein they pass'd over to Ireland, hither to Corke Yougall, or Lismore, where they have Houses, and arrived safe there within a while after. After they had resided in England the most part of two yeares and 6 months, excepting a little while that my Lord of Corke and his two Sonnes went over into Ireland hither the last summer or the summer before, but they came quicklie into England againe. And now that they all went into Ireland did the Earle of Corke's eldest Sonnes Wife, she that was the Ladie Jane Seymore, and youngest Daughter to the widdow Dutchesse of Somerset and her deceased husband the Duke, goe over also into Ireland with her Husband, this Charles Boyle Lord Dungarvan, by whom she hath had one Child alreadie (a Daughter), which she left behind her at London with her Mother, it being not a yeare old.

And it was the first time that ever this Ladie Dungarvan came into Ireland or went beyond the Seas. And her sister, Marie, is now beyond Seas in Turkie at Constantinople.

But they came into England againe in the yeare 1663, and so to there House in Whitefryers where, and in other places in England they continued till theire second Daughter Elizabeth came to be married the 11th of Aprill in that yeare to my eldest Grandsonne Nicholas, Lord Tufton, who by the death of his Father the 7th of May following came to be Earle of Thanet.

And a little after that marriage, in Julie following they all came downe into the North to their House at Launsborrow [Londesborough] in Yorkshire, from whence after a while my Lord of Corke and his Ladie with most of there Children came to Bolton Abbey in Craven to lye there for a time, and in that time they went also into my Castle of Skipton and Towre of Barden for a while to see them.* And about that time did there sayd second Daughter and her Lord my Grandchild the Earle of Thanet come hither into this Appleby Castle in Westmerland to mee for a few nights.

---

* Richard Boyle, husband of Lady Anne's cousin Elizabeth (and who was also, incidentally, MP for Appleby from 1640 to 1643), had been created Earl of Cork in 1643 and Baron Clifford of Lanesborough, Yorkshire, in 1644. In 1663/4 he was also made Earl of Burlington (otherwise Bridlington).

In the Yeare of ower Lorde God in 1663

The 2nd day of Aprill in this yeare did my Grandchild Mr John Tufton come from his journie from London hither into this Barden Towre to mee, where I now kiss'd him with much joy a little before suppre, and he told me how he sett forewards on his journie from hitherwards, from his Mother and two of his sisters, Lady Frances and Lady Cecily the 26th day of March last for he and they came hither from Hothfield in Kent from my Lord of Thanet the 16th of the same month, whithere his Mother and the two Sisters returned back againe the 27th day. And when he now came hither to mee he begun to lie in the Best Roome in this Barden Towre at the end of the Great Chambre where my daughter of Northampton lay when she was last here; and his Man, John Gotchley (who was newlie come to him), in the Roome within it.

And I had not seen anie Grandchild of mine since the death of my Daughter of Northampton and three of her children till now, that I saw this John Tufton, and this was the first time that anie of mine Daughter of Thanet's children ever lay in this Barden Towre. And this Grandchild of mine was the more welcome to mee in regard he had escaped death verie narrowlie by a dangerous sickness he had in France the last yeare, which causes me to have in a thankful remembrance God's great mercies to mee, and mine.

And the sixth daie of May in this yeare being Wedensday, did I with my Grandchild Mr John Tufton and my whole family, remove from Barden Tower in Craven (after I had now layen in it ever since the 26th of September last, till now) and came the nerest way through the Haw park to Skipton Castle into the now repayred Old Buildings there, to ly now for a time in the Chamber wherein myself was borne. For though thatt and the cheife partes of the Castle were pulled down by the demmaunds of Cromwell in 1648, yet did I cause it to be rebuilt as it now is in the yeares 1657, 1658 and 1659. And I was not in this Skipton Castle since the 9th of December in 1659, where I went out of it in hast to lye first of all in Barden

SKIPTON CASTLE, Yorkshire, Lady Anne's birthplace, engraved by G. Stow from a drawing by N. Whittock (eighteenth century)

Tower, till this time, that I came now to ly in it againe. And though I was neer the said Castle of Skipton and about the Walles of it with my Blessed Mother about the 12th of October in 1607, when we were then in our journey out of Westmerland towards London, yet I did not come to ly in this Old part of the Castle wherein I was borne, since I was carryed out of it when I was about eight weeks old, [with] my Father and Mother and my Brother Robert, Lord Clifford from thence towards London, till this sixth day of May. And it is to be accounted a great and wonderfull providence of God that now, in the 73rd yeare of my age I shold ly againe in thatt Chamber wherein I was borne into the World.

And the 25th of Januarie in this yeare of 1663 as the same beginnes on New Yeares day, dyed that Mr John Turner, the Recivor of my Jointure Rents in the Isle of Sheppey in Kent, who was Husband to Mrs Elizabeth Turner that was a Nichols and had served me so many yeares; and he dyed in his House at Ramsbury in Wiltshire.

And the 22nd daie of May in this yeare did my Grandchilde Mr John Tufton goe away from mee and us here, out of this Skipton Castle over Cotter and those wayes into Pendraggon Castle in Westmerland, that being the first time that either he or any grandchilde of myne ever lay in that Castle. It was lately repayred by mee. And from thence he went into Appleby Castle and lay there two nights, and the next daie he went to Brough Castle where he lay one night. This being also the first time either he or any Grandchilde of mine lay in that Brough Castle, for I repayred it but lately. And from thence the daie after, he rood through Whinfell Park into Brougham Castle where he lay one night. And while he was now in Westmerland hee went also into Lowther as well as Acrous Link and other places, and was att the Loys raid on Inganby moore, and came home well againe to mee (I thank God) the 29th daie of the same month following. And Hee had not bene in Westmerland since the 25th daie of June in 1658, that hee went hence from Brough Castle towards London, till now.

The 24th day of Julie in this yeare did Mrs Elizabeth Turner the widdow that had served me so manie yeares come from her journie from London and from York, hither to Skipton Castle into the Chambre where I was borne into the world. Soe she lay here 18 nights, the first 7 or 8 nights in the best chamber in the great halfe-round Tower, and the rest in the Chamber called Mrs Widdringtons Chamber below. And I had not seene her since the 9th of May 1660: that she and her Husband Mr John Turner and there Daughtre went away then from mee from Barden Tower in Craven towards London, till now. And I never saw her Husband since, for he dyed in his House at Ramsburie in Wiltshire the 25th day of Januarie last.

And there came now hither with her Mr William Edge, the Receiver of my Sussex Jointure Rents, and he lay in the Withdrawing Chambre next the Gallerie, the time of his staying here saving 6 nights, that he went to Manchester in Lancashire amongst his friends and Kindred. And the 11th day of August following, hee and Mrs Turner went away from hence from mee and my Daughter of Thanet and us here, onwards on their journie towards London.

And the third day of August this Summre being Munday did my Daughtre the Countesse of Thanet with four of her younger Sonnes – Richard, Thomas, Sackville and George Tufton, and her Daughtre Ladie Frances Tufton come hither from their journie from Yorke and from London hither into Skipton Castle in Craven to mee about 8 a clock at night, into the chamber where I then lay, and wherein I was borne into the world; and I then kiss'd them all with much joy and comfort. It being the first time that I saw my Daughtre of Thanet or these four younger Sonnes of hers in Skipton Castle or in Craven, for it was the first time that my Daughtre of Thanet or these her four younger Sonnes ever came into Craven. Neither did I see her daughter Ladie Frances Tufton since she went from me from Skipton Castle ye 10th of September 1659 till now. Nor had I seen my three Grandsons Richard, Thomas and Sackville since they went away with their Mother, my Daughter of Thanet, from Brougham Castle in Westmerland from mee the 6th day of September 1658 till now. Nor had I seene my said youngest grandsonne George Tufton since the 28th of Julie 1656, when he then went away from me from the sayed Brougham Castle with his Mother and his three youngest Sisters towards London till now. And I had not seene my Daughter of Thanet her selfe since she went from mee from Appleby castle in Westmerland towards London with her three youngest Daughters, Ladie Cecily, Ladie Marie and Ladie Anne Tufton on the 20th day of August 1661 till now.

Soe as this journie of hers now this August from London to Skipton Castle to mee was the fifth journy she had taken into the North to see me, for she had bin four severall times with me before in Westmerland.

And my Daughter of Thanet and these four younger Sonnes of hers and her Daughter Ladie Frances, continewed to lye with me in the sayd Skipton Castle, herself and her Daughter Frances lying in the two best Rooms in the Cheife round towre in the Old Building in Skipton Castle newly repayred by me. And her two younger Sonnes Sackville and George lying in the upper great round Roome at the end of the Gallerie; and their Brother Thomas in the round Roome below it, where I formerly used to lye my selfe. And there Brother Richard lying with his brother John Tufton in the greate Roome over the Gatehouse all the time, (save one night that he lay in the withdrawing Roome next the Gallerie), for this Brother John Tufton mett his Mother and four Brothers and sister at Yorke and came hither to Skipton Castle with them and continued to lye in it as formerlie all the while they stayed here.

And the 10th day of this August my Daughter of Thanet and those five younger Sonnes of hers and her Daughter ladie Frances went from Skipton Castle into Barden Towre to see it, which was the first time that she or her four younger Sonnes ever came into this Barden Tower. But they all came back againe the same night to mee at Skipton Castle. And soe after they had layen here 12 nights, on the 15th day of the said August about 10 a clock in the forenoon (after I had first kiss'd her and then her Children in the Chamber wherein I was borne) they went away from mee out of this Skipton Castle onwards on their journie towards London. And my Grandchilde her Sonne John Tufton went also with his Mother and his Brothers and Sister the first daies journie to Wetherby, but returned back againe to me at Skipton Castle the 17th day of that August, at night. And the 22nd day of the sayd August my Daughter of Thanet and those four younger Sonnes of hers with her daughter Ladie Frances Tufton came all well to Thanet House in Aldersgate Street at London where they now lay for two nights together, because the next daie was Sundaie, and on the 24th day they went from thence downe into the Countrie towards Hothfeild House in Kent, whither they came well the next day being the 25th day, to my Lord of Thanet and his three youngest Daughters.

The 29th day of this August did Sir Thomas Twisden and Sir Christopher Turner, the Kings two Judges of Assize appointed this yeare for the Northerne Circuite, come from their journy from Carlisle into my Castle of Appleby in Westmerland where they lay for 4 nights together; Judge Twisden in the Barons Chamber and Judge Turner in the best chamber in Caesars Tower. In which time they kept the Assizes in the Moot Hall in Appleby Towne. And the 2nd of September following being Wednesdaie, they went away from thence to Kendall in the same Countie where they lay that night. And ye next day to Lancastre where they finished the Circuite.

And the 7th day of September in this yeare did my Grandchild Mr John Tufton ride away from this Skipton Castle from me and us here with his Man John Goatley towards London, and so into Kent to his Father and Mother and manie of their Children, and I did not see him againe till after his Father's death which was on the 7th of May 1664; for he came to mee the 8th of Jullie following, that he came from his journy from thence and from London hither into this Appleby Castle in Westmerland to mee.

LADY MARGARET SACKVILLE with her husband JOHN TUFTON (1609–64), 2nd Earl of Thanet, by an unknown artist

And ye 30th of this September (a little before my Removall hither) did my Coz. Philip, Lord Wharton and 3 of his Daughters by his second wife, viz: Anne, my God-daughter, and Margaret and Mary, came from his House called Hileigh Mannor in Yorkshire to this Skipton Castle to mee, where they lay 2 nights together, and then went home to Hileigh Mannor aforesaid.

And the 6th day of this October in 1663 after I had layen in Skipton Castle in the Chamber wherein I was borne (just a month after my coming from Barden Tower) did I remove from thence onwards on my journie towards Westmerland, so as I went to Mr Cuthbert Wades House in Kilnsey and lay there that night. And the next day from thence through Kettlewelldale, upp Buckden Rakes and over the Staks into Wensleydale to my Cozen Mr Thomas Metcalfes house at Nappa, where I lay also that night. And the next daie being the 8th daie from thence I went over Cotter in my Coach (where I think never Coach went before) and over Hellgill Bridge into Westmerland, so by the Chappell of Mallerstang (I lately repayred) I went into this Pendraggon Castle to lye in it again.

And this was the first time I was ever in Kettlewell dale, or went over this Buckden Rakes or the Stake or Cotter or any of the places wherein, yet God pleased to preserve me in that journy. And I was not in Westmerland since the 25th of October till now. Soe I now kept Christmas here in this Pendragon Castle this yeare and this was the first time that I ever kept Christmas or any of my Ancestors before mee for 300 yeares before or more. And I now lay in it till the 27th of Januarie that I removed from thence into Appleby Castle in Westmerland.

And while I lay in Pendragon Castle was my Sonne in law John Tufton Earle of Thanet committed prisoner to the Fleet at London, the 21st of December about the Businesse of Sackville College in Sussex,[*] in which Imprisonment he continued to lye till the 21st of Januarie next after that he was released thence, and came home againe to his House in Aldersgate Streete to my Daughter his Wife and some of their Children.

---

[*] Sackville College at East Grinstead in Sussex had been founded by the 2nd Earl of Dorset and completed by Richard, the third earl, as an almshouse for thirty-one poor persons of the area. The intention was to finance it with income derived from the Sackville estates, but when the profligate third earl died in 1624, having spent £40,000 during his lifetime and leaving debts of £60,000, the college finances from then onwards became very precarious. In consequence the trustees sued the family and after various vicissitudes the Earl of Thanet, Dorset's son-in-law, was arrested for contempt of this order and spent two months in the Fleet Prison until he relented and settled some of the monies owing to the college. The problem of the college finances remained unresolved until 1700.

In the yeare of our Lord God 1664

The 27th day of Januarie in this yeare about 10 a clock in the forenoone did I goe out of Pendraggon Castle in Westmoreland in my Coach drawn by 6 Horses, and most of my familie with me on Horsback into Applebie Castle in Westmerland, after I had layen in the said Pendraggon Castle ever since the 8th of October last, that I came to it with my familie from my journy from Skipton Castle in Craven untill now. And now I beganne to lye in the chamber in this Appleby Castle where I used formerly to lye, and where I had not beene since the 18th of October in 1662 till nowe. And in here I now continued to lye till the 16th of September following that I removed from thence into Brough Castle in the same Countie where I lay 8 nights, viz: till the 24th of that September, and then returned back from thence to this Appleby Castle againe.

And before I came away from Pendraggon Castle did I upon the 12th day of this Januarie purchase of Reynold Cocke of Cawtley neere Sidbergh in Yorkshire, Landes to the value of £11 per annum for which I payed two hundred and twentie poundes, which Landes I gave for the maintenance of a parson qualified to read praiers & the Homilies of the Church of England & to teach the Children of the Dale to write and read English in Mallerstang Chappell for ever, and I did putt in, to officiate in the sayd Chappell of Mallerstang, Rowland Wright who had bin at the same Chappell some 3 or 4 yeares before, to teach Scollres there.

And the 17th day of this Month being Thursdaie, in the evening did Sir Thomas Twisden one of the Judges of the Court of Common Pleas at Westminster, and Sir Christopher Turner one of the Barons of the Exchequer, come hither from Kendall and so from Lancaster the day before, to this Appleby Castle, where they stayed for 5 nights together. Judge Twisden lying in the Barons Chamber, and Judge Turner in the best Roome in Caesar's Tower; sitting here by speciall Comission from the King, upon the tryalls of divers of the Traitors in this Countie that

THANET HOUSE, Aldersgate Street, the London house of the Earls of Thanet (eighteenth century)

were ingaged in the late Plott and rising against his Majestie, so as three of them were hanged drawne and quartered here at Appleby, for otherwise except upon such an occasion the Assizes are but kept once a yeare for this Countie. And on the 22nd day they went away from hence on there journie towards Yorke to keep the Assizes there also. And I lay in my owne Chamber in this Appleby Castle all the time that these Judges now lay here.

The 11th day of Aprill being Easter Munday was my first Grandchild Nicholas, Lord Tufton married in a Chamber in Cliffords Inne in London Towne to the Ladie Elizabeth Boile, my Cozen and Goddaughter, second Daughter to Richard Earle of Corke by his wife my Cozen Elizabeth Clifford, Countesse of Corke. And my said first Grandchild and the said Ladie Elizabeth Boyle were married together by one Mr Byfield, who is Chaplain to her said father. I then lying in my own chambre in Appleby Castle in Westmerland, and this new-married Couple began first of all to lye together in that House in Whitefryers at London which was once part of the pryory there, where her father and Mother and most of there family sow lye.

And the 7th day of May being Saturdaie, about 3 a clock in the morning dyed my Sonne in Law John Tufton Earle of Thanet, in his House called Thanet House in Aldersgate Street at London, in those Lodgings that look towards the Street which he had about 20 yeares since built with freestone so magnificently, and my first child his wife the Ladie Margaret Countesse of Thanet, and their 5 younger Sonnes and 4 younger Daughters lay in this House of his when he dyed. And he was 55 yeares old the 25th of December last, before his death.

And the 11th of this month was the dead Bodie of my Sonne in law John, Earle of Thanet carried out of his House in Aldersgate Street where he dyed the 7th of that month, and so over London Bridge downe into the Countrie into the Church at Raynham in Kent, and was burried in the vault there by his Father and Mother and his second Childe my Grandchild the Ladie Anne Tufton. His Brother and his five younger Sonnes and his Daughters, Ladie Frances and Ladie Cecily Tufton being there present at his Burrial, but his eldest Sonne was not.

And I lay in my owne chambre in Appleby Castle in Westmerland both when he dyed and when he was burried.

And the 8th day of July following did his second Sonne, my Grandchild John Tufton come from his journie from Thanet House in Aldersgate Street in London Towne, from his Mother and some of his Brothers and Sisters, hither to Appleby Castle to mee to my great joy and comfort, I haveing not seene him since the death of his father, my

Sonne in law John, Earl of Thanet not 8 monthes before, till now. For the 7th day of September last 1663 this Grandchilde of mine went from Skipton from mee onwards on his journie towards London. And now in this journie of his from thence hither he lay two nights by the way (viz: the 5th and 6th of this month), in the highest Chamber in the great round tower at Skipton Castle, over the Chamber at the end of the Long Gallerie there wherein I formerlie used to lye. And the 7th day at night he lay in the Inne at Kirkby Lonsdale from whence the next day, (as aforesaid), he came hither to Appleby Castle where he now continued to lye till the 2nd day of the month following, that he went with his Mother and his three youngest Sisters from mee to Brougham Castle and lay there with them 4 nights – viz: till the 24th of the same month, that he came back againe hither with them to this Appleby Castle, from whence after he had layen two more nights in it, on the 26th day he went away from mee and from his Mother and Sisters up towards London about four daies before they went. And he came to Thanet House in Aldersgate Streete the 2nd day of the month following.

The 29th of this Julie did my Grandchild Nicholas Tufton, Earle of Thanet and his wife my Cozen and Goddaughter the young Countesse of Thanet, come hither to mee and to his Brother John Tufton into my chamber in this Appleby Castle in Westmerland about 7 a clock in the eveninge, where I kiss'd them both with much joy and comfort. It being the first time I saw any Grandchild of mine that was an Earle, neither had I seene him since I saw him in the Court of Appleby Castle when he went away from here with his father and mother towards Croome in Worcestershire, and from thence up to London in 1653, till this day. And it was the first time this new married wife of his ever came into Westmerland; neither had I seene her since I saw her and her Father and Mother the Earle and Countesse of Corke and her Brothers and Sisters, in Craven in 1650, when they were then with mee at Skipton Castle and I with them at Bolton Abbey till this time.

And this Earle my Grandchilde and his wife came now hitherr to mee from Launsborough Yorke and Topcliffe, and came today over Stainmoore hither, lying the night in the poore Inne at Bowze [Bowes]. And by the way hither from Bowze they went into Brough Castle for a while to see itt.

And now my said Grandchilde the Earle of Thanet and the Countesse his Wife, continued to lye in this Appleby Castle for 11 nights together in the Barons Chamber. And whilst they now lay here they went into Brougham Castle for a good while and into Eden hall, Lowther hall and Ackorn Banke. And hee and his Brother John Tufton went into

Pendraggon Castle to see it, but his wife did not goe with him, she being a little indisposed that day. And upon the 9th of August following, after I had then kiss'd them in my Chamber in Appleby Castle did this Earle of Thanet and the Countesse his wife with their Companie goe away againe from hence out of Westm'land over Stainmoore into the Inne at Catterick Bridge, towards Yorke and Launsburgh [Londesborough], but my Grandchild John Tufton returned back againe to mee at Appleby Castle after he had brought his Brother and Sister onwards upon their journie as far as Brough. And, some two dayes after, my said Grandchild the Earle of Thanet and his wife met my Lord of Corke and his wife about Yorke, and went with them to their House at Launsburrough, for they were lately come from Bolton Abbey and out of Craven thither againe.

The 16th daie of August in this yeare about 6 or 7 a clock in the eveninge did my Daughter Margarett Countesse Dowager of Thanett with her three youngest Daughters Ladie Cecilie, Ladie Marie and Ladie Anne Tufton and their companie come from their Journie from London over Stainmoore and those waies hither to mee and my Grandchild John Tufton, into this Appleby Castle in Westmerland, where I now kiss'd them with much joy and comfort. It being the first time I saw this Daughter of mine or any of her Daughters since she was a widdow by the death of her Lord the late Earle of Thanet (who dyed the 7th of May last) or in some time before, for I had not seene her since the 15th of August last in 1663; that she went awaie from mee from Skipton Castle in Craven with her four youngest Sonnes, Richard, Thomas, Sackville and George Tufton, and her daughter Ladie Frances Tufton up towards London, up untill now. Nor had I seen these youngest Daughters of hers since the 20th daie of August in 1661, that they went away from mee from this Appleby Castle in Westm'land up towards London with my said Daughter their Mother (who had bin then here to see mee with them) till now. And now they continued to lye in the Barrons Chamber here for four nights together.

And the 20th day, by reason of the two Judges comeinge hither to keepe the Assizes, they went from hence with my Grandchilde John Tufton into Brougham Castle in this Countie where they lay for 4 nights more during the time of the Assizes, my Daughter of Thanet and her youngest Daughter Ladie Anne lying in the Chamber there wherin I formerly used to lye, wherein my noble Father was borne and my Blessed Mother dyed, which was the first time that shee or any of her Children ever lay in that Chamber, and Lady Cecilie and Ladie Marie lying in the Middle Chamber of the great Tower there and their Brother

John Tufton lying in the Barons Chamber there. And my Daughter of Thanet had not bin in Brougham Castle since the 6th of September 1658; that she went from thence from mee with her Sonnes Richard, Thomas and Sackville Tufton up towards London, till now, this 20th of August, nor had her sayd three youngest daughters beene in that Castle since the 28th of Julie 1656, that they went from thence with their Mother my said Daughter up towards London, untill now. And this was the first time that any of them lay in that Castle when I lay not there my selfe. But on this 24th day of August when those 4 nights were past, they and their companie came from thence back againe into this Appleby Castle where they lay for 6 nights more, all save my grandchild John Tufton, who lay but 2 nights more in this Castle. For the 26th day he began his journie from hence up towards London (as aforesaid). And upon the 30th day of the same August, my Daughter of Thanet and her sayd three youngest Daughters and their Companie, after I had first kiss'd them as taking my leave of them, went away from mee out of this Appleby Castle about 8 a clock in the morninge, onwards on their journie towards London againe, whither they came safe and well the 8th day of the month following, to Thanet House in Aldersgate Street in London Towne to lye there in it for a time.

And the 20th day of this August being Saturdaie, in the evening did the two Judges of Assize for this Northern Circuite, Sir Thomas Twisden and Sir Christopher Turner come hither from Carlisle and Newcastle and those places to keep the Assizes here at Appleby for the Countie of Westmerland as usual. And they lay here in this Appleby Castle for 4 nights together, Judge Twisden in the Barrons Chamber and Judge Turner in the best Roome in Caesars Tower. In which time they kept the Assizes in the Moothall in Appleby Towne, where Robert Atkinson, one of my Tennants in Mallerstang, and that great Enemie, was condemned to be hang'd drawn and quarter'd as a Traitor to ye King, for having had a hand in the late Plotte & Conspiracie, so as he was executed accordingly the first Day of the Month following. And the 24th of this August being Wedensday the said two Judges went away from hence to Kendall in this Countie, where they lay ye night and next day to Lancaster to keep the Assizes there and to finish their Circuite. I lying in my owne Chamber in this Appleby Castle all the time of those Assizes.

The 16th day of September in this yeare after I had layen in my owne Chamber in this Appleby Castle in Westmerland ever since the 27th of Januarie last, that I came into it from Pendraggon Castle, did I remove with some of my familie out of my said Castle of Appleby into my Castle of Brough in the same Countie where I lay for 8 nights together, viz: the first four nights in the uppermost Chambre of that they call the Clifford's Tower there, and the other 4 in the middle Chamber of the great Roman Tower there. And when they were past, on the 24th of the same month I returned back into my Castle of Appleby againe into my Chambre in it while I now continued to lye for 31 nights. And when they were past, on Tuesdaie the 25th of the month following I removed from Appleby Castle into Brougham Castle in the same Countie.

And I had not beene in Brough Castle aforesaid since the 18th day of September 1662 till this 16th day.

The 8th day of Julie in this yeare, after they had taken their leaves of their Mother and most of their younger Brothers and Sisters a day or so before at Thanet House in Aldersgate Street in London Towne, did my two Grandchildren Mr Sackville Tufton and Mr George Tufton imbarque themselves at Dover in Kent, and so sayled over the seas into France, whither they came safe and well to Paris, within a while after. This being the first time these twoe Grandchildren of mine were ever beyond the seas or out of England. And Sir Thomas Billingsley who had served their Grandfather of Dorset, went along with them as their Governour. And after a short stay in Paris they went away thence to Sedan.

The 25th day of October in this yeare being Tuesdaie, after I had layen in Appleby Castle in Westmerland ever since the 27th of Januarie last past that I came to it from Pendraggon Castle (excepting only 8 nights that I lay in Brough Castle), did I this 25th day of October aforesaid remove with my familie out of my said Castle of Appleby into my Castle of Brougham in the same Countie, where I had not layen since the first of August in 1662 till now ; and where I now continued to lye in the Chamber where my Noble Father was borne and my Blessed Mother dyed, till the 1st day of August in the yeare following, that I removed from thence to Appleby Castle with my familie to lye there in it for a time. So as I now continued to lye in this Brougham Castle for 9 months together and seven daies over.

In the yeare of
ower Lorde God in 1665

The 23rd of Februarie in this yeare betweene 11 and 12 a clock in the forenoone was my Grandchild the Ladie Frances Tufton now second Daughter to my Daughter of Thanet and her deceased Lord, married in the Chappell in Thanet House in Aldersgate Street at London by Mr Hinde, my Daughter of Thanet's Chaplaine, to Mr Henry Drax. Which Grandchild of mine had bin once or twice in the Low Countries for the cure of Ricketts. But thanks be to God she came now to be well married. And after she and her sayde Husband had layen in Thanet House in Aldersgate Street some 8 or 9 nights, they went away from thence into her Husbands House in Lincoln's Inne fields to live there in it for a while, and afterwards they went into his owne House at Hackney, some 3 or 4 miles from London to live there in it. I lying at this time of her marriage in Brougham Castle in Westmerland in the Chamber there wherein my father was borne and my blessed Mother dyed. And she dyed in labour of her first child (to my griefe) at Buckwell in Kent ye 22nd of November following, ye Child dying in her a little before, and she and it were buryed together in Rainham Church in Kent ye 15th of December after.

About the 29th of June in this yeare being St Peter's Day, did our Queen Marie, the Frenchwoman, Queen Dowager and Mother of our King Charles the second, goe out of Somersett House and out of London Towne cross over the Thames to Lambeth, and soe by easie journies to Dover in Kent. Her two Sonnes, our King Charles and James Duke of York, Prince Rupert, the Duke of Monmouth and many others of the Nobillity bringing her onwards on her journie as far as Dover aforesaid, where they then all tooke their leaves of her as she was on shipboard on the Seas, from whence she cross'd the seas in one of ye Kings shippes and landed safely at Calais, and from thence went to Paris in France in the beginning of the Julie following. And this Queen Marie had stayed in England ever since the 28th of July in 1662, that she then came out of

The Kendal Diary, 1650–1675

France into England, this being the eleventh or twelfth time that she hath pass'd and repass'd the seas to and fro between England and beyond the seas; so as from her first coming into England to this going over of Hers now into France was just 40 yeares. And some few daies before her going from London this Queen Dowager took her leave of Queen Katherine, Her Sonne our Kings Wife, at Hampton Court.

And in this yeare 1665 and the begining of the yeare following, was there a great Plague in the Cittie and suburbs of London, whereof there dyed for severall weekes together above 8,000 a week, the like whereof was never known in London before.

The first day of August this yeare, I had layen 9 months and 7 daies over in Brougham Castle in Westmerland in the Chamber where my Noble Father was borne and my Blessed Mother dyed; did I then remove with all my family out of the said Brougham Castle into my Castle of Appleby in Westmerland. And I came by the way thither through some part of Whinfield Parke, where I had not bin since this day three yeares till now. And now I continued to lye in this Appleby Castle till the 10th of November followinge, that I removed from hence with my familie into Brough Castle in the same Countie.

And this first of August also did my Daughter of Thanet and her three youngest daughters, Cecilie, Marie and Anne with her family remove from out of their hyred house at Epsome in Surrey, where they drunk the waters, into Bolebrooke House in Sussex, her House of Inheritance by her Father, where they continued to lye.

And this was the first time my Daughter of Thanet came to lye in that Bolebrooke House after she was first a Widdow, or in a great many yeares before. And the first time her three youngest daughters were ever in it. And her 4 Sonnes that are now in England and her Daughter Ladie Frances Drax and her Husband came hither to see her for a time in the sayd Bolebrooke House, where she had bin deliver'd of her first Sonne, now the Earle of Thanet, whose wife came there also hither with him to see her.

The 19th day of August did Sir Richard Rainsford, one of the Barons of his Majesties Exchequer and now Judge of Assize for this Northerne Circuite, come hither from Carlisle to keep the Assizes here at Appleby, where he now continued to lye in the Barrons Chamber for some 5 nights together, viz: till the 24th of this month, that he went from hence to Kendall, and the next day to Lancaster to keep the Assizes there also, and so to finish his Circuit. And my Cozen Sir Philipp Musgrave and his Sonne Christopher, and my Cozen Sir John Lowther lay here also most part of the Assizes. And whilst the Assizes were kept here did my Cozen Charles Howard, Earle of Carlisle, and young Mr Fenwick that married his eldest Daughter, come hither to me into this Appleby Castle the 21st of this monthe, and lay here that night in the great Tower, as they were in their journie to Yorke to attend the Duke of Yorke there; which was the first time I saw my said Cozen the Earle of Carlisle since he was Ambassador for our King in Muscovia, Sweden and Denmarke, or some 5 or 6 yeares before, till now.

The 10th day of November this yeare being Fryday, after I had layen in Appleby Castle in Westmerland ever since the first of August last, being 3 monthes and some 9 daies over, in the Chamber in it where I formerly used to lye and wherein I have layen long since with my Blessed Mother when I was a Mayd, did I remove from thence with my familie out of my said Castle of Appleby into my Castle of Brough in the same Countie, where I had not bene since the 24th day of Septembre in the last yeare 1664, till this day. And where I now begun to lye in the highest Round Chamber on Clifford's Tower till the 19th day of Aprill following, that I removed from thence with my familie into Pendragon Castle in the same Countie. And during the time I lay in this Brough Castle did I keepe my Christmas in it, which was the first Christmas I ever kept in the said Castle, nor had any of my Ancestors done it since the yeare 1521; it being then burnt downe when Henry, Lord Clifford, my Fathers Grandfather then lay in the sayd Castle about 2 yeares and somewhat more before ye sayd Henrie Lord Cliffords death.

The 22nd of the said November, about one a clock in the afternoon, (to my unspeakable greife), dyed my dear Grandchild the Ladie Frances Drax who was my Daughter of Thanets third Daughter but sixth Child, and was borne in her Fathers House in Aldersgate Streete in London Towne the 23rd of March in 1642, as the yeare begines on New yeares Day. I then lying in a hyred house in the Cittie of Bath in Sommer-settshire. And she was married in the same Thanett House the 23rd of Februarie last to Mr Henrie Drax. And she dyed, (as aforesaid), the 22nd of November in a hyred house at Buckwell in Kent nere Hothfeild being then in labour of her first Childe which was a Sonne of whom she could not be delivered, for the Childe was dead within her a few houres before her owne death. And whilst she was in labour did my Daughter of Thanet her Mother, beginne her journie from Bolebrooke in Sussex towards Buckwell aforesaid to see her. But hearing of her death before she came hither, she returned immediately back to Bolebrooke againe where she lay when her sayd Daughter was buryed, which was on the 1st of December, being the month next following; and the Childe was burryed then together with her in the Vault of Raynham Church in Kent by her father and Grandfather. There being present at this Buriall severall of her Brothers and Sisters, as namely, ye Earle of Thanet and his ladie, Mr John Tufton, Mr Richard, Mr Thomas and Ladie Cecily Tufton, and also manie of their Neighbours and Relacons. And both when she dyed and was burried did I lye in my owne Chamber in Cliffords Tower in Brough Castle where I heard first of all the sad newes of her death, the 6th day of the said December.

In the yeare of
ower Lorde God 1666

The 2nd day of Januarie about 6 or 7 a clock in the evening did there a great fire happen in the highest Chamber but one in ye great Round Towre here in this Brough Castle in Westmerland, which burnt a Bedd and the Curteins and Vallance and all ye furniture belonging to it and a tapestry Hanging that hung behind the Bed. But before it gott any further hold it was by Gods mercifull Providence discovered and quenched, so as the Towre it selfe received no harme. And I then lay in my owne chambre in Cliffords Tower in the sayd Castle.

The 19th day of Aprill in this yeare did I remove with my family out of Brough Castle in Westmerland and so went through Wharton Parke neere Wharton Hall into my Castle of Pendraggon in the same Countie, after I had layen in the said Brough Castle in the uppermost Roome of Cliffords Tower there ever since the 10th day of Novembre last till now, being five months and some 9 dayes over. At the time of my now lying in Brough Castle dyed my deare Grandchild the Ladie Frances Drax, the 22nd of November in a hyred House of her Husbands at Buckwell in Kent neare Hothfeild (as is above mentioned). And the sayed 19th day in the morning before I came away from the sayd Brough Castle, did I go for a while into the great Roman Tower there into the best Roome in it, where I used sometimes to lye, and into the lower roome where Gabriell Vincent dyed the 12th day of Februarie before, to my great greife and sorrow. And I had not bin in that great Roman Tower since the 24th of September in 1664 (when I had then layen in it for 4 nights, and removed thence to Appleby Castle, till now) that I came into it againe for a while. And I had not bin in this Pendraggon Castle since the 27th of Januarie in 1664, till this 19th of Aprill that I now came into it againe, where I continued to lye in my owne Chamber there that looks to the South and West, till the 6th of August followinge that I removed from thence with my familie towards Skipton Castle in Craven.

And a little before my comeing away from Brough Castle in the latter end of March or begining of Aprill, did my two Grandchildren Mr Sackville Tufton and his Brother Mr George Tufton with their Governor Sir Thomas Bellingsley goe from Sedan in France into upper Germanie to the Prince Elector Palatine's Court at Heidelberg. And the reason of this was because of the Warres that are now between England and France.

And the 6th day of this August after I had layen in Pendraggon Castle ever since the 19th of Aprill before, did I remove out of ye sayd Pendraggon Castle and went into the Chappell of Mallerstang by the way for a while, it being the first time I was ever in that Chappell. And so over Cotter and those dangerous Wayes into one Mr John Colebys House near Bambrigg in Winsdale, where I lay that night with my women Servants and some 3 of my Menservants, my other servants lying at Askrigg and Bambrigg. And this was the first time I ever lay in the sayd house. And the next day being the 7th of August I went over the Stake and downe Buckden Rakes and so into Mr Cuthbert Wayds House at Kilnsey, where I lay in it that night (having layen in it one night before in my former remove from Skipton Castle to Pendraggon Castle in Westmerland). And from thence the next day being the 8th of the month, I came safe and well into my said Castle of Skipton in Craven, and so into my owne Chamber in it wherein I was borne into the World, where I now continued to lye for 5 months and two daies over, that is to say from the 8th of August till the 10th of Januarie following that I removed with my familie from thence to Barden Tower in Craven to lye in it for a time.

And I had not bene in those Wayes over Cotter and the Stake since the 6th, 7th and 8th dayes of October in 1663 till now, neither was I in Skipton Castle since the sayd 6th of October 1663 till now.

The 27th day of this August being Munday, did my Daughter Margaret Countess Dowager of Thanet, with her three youngest Daughters, Ladie Cecily, Ladie Mary and Ladie Anne Tufton come hither to mee from their journie from London, and today from the Inne at Wetherby into this Skipton Castle a little before Supper time, where I kiss'd them all with much joy and contentment in the Chamber here wherein I was borne into the World. I having not seen anie of them since the 30th day of August in 1664 – when they went away from mee from Appleby Castle in Westmerland back towards London, till now. And now they continued to lye here in this Castle for 12 nights together, my Daughter and her Daughter Ladie Cecily in the middle round roome at ye end of the long Gallerie here (where formerlie I used to lye myselfe), and Ladie Marie and Ladie Anne in the Roome above it, which was the first time since my Daughter of Thanet or these three Daughters of hers ever lay in that Round Tower, though her Daughter Ladie Frances Tufton (since deceased) had layen in it when she was here. And this is the seventh time that my sayd Daughter hath come into the North to see me, whereof she hath bin 5 times with mee in Westmerland and this is the second time she hath bin with mee here at Skipton. But it is the first time these three youngest Daughters of hers were ever here, though they had bin with mee before in Westmerland, both at Brougham Castle and Appleby Castle. And the 31st of this month during their stay here, these three young Ladies my Grandchildren, with their three women, Mrs Jane Paulett, Mrs Bridget Billingsley and Katharine Poston, went in my Daughter their Mothers Coach with 6 horses out of this Skipton Castle into my Tower of Barden where they dined, and from thence into Mr Sheffield Clapham's House at Beamsley where they stayed a while, and from thence into my Blessed Mothers Almeshouse at Beamsley, and returned back againe into this Skipton Castle a little before Supper, this being the first time that any of my sayd Grandchildren were ever in Barden Tower, Beamsley hall or in the Almeshouse at Beamsley which was founded by my Blessed Mother.

And when these 12 nights were past my Daughter of Thanet and her sayd three Daughters and their Companie went away from hence from mee (after I had first kiss'd them on taking my leave of them) and so from this Skipton Castle on the 8th day of September following about 9 a clock in the morning, onwards on their journie towards London againe.

And the first day of June in this yeare whilst I lay in Pendragon Castle with my family, did Mr William Russell, second sonne to my Cozen, ye now Earle of Bedford and his wife, come from his journy from their House at Woburne in Bedfordshire thither to Pendraggon Castle to mee, where he lay that one night and the next day he continued his journy into Scotland calling by the way at Naworth Castle in Cumberland to see my Cozen the Earle of Carlisle and his Ladie, who is his Cozen. And this was the first time that ever my said Cozen Russell was in Westmerland or in anie parte of my Inheritance, or so far Northwards. And about the latter end of that month or the next after he came well home againe to his Father and Mother in their sayd House att Woburne in Bedfordshire.

And whilst my Daughter of Thanet and her sayd 3 youngest Daughters were with mee here at Skipton Castle did the two Judges of Assizes for this Northerne Circuite, Sir Christopher Turner and Sir Richard Rainsford, two of the Barons of His Majesties Exchequer, come into Appleby Castle in Westmerland the 1st day of this September in the evening (being Saturday) where they now lay for 4 nights together. Judge Turner in the Barrons Chamber and Judge Rainsford in the best Roome in Caesars Tower. And after these 4 nights were past and that they had ended the Assize there at Appleby, those two Judges went away from thence on Wedensday following being the 5th of that month about 2 a clock towards Kendall, where they lay that night, and the next day to Lancaster to keep the Assizes there also, and so to end their Circuite.

The 2nd day of this September being Sunday, about 2 a clock in the morning, whilst my Daughter of Thanet and her three youngest Daughters lay here in Skipton Castle with me, and whilst the sayd Judges of Assize for this Northerne Circuite lay in my Castle of Appleby in Westm'land to keepe the Assizes in the Towne there, did a great fire break out in severall places and Houses within the Walles of the Citty of London, which continued raging there for about 4 dayes together before it could be quenched. And in that time consumed and burnt downe not only Baynards Castle, but Great Dorsett House and Little Dorsett House (in which place I had spent much of my time when I was Wife to my first and second Husbands), but also did consume that ancient and Noble Church of St Paules in London, and the whole streets of Cheapside, Blackfryers and Whitefryers and all the Houses between that and ye River of Thames. But in all this desolation Thanet House in Aldersgate, my Daughter of Thanets Jointure House was then preserved.

In the yeare of ower Lord God 1667

The 10th day of Januarie in this yeare (after I had layen in Skipton Castle in that chamber within the walles of it wherein I was borne into the world, ever since the 9th day of August last) did I remove from thence with my family, and so went through the Haw Parke and by Skibden and Halton and those waies, I in my Hors Litter and some of my Cheife women in my Coach, into my House or Towre of Barden in Craven, where I had not bin since the 6th day of May in 1663, till now. And where I now continued to lye (in the same chamber I formerly used to lye in) till the 29th day of Julye following that I removed from hence with my familie towards Pendraggon and Appleby Castles in Westmerland.

And so this late Christmas did I lye all the time of it in my owne chambre within the old Walles of Skipton Castle, wherein I was borne into the world, which was the first Christmas I ever kept in that chamber since I was borne, though I had layen for severall Christmases since I was last a widdow, by the death of my Lord the Earle of Pembroke, in the other part of that Castle which was built by my great Grandfather of Cumberland, viz: in the middle chamber in the great round Tower at the East end of the Long Gallerie there.

And about the beginning of June in this year 1667 did my Cozen Elizabeth Clifford, Countesse of Burlinton and Corke and the Earle, her husband, and their youngest daughter (save one), the Lady Anne Boyle, come from there house called Barkshire House at St James's at London, downe to there house at Launsborough in Yorkshire to lye in it for a time.

And about the 19th day of the said month of June did the said Richard, Earle of Burlington and Corke goe from his said house at Launsborough from his wife and his Daughter Anne, and two of his Sonnes Children, either to Chester or to Leverpool in Lancashire, from where hee cross'd the seas in shipe to Dublin in Ireland, and after some stay there hee went to some of his owne houses there in Ireland.

The Kendal Diary, 1650–1675

And about the —— [blank in manuscript] day of this June did my Grandchilde Nicholas, Earle of Thanet and his wife come from ther house at Hothfeild in Kent to Gravesend in the same Countie, and from thence by Water in a Barge up to London, where they lay two or three nights in a Lodgeing there. And then hee went downe againe to his said House of Hothfeild. But his wife came downe from London to Launs-borough House in Yorkshire to her Mother and sister Anne and two of her eldest Brothers Children for a time.

And the 29th day of this June, at night, the said younge Countesse of Thanet came from Launsborough in Yorkshire and from Yorke to mee at Barden Tower in Craven in that County, where she staid with mee for 4 nights together – Shee and her two Women lyeing in the two low Roomes at the West end of the great chamber there over the kitching; and when those 4 nights were past, shee and her Company went away from thence from mee and my family back to Launsborough againe. And from thence, about Michaelmas following, she went with her Mother, the Countesse of Cork and Burlington up to London to her father, where after a short stay at Barkshire House with them, the sayd young Countesse of Thanet went from thence downe to Hothfeild House in Kent to her Lord.

And the 29th of July in this yeare (after I had layen in my House or Tower of Barden in Craven ever since the 10th day of Januarie last, being 6 months and some 19 daies over) did I remove thence with my familie towards my Castle of Pendragon in Westmorland, so as that day I went into one John Symondsons House of Starbotten in Craven, where I lay that one night, (which was the first time I ever lay there), and from thence, the next day being the 30th day, I went up Buckden Rakes and over the Stake and so out of Craven into Mr John Colebyes House in Wonsedale [Winsdale], where I lay that one night, (which was the second time I had layen there), and from thence the next day, being the 31st, I went up Cotterhill and over Hellgill Bridge and by Mallerstang Chappell and those wayes into my said Castle of Pendraggon where I had not beene since the 6th day of August last in 1666, untill now; and where I now continued to lye in the chamber within the great chamber there, the windows whereof are towards the South and West, but for 8 nights together.

And when they were past, on the 8th day of August I removed from my said Castle of Pendraggon with my family into my Castle of Appleby in the same County – where I had not been since the 10th day of November in the yeare 1665, till now; and where I now continued to lye in the same chamber I used to lye in till the 18th day of October

BARDEN TOWER, Yorkshire, engraved by N. Whittock from a drawing by J. Rogers (eighteenth century)

following, that I removed from thence to Brougham Castle to lye in it with my family for a time.

And in all these late Journies of mine from Skipton to Barden and from thence to Pendragon and so to Appleby, I ridd all the way in my Hors Litter.

And the 24th day of this August beinge Saturday, in the eveninge did the 2 Judges of Assize for this Northerne Circuite, namely Sir Christopher Turner and Sir Richard Rainsford, 2 of the Barons of his Majesties Exchequer, come from the City of Carlisle in Cumberland from holding the Assizes there, hither into this Appleby Castle in Westmerland, where I and my family now lye, and where they now lay for 4 nights together; Judge Turner in the best Roome in Caesars Tower, and Judge Rainsford in the Baron's Chamber. And after those 4 nights were past the Assize here at Appleby being ended, they went away from hence from mee on Wednesday the 28th of this month about 11 a clocke towards Kendall, where they lay that night, and the next day they went to Lancaster to keepe the Assizes there also, and to end there Circuite. And these 2 Judges have come the Circuit severall times before.

And my Cozens Sir Philip Musgrave of Edenhall in Cumberland and Sir John Lowther of Lowther in this Countie lay here also most part of these Assizes as usuall.

And presently, after the Assizes ended, was the peace proclaimed in Appleby as elsewhere throughout the Kingdome, which had bin concluded of but the last month at Breda betwene our King Charles the second, (by his Ambassadors Denzill, Lord Hollis, and Mr Henrie Coventrie) on the one part, and the States of the United Provinces and the 2 Kings of France and Denmark on the other part, to the generall good of Christendom and the joy and satisfaction of our King and all his good Subjects, after there had bin hotte Warres between them by Sea for almost 3 yeares last past.

And the 18th of October in this yeare after I had layen in Appleby Castle in Westmerland in the chamber wherein I used to lye ever since the 8th day of August last, being two months and some 10 daies over, did I remove from thence in my Horslitter with my family, going along the usual high Road, and not through Whinfeild Parke, into Brougham Castle in the same Countie, in which Castle of Brougham I had not bin since the 1st day of August in 1665 till now, and where I now continued to lye as I used to do in the Chamber wherein my Noble Father was borne, and my Blessed Mother dyed, till the 26th day of June next following, that I removed from thence back againe to Appleby Castle aforesayd, to lye there in it for a time.

In the yeare of our Lord God in 1668

The 12th day of Februarie in this yeare, I then lying in Brougham Castle in Westmerland, I first of all came to know that my Grandchild Ladie Cecilia Tufton, my Daughter of Thanets fourth Daughter and seaventh Child, was married to Mr Christopher Hatton oldest Sonne to Christopher, Lord Hatton of Kirkby in Northamptonshire, privately on the 12th day of Februarie in the last year 1667; as ye same beginnes on New Yeares Day, I then lying in Barden Tower in Craven. And that they were married together by Dr Evans one of ye Dutchess of Yorkes Chaplains in Sir Charles Littletons House in the Minories, he that is Cup Bearer to the King; none but he and his Lady being present at the marriage.

And on the 2nd day of March this yeare when I also lay in Brougham Castle, my Grandchild Mr Thomas Tufton was chosen Burgess for the Towne of Appleby to serve in the House of Commons in Parliament then assembled, and sitting in Parliament at Westminster in the place of Mr John Lowther, eldest Sonne to my Cozen Sir John Lowther, which Mr John Lowther dyed but a while before at London. Soe as this Thomas Tufton my Grandchilde beganne first of all to sit in the sayd House of Commons at Westminster as a Member there on the 10th day of March instant; which Parliament had begun to sitt againe the 14th day before. He being the first Grandchilde of mine that ever sate in that House of Commons in the Parliament at Westminster.

The 11th day of May in this yeare did my old Servant Mrs Elizabeth Gillmore, whose first Husband was Mr John Turner, come from her Sonne in Law Mr Killaways at Wirk in Wiltshire to an Inne at Redding in Barkshire, and from thence next day to London, where she stayd till the 5th day of the month following, in which time her second husband Mr John Gillmoore with there Mayd and a man call'd John Walker and one Thomas Kingston, came up thither with her. And from thence the same 5th day of June they came downe together in a hired Coach towards Yorke, whither they got well the 9th day; and there my Servants George

Goodgion and John Hall by my appointment mett them with some of my Horses to bring them from thence hither to Brougham Castle. And accordingly they sett forth from York the 11th day, and came that night to Greta Bridge, and the next day over Stainmoore and by Brough Castle into my Castle of Appleby where they lay all night, Mrs Gilmoore and her Husband lying in the Barons Chamber there; and from thence the 13th of this June they came by Julian Bower (where they alighted to see all the Roomes and places about it), and so though Whinfield Parke hither into this Brougham Castle to mee, where I kiss'd Mrs Gilmoore, I having not seen her since the 11th of August 1663, when she had bin for a while at Skipton Castle with me, till now this 13th of June.

The 26th of June in this yeare after I had layen in Brougham Castle in the Chamber there wherein my Noble Father was borne and my Blessed Mother dyed, ever since the 18th of October last, being 8 monthes and some 8 daies over, did I remove from thence in my Horslitter, (my women riding in my Coach drawn with six Horses, and my Men-servants on horsback), through Whinfeild Park, and by the Harts Hornetree, and by ye House called Julians Bower in my said Parke to see it, (though I did not alight to go into it), and so from thence through Temple Sowerby, Kirkbythure, Crackenthorp and over Appleby Bridge into my Castle of Appleby in the same Countie, where I now began to lye in ye same chamber wherein I formerly used to lye and now lay in till the —— [blank in manuscript].

The 21st of July in this yeare did my Daughter the Countesse Dowager of Thanet with her 2 youngest Daughters, Lady Mary and Lady Anne Tufton go out of Thanet House in Aldersgate Street (leaving there behind them Mr Sackville Tufton her youngest Sonne save one and her Daughter Lady Cecily Hatton and her Husband) and so out of London Towne downe into the Country towards Croome House in Worcestershire. And having layen 2 nights by the way, the first at Wickham in Buckinghamshire and the second at Anston in —— [blank in manuscript] they came safe and well thither to Croome the 23rd of that month, to her daughter the Lady Margaret Coventry and her Lord and ther 2 children, where they stayed with them for 7 nights together, viz: till the 30th of the same month. And then returned from thence back towards the sayd Thanet House at London againe, whither they came well the 1st of August following, having layen 2 nights by the way, the 1st at Stow-in-the-Wold in Glocestershire, from thence going by Oxford to see the most remarkable things there, and the next night at Titsworth in —— [blank in manuscript]. And her Daughter the Lady Margaret

Coventry with her Daughter Margaret came up thither with them that journy from Croome leaving behind them my Lord Coventry and his eldest and now only Sonne.

And on Friday the 31st of this July did my eldest Grandchild Nicholas Tufton, Earle of Thanet, come hither into this Appleby Castle in Westmerland late in the evening so as I saw him not till the next day in the morning, that he came up to mee in my Chamber, when I kiss'd him with much joy and comfort, I having not seene him since the 9th of August 1664 when he had bin here with mee with his wife, my Cozen and God-Da.; and that they then took their leaves of me in this same chamber of mine, and went towards her Father, the Earle of Burlington and Corke's House at Lonsborrow in Yorkshire, and so to their owne House at Hothfeild in Kent, untill now. And now this Earle my Grandchild came from his journy from the sayd Hothfeild House, and by the way from the Lord Viscount Dunbarrs House in Holdernesse and from Starbarrow Hills and Bolton in Yorkshire, and today from the Inne at Kirkby Lonsdale in Westmerland hither into this Appleby Castle as aforesaid; where he now continued to lye in the Barons Chamber 7 nights together, and when they were past, on the Friday following being the 7th of August, betimes in the morning before I saw him (He having taken his leave of mee the night before in my Chamber), went away againe from hence with his Companie by the same waies that he came onwards on his journy back towards his sayd House at Hothfeild to his Wife.

And the 8th of this August being Saturday, in the evening did the two Judges of Assize for this Northerne Circuite, namely Sir Christopher Turner and Sir Richard Rainsford two of the Barons of his Majesties Exchequer, come from the City of Carlisle in Cumberland from holding the Assizes there, hither into this Appleby Castle in Westmerland, where I and my family now lye, and where they now lay for 4 nights together. Judge Turner in the Best Roome in Caesars Tower, and Judge Rainsford in the Barons Chamber; and when they were past, (the Assizes at Appleby being ended), they went away from hence from mee on Wedensday the 12th of this month to Kendall, where they lay that night, and the next day they went to Lancaster to keep the Assizes there also and so to finish there Circuite. And my Cozen Sir Philip Musgrave* of Edenhall in Cumberland

---

* Sir Philip Musgrave (d. 1678), whose grandmother Joan was the daughter of Thomas, Lord Clifford, was the son of Sir Richard Musgrave and Frances, daughter of Philip, Lord Wharton, of Wharton Hall. Sir Philip married Julia, daughter of Sir Richard Hutton of Goldsborough, Yorkshire.

The Kendal Diary, 1650–1675

and my Cozen Sir John Lowther[*] of Lowther in Westmerland lay here also in this Castle most part of these Assizes, as was usuall.

And on Munday the 21st of September in the afternoone, my Grandchild Mr Thomas Tufton, the fourth Sonne and seventh child to my Daughter the Countesse of Thanet and now one of our Burgesses in Parliament for the Corporation of Appleby came thither into this Appleby Castle in Westmorland, and so up into my chamber to see mee, where I kiss'd him with much joy and comfort, I having not seen him since the 15th of August in 1663, when he with his Mother and some of his brothers and his Sister Lady Frances went from Skipton Castle from mee up towards London, untill now. And now this Grandchild of mine came from his Journy out of Kent and so by London, York, Rippon and today from ye Inne at Bowze in Richmondshire hither into this Appleby Castle (as aforesaid), where he now lay in the Barons Chamber for 10 nights together, during which time he went to visitt severall of the Gentry, my Neighbours and Freinds in the Country, and on the 23rd of this September to Akornbank to Mr John Dalston his fellow Burgesse, and to my House at Julian Bower in Whinfeilde parke; and the 24th day to Edenill [Edenhall] in cumberland to my Cozen Sir Philip Musgrave, and the 25th to the Sheriff Mr Thomas Gabetis' House at Crosby, to Lowther Hall to my Cozen Sir John Lowther, and so to my Castle of Brougham to see it. And the 26th day to Howgill Castle to the Widow Lady Sandford and Sir Richard Sandford her eldest Sonne and ye rest of her children. And the 28th day being Monday, to my Castles of Pendragon and Brough to see them; at none of which Houses and Places he had ever bin before, except at Brougham Castle where he had bin once with mee for a time in August and September in 1658 with his Mother and some other of her Children. And when those 10 nights were over, on Thursday the 1st of this October in the morning, before I saw him, he having taken his leave of mee the night before, went away againe from hence by Brough and over Stainmoore into the Inne at Bowze aforesaid where he lay one night, and so continued his Journy up towards London.

And the 9th day of October in this yeare being Fryday, about 4 a clock in the morning in Thanet House in Aldersgate Street, London, where her husband Mr Christopher Hatton, and her Mother my Daughter of Thanet and most of her younger Children then lay, was my Grandchild

---

[*]   Sir John Lowther (b. 1605; MP for Westmorland, 1628–60) was a great great grandson of Sir Hugh Lowther and Dorothy, daughter of Henry, Lord Clifford ('The Shepherd Lord'). Sir John married Mary, daughter of Sir Richard Fletcher of Hutton, Cumberland. Their son, also John, was MP for Appleby (1661–7) and father of the 1st Viscount Lonsdale.

the Lady Cecilia Hatton deliver'd of her first Child, which was a Daughter, and was christened the 18th of that month being Sunday, by the name of Anne; myself a Deputy, and my said Daughter the Countess Dow'r of Thanet being the two Godmothers, and Christopher Lord Hatton of Kirkby, Grandfather of ye said Child being the God-father.

And I lay all this Christmas in this yeare in my owne Chamber in Appleby Castle in Westmerland, where I used to lye.

In the Yeare of
our Lorde God in 1669

The 22nd of March in this yeare the Prince of Tuscany who is the oldest Sonne to Cosmo de Medici ye great Duke of Florence in Italy, and some yeares married the then Duke of Orlean's Daughter by his second Wife, by whom he hath already had some Children, came from his voyage from Corunna and from his visits of severall Princes in Christendome at their severall Countries, hither into England, landing at Plimouth in Devonshire. From whence the 27th of the same month he went to Exeter, and so by continued dayes journys to Salisbury in Wiltshire, where whilst he lay he was magnificently entertain'd the 2nd of ye month following by the new Earle of Pembroke at his House at Wilton in that County; and the 5th of the same month he arrived safe at London and came to the Court at Whitehall to the King and Queen and the Duke of Yorke. Where he lay for some time in the House called the Pol Mol near St James', and then went to see ye Universities of Oxford and Cambridge and other remarkable places in this Kingdom. And on Fryday the 4th of June following, having before taken his leave of our said King and ye rest, he came to Harwich where he imbarqued for Holland.

And the 29th of May in this yeare did my Daughter the Countess Dowager of Thanet and her Sonne Sackville Tufton and her two youngest Daughters, Lady Mary and Ladie Anne Tufton, go from Thanet House in Aldersgate in London Towne from her Daughter Ladie Cecily Hatton and her Husband and their little Daughter Anne, down into the Country to Bolebrooke House in Sussex, where they continued to lye till the 8th of the month following, and then return'd back againe to her said House in Aldersgate Street to lye in it as before.

And on Fryday the 4th of June this yeare did our Queen Katherine, wife to our new King Charles the second, in her lodging in the Court at Whitehall near Westminster and London, miscarry of a Child, which She had gone about 9 weekes with all to her great Griefe, this being the third Child that she hath miscarried of.

The 5th of this June did my Cozen and Godsonne Mr Edward Russell, third Sonne to the new Earle of Bedford, come from his journy from his sayd father's House at Woburn in Bedfordshire, from him and his Ladie and some other of their Children and their family, hither into this Appleby Castle in Westmerland late in the evening, so as I saw him not till the next morning that he came up into my Chamber to mee where I then kiss'd him; it being the first time I ever saw him in any part of the Landes of my Inheritance, or that ever he was so far Northwards. Though his older Brother William, the second Sonne, had bin with me before at Pendragon Castle in this Countie in June 1666. And this Mr Edward Russell now lay here in the Baron's Chamber for 10 nights together, in which time he went to see my Castles of Brougham, Brough and Pendragon and other chiefe places in this Countie. And on Tuesday the 15th of this month, in the morning after he had taken his leave of mee, he went away from hence by Brough and over Stainmoore and those Waies, (though in his journy hither he came by Lancaster and Kendal), and so went now onwards on his journy home towards the sayd Woburn House in Bedfordshire, whither he came safe to his Father and Mother and some of their Children about them.

And the 7th of this June whilst my said Cozen and God Sonne Mr Edward Russell was here, did my Grandchildren Mr John and Mr Richard Tufton, second and third Sonnes to my Daughter the Countess Dowager of Thanet, come hither into this Appleby Castle in Westmerland to mee, where I then in my owne Chamber kiss'd them both with much contentment, I having not seen my said Grandchild John since the 26th of August 1664 when he went away from hence from mee and from his Mother and three youngest Sisters (who were then also here with mee), onwards on his journy towards London untill now, nor had I seen his Brother Richard since the 15th of August 1663 (which was almost 9 months before his Father dyed), when he went away from Skipton Castle in Craven from mee with his Mother and some of his Brothers and his Sister Lady Frances, up towards London untill now; and now these two Grandchildren of mine came from their journy from Great Chart, neere their eldest Brother the Earle of Thanet's House at Hothfield in Kent, and from London after some six weekes stay there, and today from Bows and over Stainmoore by Brough and those Waies hither into this Appleby Castle (as aforesaid), where they now lay together in the Green Chamber which is under the Withdrawing Roome, for 7 nights together. In which time they went with my said Cozen Russell to my Castles of Brougham, Brough and Pendragon, to show him them and some other remarkable Houses and Places in this

Countie. And when those 7 nights were past, on Monday the 14th of this month in the morning, after they had taken their leaves of mee and my sayd Cozen Russell (who stay'd with mee a day longer), they went away from hence by the same waies they came, onwards on their journy towards London. And this was ye first time that ever my Grandchild Mr Richard Tufton was in Pendragon Castle aforesaid, whither he went with his Brother and Mr Edward Russell the 11th of June.

And the 11th of this June whilst my said Grandchildren and my Cozen and Godsonne Mr Edward Russell were here, there came hither to mee to Appleby Castle from his owne House at Edlington in Yorkshire, over Stainmoore and those waies, my Cozen Sir Thomas Wharton who is second and only Brother to the now Lord Wharton. And this Sir Thomas now lay with us for 2 or 3 nights in Caesars Tower here, which was the first time he ever lay in that Tower; and about the 16th of June he went away againe.

And the 20th and 21st of May in this yeare did my Grandchild George Tufton, youngest Sonne to my Daughter, Countess Dowager of Thanet, take his leave of her and some of his Brothers and Sisters at Thanet House in Aldersgate Street in London Towne, and go from thence to Dover in Kent and after some four dayes stay there for a fair winde, he took shipping for France, in which Shippe he went well and safe to Rochell in France, where he arrived safe about the —— [blank in manuscript] and from thence he went to Bourdeaux and so to ye Baths called the Mudds in France. And about the beginning of September following he came from the hott baths in France, upon the frontiers of Spain, took Shipp at Rochell, and landed the 19th day at Dover in Kent, and so came safe to his Brother Mr John Tufton's House in Kent and from thence to his eldest Brother, the Earle of Thanets House at Hothfield in that Countie, and so to Bolbrooke House in Sussex to his Mother, and his two youngest Sisters, to stay there with them for some while. But my said Grandchild received little or no benefit from the said Baths.

The 3rd of August in this yeare being Tuesday, about 6 a clock in the evening, did my Daughter Margaret, Countess Dowager of Thanet with Mr Sackvill Tufton her youngest Sonne and her 2 youngest Daughters, Lady Mary and Lady Anne Tufton, and their Company come from their journy from my said Daughters House call'd Thanet House in Aldersgate Street at London, and this Day came over Stainmoore and those Wayes hither into this Appleby Castle in Westmerland, and so up in to my Chamber to mee, where I now kiss'd them with much joy and comfort. I having not seen this Daughter of mine nor her said youngest daughters since the 3rd of September in 1666, when they, with Lady Cecily another of her Daughters went away from mee from Skipton Castle in Craven (where I then lay) back towards London againe, untill now. Nor had I seen her Sonne Sackvill Tufton since the 18th of August 1663 when he, with my sayd Daughter his Mother and three of his Brothers, namely Richard, Thomas and George, and his Sister, Lady Frances (since deceased), went away from mee from Skipton Castle aforesayd, back towards London againe untill now.

And now they continued to lye here (my Daughter with her youngest Daughter Lady Anne in the Baron's Chamber, and Lady Mary with her Woman in the Sheriffs Chamber neare to it, and Sackville Tufton in the best Roome in Caesars Tower here) for 10 nights together. In which time viz: on Munday the 9th of this August they went in my Coach to my Castle of Pendraggon in this Countie to see it, which was the first time my Daughter or any of these her 3 children were ever in it, though most of her other Children had bin in it before. And on Friday the 13th of this month about 9 a clock in the morning after I had kiss'd them as taking my leave of them, they with their Company went away from hence from mee to Brough, my said Grandchild Mr Sackvile Tufton going a little before to see my Castle there, and the Roman Tower, for he had never bin in them before. And afterwards meeting his Mother and Sisters and their Company againe, they rid together over Stain moore, and so onwards on their journy towards London, whither they came safe and well to Thanet House in Aldersgate Street there the 21st of that month, and lay there in it for a time.

And the 21st of this August being Saturday, in the evening did the two Judges of Assize for the Northern Circuite, namely Sir Christopher Turner, one of the Barons of his Majesties Exchequer (who hath come hither often on the same occasion) and Thomas Waller Esq Serjeant at Lawe, come from the City of Carlisle from holding the Assize there, and so out of Cumberland over the River neare Brougham Castle, hither into this Appleby Castle in Westmerland, where I and my family now lye, and where they now lay for 4 nights together, Judge Turner in the Baron's Chamber and Serjeant Waller in the best Roome in Caesars Tower. And when they were past (the Assizes in Appleby being ended) they went away from hence from mee on Wednesday the 25th of this month to Kendall where they lay that night, and the next day they went to Lancaster to keep the Assizes there also and to finish their Circuite. And my Cozen Sir John Lowther in this County lay here also in this Castle most part of the time of these Assizes as usual.

And a little before this, on the 14th of May last did there come into this

The Kendal Diary, 1650–1675

Appleby Castle in Westmerland to mee from their journy out of Darbyshire, Sir Francis Rodes and his Sister Mrs Jane Rodes, whose Mother was the Widdow Lady Rodes my Cozen-German. She having bin the youngest Daughter to my Uncle of Cumberland, and this was the first time I ever saw any of his generacon in Westmerland. And with them there came hither to me Mr Roger Molyneux who had bin a Colonell, and now also lives in Darbyshire. So these three lay here three nights, and on the 17th of this month they went away from hence from mee back againe towards their owne homes in Darbyshire.

And the 26th of August in this yeare being Thursday about Noone, did my Grandchild the Ladie Margaret Coventrie and her two Children now only living, namely Mr John and Miss Margaret Coventry, and their company come from their journy from her Lords House call'd Croom in Worcestershire, from whence they set forth on Thursday the 19th instant, and came by Nottingham, Doncaster and over Stainmoore, and today from Brough in Westmerland hither into this Appleby Castle in the same Countie, and so up into my Chamber to mee, where I now kiss'd them with much joy and contentment; this being the first time that ever any of them were in Westmerland, or in any partes of ye Lands of my Inheritance. And also the first time that ever I saw any to whom I am Great-Grandmother; and I had not seen my Grandchild the Lady Margaret Coventry since she was marryed, nor in a good while before. For I had not seen her since about the beginning of July in 1649, when she was with mee at Baynards Castle in London, a little before I came quite away from thence hither into the North, to Skipton and Westmerland, untill now.

Gen. 48.11.

And now they continued to lye here (my said Grandchild the Lady Margaret Coventry in the Baron's Chamber) and her Daughter Miss Margaret Coventry and her Mother's Gentlewoman in the Sheriff's Chamber nere to it, and Mr John Coventry in the Green Chamber which is under the withdrawing Room, for eight nights together. In which time, viz: on Monday the 30th of this August they went in their Coach from hence to Julian Bower in Whinfeild Parke to see it, and from thence by the 3rd Brother Tree in that Parke into Lowther Hall to my Cozen Sir John Lowther and his Lady where they dined, and from thence after Dinner, they went into my Castle of Brougham in the Countie to see it, but came back againe the same night hither into this Appleby Castle. From whence on Friday the 3rd of the month following, about 9 a clock in the morning, after I had kiss'd them and taken my leave of them, they with their Company went from mee by Brough and over Stainmoore and those Waies to the Inn at Greta Bridge, and the next day to the City of York to see it, where they lay 2 nights (the next day being Sunday). And on Munday the 6th of the same September they continued their journie from thence homewards, towards her Lords House at Croome in Worcestershire, whither they came safe and well, I thank God, to her Lord and Husband; the 9th of the same lying by ye Way (amongst other places) in the City of Coventry in Warwickshire.

Jer. 29.6; 30.19. Ps. 116.12, 13, 14.

The 10th day of September in this yeare, being now Friday, dyed Henrietta Maria, Queen Mother of England in her House called Colombe in France, some 4 miles from Paris; which House she had lately caused to be built Her Selfe; who, if she had lived till the 16th of November following would have bin 60 yeares old. She came first into England and was married in July 1625 to our King Charles the first, who was afterwards unfortunately beheaded ye 30th of January in the year 1649 – as the same begins on New Yeares Day; during which time she had many children by Him, and amongst the rest, our now King Charles the Second. She was a Woman of excellent perfections both of Mind and Body; and was youngest Child to Henry of Bourbon the Fourth, King of France, who was treacherously killed when she was about 5 months old.

And on Wednesday the 10th of November following in this yeare (according to the account of the Church of England) was performed the solemne funerall service for the said Queen Mother in the Abbey Church at St Dennis near Paris in France, where Her dead Body was then buryed after the form and magnificence as had bin formally used at the funerall of the Queen Mother of France.

Job 7.1. Eccles. 3; 8.6.

And the 7th of this September being Tuesday about 5 or 6 a clock in the evening, did my Sonne in Law James Compton, Earle of Northampton, with his Company come from his journey from his owne House at Castle Ashby in that Countie, from my Grandchild the Ladie Alethea Compton his Daughter, and from his second wife and his children by her, hither into this Appleby Castle in Westmerland; for he sett forth from Castle Ashby aforesaid on Tuesday the 31st of the last month and lay two nights by the Way, viz: the 4th and 5th day of this month (the latter being Sunday) in my Castle of Skipton in Craven, the highest Chamber in ye Great Round Tower there, in which Castle he had not bin since the 11th of April 1662, as he was on his journey to Brougham Castle to mee, till now.

And the 6th day from thence he came to Kirkby Lonsdale and so the 7th day (as aforesaid) hither into this Appleby Castle to mee, where I now kiss'd him in my owne chamber, I having not seen him since the 19th of May in the sayd yeare 1662, when he was then newly a Widdower by the death of my dear Daughter his first wife; and when he then went from mee from Brougham Castle aforesaid, through Craven by Barden Tower and those wayes up towards London and the Southern Partes, untill now.

And now he lay here for 3 nights in the Baron's Chamber, viz: till the 10th of this September, that he went from hence onward on his journy towards Niddsdale in Scotland to see his Aunt the Countess of Niddsdale, where he also lay 3 nights, and 2 nights by the way at Carlisle in his going and coming. And on the 15th instant returned back hither to Appleby Castle aforesaid to mee, where he lay in the Baron's Chamber for 5 nights more; and when they were past, on Munday ye 20th of this month in the morning, before I saw him (for he took his leave of mee in my chamber the night before) he went away againe from hence with his Company by Brough and over Stainmoore and those wayes, onward on his journy towards his sayd House at Castle Ashby in Northamptonshire.

And the 9th of this September in the forenoone, whilst my Lord of Northampton was here (so as it was now their fortune to meet together here) did my second Lord the Earl of Pembrokes youngest Sonne but one, called Mr James Herbert, with one Mr Thomas Saunders, come from their Houses in Oxfordshire to mee in this Appleby Castle in Westmerland, where I now kiss'd them both, it being the first time that I ever saw any of my second Husbands Children in Westmerland, or any parte of my Inheritance; and they now lay in Caesars Tower here for 3 nights together; and on Tuesday the 14th instant betimes in the morning, before I saw them, they (having taken their leave of me the night before) went away from hence over Stainmoore to the City of York, and so onwards on their journy towards Oxfordshire againe.

And about the latter end of August in this yeare did my Daughter the Countess Dowager of Thanet's two youngest Daughters, Lady Mary and Ladie Anne Tufton go from her, out of her House called Thanet House in Aldersgate Street by reason the small pox was then so rife in that part of London, down into the Country to Bolebrook House in Sussex; whither their said Mother my Daughter went down to them the 6th and 7th of the month following, to lye there in it with them for a time, viz: till the 16th of November following (as hereafter written) that she and they returned back to Thanet House aforesaid to lye there in it againe as before.

And the 1st day of October this yeare did there come hither to me at

Appleby Castle from their House not far from Narworth Castle in Cumberland, Edward Lord Morpeth (eldest sonne to my Cozen Charles Howard, Earl of Carlisle) and his Ladie who was one of the younger daughters of Sir William Vurdale [Uvedale] by his second wife Victoria Carey, and widdow of one of the Berkeleys that was killed in the late Warres. So she and her Husband lay that one night in the Barons Chamber and the next day in the morning before I saw them, they and their Companie went away onwards on their journy towards London.

And the 19th of this October about 11 a clock in the forenoon did I and my family remove out of Appleby Castle to Brough Castle in Westmerland, and coming out of my owne chamber there I pass'd through the great chamber and went into the Chappell and through the Hall, took my Litter at the Hall Doore in the Court, and so passing through the Towne of Appleby over the Bridge and Sandford Moore, went through Warcop Towne into the sayd Brough Castle.

And I had continued to lye in the sayd Castle of Appleby in my chamber there from the 26th of June 1668 till the time of my now Removall, being a yeare and 4 monthes wanting some 7 or 9 daies. And I had not layn in Brough Castle since the 19th of Aprill 1665 being 3 yeares and six months compleat. And I now began to lye againe in the Round Tower called Clifford's Tower in the upper Roome next the Leads in that Brough Castle, where I did alwaies used to lye since the repair of that Castle, excepting some four nights that I lay in the Roman Tower. In which Chamber of mine in Clifford's Tower I now continued to lye for 28 weekes together, viz: till the 3rd of May in the year following that I removed from this Brough Castle into my Castle of Pendragon in the same Countie to lye in it for a time.

And the 16th of November in this yeare did my Daughter Margaret, Countess Dowager of Thanet with her two youngest Daughters Lady Mary and Lady Anne Tufton, after they had layen in Bolebrooke House in Sussex ever since the latter end of August and beginning of September before, remove from thence up to London againe to my said Daughter's House called Thanet House in Aldersgate Street, there to her Daughter Lady Cecily Hatton and her Husband and their little Daughter Anne, and to her youngest Sonne George Tufton, who then also lay there though he had bin downe at Bolebrook aforesaid with his sayd Mother and Sisters but a little before, when he was then but newly come from his journy from the hott Baths in France, near to the Borders of Spaine, which he went to make use for his lameness, though it seems they did him little good.

In the yeare of
our Lord God 1670

The 3rd day of May in this yeare after I had layen in Brough Castle in Westmerland in the highest chamber in Cliffords Tower there, ever since the 19th of October last, being 6 monthes and some 14 daies over, and after I had bin a while in the fornoone in the Roman Tower there to see it, did I remove from thence in my Horslitter, my women riding in my Coach drawn with 6 Horses and my Menservants on horsback, through Brough Sowerby and Kirkby Stephen and within sight of Wharton Hall (though not through the Parke there) I came safe and well into my Castle of Pendraggon in the same Countie, and so up into my owne chamber in it wherein I formerly used to lye and where I now continued to lye till the 3rd day of August following, that I removed from thence into my Castle of Appleby in the same Countie to lye in it for a time.

The 29th day of Aprill in this yeare was Cardinal Paulus Emilius Abieri elected and proclaimed Pope at Roome, by the name of Clement the tenth, after there had bin a vacancy ever since the 9th of December last, which was the longest vacancy that hath bin in ye Papacy since the reign of Henrey the 4th, Henrey ye 5th and Henrey the 6th.

The 16th of May in this yeare being Munday, did the Princess Henrietta wife to the Duke of Brabant, who was the youngest Daughter to our late King and Queen and youngest sister to our now King Charles the second, come from her journy out of France from the said Duke, her husband, and so from Dunkirke over Sea into England, and landed at Dover in Kent, whither our King, her Brother, with the Duke of York and Prince Rupert went to meet her, and afterwards on the 18th instant the Queen went also towards Dover to visit Her. And after this Princess Henrietta Maria had made a short stay there she returned back into France, and being arrived at St Clou which is within 4 or 5 miles of Paris, she was taken ill with a sudden and violent distemper (thought to be a kind of bilious cholic), whereof she dyed there on Monday the 20th of the month following about 4 a clock in the morning; which sad news was brought into England to Whitehall the 22nd of the same month by expresse from Mr Montague our King's Ambassador at Paris, to the great griefe of His Majestie and the rest of Her Relacons.

The 20th of this May being Friday, before 9 a clock in the morning was my Grandchild the Lady Cecily Hatton delivered of her second Child which was also a Daughter, in Thanet House in Aldersgate Street in London Towne, where she and her Husband then lay; which child was christened the next day by the name of Margaret; her two Grandmothers (namely my Daughter Margaret, Countess Dowager of Thanet and my Lord Hatton's Lady) being her Godmothers, and my Lord Fanshaw the God father.

The 10th day of June in this yeare being Friday did my deare Grandchild the Lady Alithea Compton, youngest and only surviving child to the now James, Earle of Northampton* by my deceased Daughter, his first wife, come from her journy from her said Mother's House at Castle Ashby in Northampton-shire, from him and his new wife, and their children and family, hither into this Pendraggon Castle in Westmerland to mee, whereof now I kiss'd her in my owne chamber with unspeakable joy and comfort; it being the first time I ever saw her, though she be now 9 yeares and 3 months old wanting some 4 days. And this Grandchild of mine set forth from Castle Ashby aforesaid on Thursday the 2nd of this month in her Coach (attended by 4 Gentlewomen, a Gentleman and other servants and also by Collonell Carr, that lives at Skipton in Craven) and so came by Stamford, Newark, Doncaster, Wetherby, Knaresborough and by my Almshouse at Beamsley (which she went into to see it) into my Castle at Skipton in Craven where she lay 2 nights in the highest Roome of the great round Tower at the end of the long Gallery there (where her father and Mother had layn formerly) and in that time, viz: ye 8th instant, went for a while into my House or Tower of Barden to see it; and the next day, being the 9th day, she came from Skipton to Kirkby Lonsdale, where she lay one night, and from thence the 10th day (as aforesaid) came safe, God be thanked, hither into this Pendraggon Castle to mee, where she now lay in that Chamber over the great Chamber which hath windows to ye East and South, for 33 nights together, during which time, viz: the 1st of July, she went with her gentlewomen and my 2 gentlewomen to Hartley Castle to my Cozen Mr Richard Musgrave and his Wife and Daughter for a while, and to Kirkby Stephen and Wharton Hall to see those places, but came back againe to mee about 6 a clock the same evening. And another time she went to Mallerstang Chappell which I, not long since had caused to be new-builded.

* James, 3rd Earl of Northampton, married secondly Mary, eldest daughter of 3rd Viscount Campden in 1664.

The Kendal Diary, 1650–1675

And the 13th of July this Grandchild of mine, after I had kiss'd her, and she had taken her leave of mee, and after she and her company had layn here ever since the 10th of last month, went from hence to my Castle of Brough to see it, and the Roman Towne there, and so from thence over Stainmoore onwards on her journy towards Castle Ashby in Northamptonshire, whither she came safe and well (I thank God) the 23rd of ye month, to her father.

Jer. 29.6; 30.19. Ps. 116.12, 13, 14.

And the same 10th of this June, a little after she was gone hither, did my deare Grandchilde Mr Thomas Tufton, 4th Sonne and 7th Child to my Daughter Margaret, Countess Dowager of Thanet, and now one of the Burgesses of Parliament for the Corporation of Appleby, come from his journy from London and the Southerne partes and today from the Inne at Greta Bridge, and so over Stainmoore hither also into this Pendraggon Castle in Westmerland to mee, and so up into my Chamber where I kiss'd him with much joy and contentment, I having not seen him since the 30th of September 1668; that he went the day following from Appleby Castle (where I and my family then lay) up towards London, untill now. And now he lay in this Pendraggon Castle in the Chamber over the Great Chamber which adjoins to my Grandchild Lady Alithea's, for 19 nights together, in which time, viz: the 13th of this month, he went to see severall remarkable places about this Castle, as namely Wilbor Fell, Hugh Seat Morvill and Holgill Bridge. And the 16th of this month he went to Edenhall in Cumberland to my Cozen Sir Philip Musgrave calling by the way at Acornbank in this Countie to see Mr John Dalston.

And ye 18th of this month he went to Kendall in this Countie to see it, and into the ruinous Castle and the church there, and to Mr George Sedgwick's House at Collinfield, where he dined with him, and came back also the same night into this Pendraggon Castle againe, from whence on Munday the 20th instant, betimes in the morning before I saw him he went away onwards on his journy into Scotland (by the City of Carlisle and those Waies) and saw most of the remarkable Cities and places in that Kingdome – as namely Dumfries, Douglas Hamilton and the Duke's Palace there (where he was nobly treated) and from thence went to ye City of Glasgow where he gave a visit to ye Archbishopp at ye Castle, and saw ye University there; and thence to ye Towne and Castle of Dumbarton, thence to ye Towne of Stirling, thence to ye City of Edinburgh, thence to a place called Bask Island (which is so remarkable for Soland Goose). And from thence out of Scotland he returned back by ye Towne of Berwick upon Tweed, Newcastle and Barnard Castle hither into Pendraggon Castle to mee, the 7th of ye month following, where he lay for about 11 nights more. In which time, viz: ye 15th of ye same July, he went with some of my chiefe folk through Whinfield Parke and by my Castle of Brougham into Dacre Castle in Cumberland, thence to Dunmallord Hill and so down to Ullswater to see those places, but they came back to Brougham Castle aforesaid where they lay that one night (my Grandchild lying in the Baron's Chamber) and ye next day from thence (by Julian Bower and ye same waies they went) and they came back into this Pendraggon Castle againe. And on the 18th of this July betimes in the morning, after I had kiss'd him and he taken his leave of mee in my Chamber he went away from hence from me over Stainmoor onward on his journy towards London.

Jer. 29.6; 30.19. Ps. 116.12, 13, 14.

The 3rd day of August this yeare being Wedensday, after I had layen at Pendraggon Castle in Westmerland (in the same chamber I formerly used to lye) ever since the 3rd of May last being just a quarter of a yeare, did I remove from thence in my Horslitter, and my family, towards my Castle of Appleby in the same Countie; so as we now went within sight of Wharton Hall, Brough Castle and Hartley Castle, and through Wateby and Soulby and over Soul by Mask to my said Castle of Appleby safe and well (I thank God) where I alighted in the Court and came through the Hall, the Chappell, the Great Chamber, the Withdrawing Roome (in every of which places I stay'd a while to see them), and so up into my owne chamber in it where I formerly used to lye, and where I had not bin since the 19th of October last, that I removed from thence to Brough Castle, and from thence the 9th of May last to Pendraggon Castle aforesaid, until the 3rd of August that I came hither againe. And I continued to lye in this Appleby Castle till the 14th day of October following that I removed thence to Brougham Castle in the same Countie with my family to lye in it for a time.

The 13th day of August being Saturdaie, in the afternoon did the two Judges of Assize for this Northern Circuit, namely Sir Christopher Turner and Sir Timothy Littleton, two of the Barons of His Majestys Exchequer, come from the City of Carlisle in Cumberland from holding the Assizes there, and so out of that Countie, over the River neare my Castle of Brougham hither into Appleby Castle in Westmerland, where I and my family now lye. And where in the Towne Hall here in Appleby those Judges now hold the Assizes for this Countie also; which was the first time that ever the said Sir Timothy Littleton came hither on this occasion, though the other hath come this Circuit for severall yeares past. And they now lay here in this Castle for four nights together,

The Kendal Diary, 1650–1675

Judge Turner in the Baron's Chamber and Judge Littleton in the best Room in Caesars Tower. And when they were past (the Assizes being ended) they went away from hence from mee on Wedensday the 17th of this month to Kendall where they lay that night, and the next day they went to Lancaster to keep the Assizes there also and so finish their Circuit.

The 8th day of September being Thursday did Mr William Edge, who had bin formerly my Domestick Servant, and is now Receiver General of my Southern Rents, come with his second and new married Wife who was a Widdow and whom I never saw before, from their journy from London where they live, through Staffordshire and Lancashire and today from Kendall, hither into this Appleby Castle to mee, where they now lay for 7 nights together in the Baron's Chamber. And when they were past, on Thursday the 15th of this month after they had taken their leave of me in the morning, they went away from hence onwards on their journy towards London againe, and I had not seen William Edge these good many yeares before, till now.

And this September whilst I lay in Appleby Castle, a little before my Removall to Brougham Castle, did my Daughter Margaret, Countess Dowager of Thanet, go from Thanet House in Aldersgate Street in London Towne down into the Country to Kirkby in Northamptonshire (which is not far from Lilford) to her Daughter Lady Cecilia Hatton and her two little children Anne and Margaret, whither she came to them the 22nd of that month. But her Sonne in law the now Lord Hatton was then beyond the Seas in the Isle of Gernsey, which Island the King lately made him Governor. And after my Daughter had layen at Kirkby aforesaid for 4 or 5 nights, she came back againe to her sayd House called Thanet House at London.

And the 14th of October, being Friday, about 9 or 10 a clock in the forenoone after I had layen in Appleby Castle ever since the 3rd of August last, that I came from Pendraggon Castle thither, did I remove with my family from thence, coming through the Withdrawing Chamber and great chamber into the Chappell for a while, and so through the Hall, took my Litter at the Hall Doore in the Court, in which I rid through the Towne of Appleby, over the Bridge and so through Crackenthorp, Kirby Thure, Temple Sowerby, Woodside and by the Hartshorn Tree (which I look'd on for a while). I came safe and well I thank God into my Castle of Brougham in the same Countie about 3 a clock in the afternoon, and bin accompanied hither by severall of the Gentrys of this Countie and my Neighbours and Tenants both of Appleby, Brougham and Penrith; and when they had taken their leaves of mee in the Hall of this Brougham Castle, I came up through the great chamber and painted chamber and the little Passage Room into my owne Chamber where I formerly used to lye, and where my Noble Father was borne and my blessed Mother dyed. And I had not bin in this Brougham Castle since the 26th of June in 1668, when I removed thence to Appleby Castle aforesaid, untill now. And I now continued to lye in my said Chamber in Brougham Castle till the 17th of August following, that I removed with my family to the said Appleby Castle againe, as the time of my stay at Brougham now was 10 months and 3 daies; in which time, viz: the 12th of December in this yeare, dyed my deare Grandchild Mr George Tufton, youngest Sonne to my Daughter Margaret, Dowager Countess of Thanet.

And before I removed (as abovesaid) from Appleby Castle to Brougham Castle, on the 8th of September in this yeare, being Thursday, was my Grandchild the Lady Mary Tufton, youngest Daughter and child but one to my Daughter Margaret, Countess Dowager of Thanet, marryed to Mr William Walter, eldest Sonne to Sir William Walter of Sarsden, not far from Woodstock in Oxfordshire, whose father was that Sir John Walter that was Lord Chief Baron of ye Exchequer in the time of our late King Charles the First. And this young couple were marryed together in St Botolph's Church in Aldersgate Street in London by Dr Wells, Minister of that Parrish, there being present at ye marriage Christopher, Lord Hatton her Brother in Law (who gave her in marriage), her Mother, my Daughter of Thanet, and the Lady Diana Curzon, Mr Cecil Tufton and his Wife and Sonne, ye Lady Dacres and her second Husband Mr David Walter, Sir Peter Killigrew and his Wife, the Lord Darcy and his wife and his Sonne and Daughter, and Mr Otley Groom Porter and others. And the said new married couple lay for 5 nights together in my Daughter of Thanet's House in Aldersgate Street aforesaid; and when they were past, the 13th of this month they went down towards their father's House at Sarsdon in Oxfordshire to live there with him.

The 24th day of October in this yeare being Munday, the two Houses of Parliament, viz: the Lords and Commons (according to their adjournment) re-assembled at Westminster where our now King Charles was then present in the House of Lords habited in his Royal Robes, and Crown upon his Head, and having taken his Place with the usual ceremonies in the Chain of Estate, His Majesty made a gracious speech, in short, to both Houses, leaving the Lord Keeper to open the particulars more at Large.

And the 27th of this October did His Highness William of Nassau, Prince of Orange, and only Child to our now King of Englands eldest Sister, now deceased, take Shipp at the Briol in Holland, in which he came

The Kendal Diary, 1650–1675

over sea into England and landed at Margate the 29th of the same month in the morning, from whence immediately He rid first to Canterbury and thence passed by Coach to Rochester where he lay that one night; and the next day, being the 30th day, He came to Gravesend, and so from thence, in a Barge of the Kings along the River of Thames to Whitehall to his Uncle our sayd King of England, and her Majestie and to the Duke and Duchesse of Yorke, who all of them receiv'd him in great demonstration of affection and joy; this being the first time that ever this young Prince came into England. And he now began to lye in those Lodgings by the Cockpit at Whitehall wherein my late Lord the Earl of Pembroke did use to lye, and wherein that Lord of mine dyed. And in a short time after this young Prince went to Windsor Castle where he lay one night, and then to both the Universities of Oxford and Cambridge and to Audleyend House to see them and other remarkable places in this Kingdom.

And on Monday the 13th of February following He, with the Earl of Ossery (whom the King appointed to attend him on the Voyage) went from Whitehall and so from London down by Rochester in Kent to Sheernesse, where His Highness took Shipping that evening in one of His Majestie's Yachts, and so passed safe and well over seas into his owne Country, viz: to the Hague in Holland to live there againe, and in other places in the Low Countries as before.[*]

And the 12th day of December being Munday, about 12 a clock at Noone (to the unspeakable grief of mee & his Mother, my Daughter ye Countess of Thanet) dyed my deare Grandchild Mr George Tufton, her youngest Sonne, in Thanet House in Aldersgate Street in London Towne. In which House he was borne into the world (or rather in Hothfield House in Kent) ye 30th of June 1650. So as he was twenty yeares old and almost six months at the time of his death, and he dyed of a wound which he got about 4 yeares since by a shott in the Warrs in Gernsey. And his dead Body was opened and inward partes view'd by a Phisician and Chirurgeon [surgeon], who wondred he should live so long after such a wound. And afterwards his Bowells being putt in again, his dead Body was buryed in the Church at Raynham in Kent by his Father and 2 of his Sisters, namely ye Lady Anne Tufton and the Lady Frances Drax. And both when he dyed and was buryed, did I lye in my chamber in Brougham Castle in Westmerland wherein my Noble Father was born and where my blessed Mother dyed.

[*] Following the Second Dutch War (1665–7), an alliance had been formed between England, Holland and Sweden, though this was negated by the Treaty of Dover (May 1670) made between England and France, resulting in the Third Dutch War against King Charles' nephew, William of Orange, two years later.

In the yeare of
our Lord God 1671

The 31st day of March in this yeare being Friday, in the King's House at St James neare Whitehall and the River Thames and nott farr from London, dyed that Anne Hyde that was Dutchesse of Yorke, in one of the chambers there, wherein had formerly dyed Queen Mary and Prince Henry. Her Husband, James, Duke of York being present at her death, and her three Children that are living (whereof two are daughters and one a Sonne) being there also in the House. And on the 5th of the month following betwixt 9 and 10 of the clock at night her dead body after it had bin opened, was accompanyed from the painted chamber in the Palace at Westminster by his Highnesse Prince Rupert who appeared as Chief Mourner, and most of the English Nobility, and was buryed in a large vault on the Southsyde of Henry the Sevenths Chappell in Westminster Abbey.

And the 17th day of August being Thursday, in the forenoone after I had layn in my Castle of Brougham in Westmerland in the Chamber wherein my Noble Father was borne and my blessed Mother dyed ever since the 14th of October last, did I go for a little while out of it into the Roome adjoining, being the middle Roome in ye great Pagan Tower, and into that part of it where my old servant Jane Bricknell dyed, and so came into my owne Chamber againe, where, after a short stay I went from thence about 11 a clock of the same day through the little Passage Roome and the Painted Chamber and the Hall down into ye garden for a while, and from thence back into ye Court of ye Castle, where I took my Horslitter in which I ridd by ye Pillar that I erected in memory of my last parting there with my Blessed Mother, and so through part of Whinfield Park to Julian Bower; and from thence, out of ye Park I went over Eden Bridge and through the Townes of Temple Sowerby, Kirbythure and Crackenthorp, and down the Step Stones and over Appleby Bridge and near ye Church, and through Appleby Towne I came safe and well (I thank God) into my Castle of Appleby in the same Countie, about 4 a clock in the afternoon, my women attending me in my Coach drawn with six horses and my menservants on horsback and a great many of the chief Gentry of this Countie and of my Neighbours and Tenants accompanying mee in this my Removall. So after I was now alighted in this Appleby Castle, I went through ye Hall up into ye Chappell for a while, and into the great chamber and so up ye greene staires and through ye Withdrawing chamber into my owne chamber where I formerly used to lye, and where I had not been ever since the sayd 14th October last, until now. And I now continued to lye in this chamber of myne for 3 months together, viz: until the 17th November following that I removed from thence with my family to my Castle of Pendraggon in the same Countie to live in it for a time.

And the 25th of this August, whilst I lay in Appleby Castle in Westmerland did my Daughter Margaret, Countess Dowager of Thanet, and her youngest Daughter Lady Anne Tufton, after they had layn some nights in Bolebrooke House in Sussex, remove with her family from thence up into her House in Aldersgate Street in London Towne to lye in it as before.

And the 2nd of September in this yeare, being Saturday, did Sir Timothy Littleton who is one of the Barons of His Majesties Exchequer and now one of the Judges of Assize for this Northern Circuit, come from the City of Carlisle in Cumberland from his fellow Judge Sir William Wild (who was detained there longer by occasion of much business), and so over the Rivers of Eamont and Lowther near my Castle of Brougham in Westmerland, where he was met by my Under Sheriff Mr Thomas Gabetis and several of my servants with my Coach and six Horses in which he came about 5 a clock in the afternoon hither into this Appleby Castle in the same Countie. And on Monday following being the 4th of the same month did the said Sir William Wild who is one of the Justices of His Majestys Court of Common Pleas and now the other Judge of Assize for this Northern Circuit, come from the said City of Carlisle, being mett by the way at Eamont Bridge by my said Sheriff and with my Coach in like manner as the former Judge was, and so came in it hither into Appleby Castle to him and mee and us here. So as these two Judges now lay here till the 6th of this month; viz: Judge Littleton 4 nights in the Best Roome in Caesars Tower, and Judge Wild 2 nights in the Barons Chamber, during which time they held the Assizes in the Moot Hall in Appleby Towne and dispatched business for the People of the Countie as usual; and on the 6th instant being Wednesday (having taken their leaves of mee in my Chamber) they went away from hence, part of the way in my Coach attended by some of my Servants, towards

Kendall intending to lye there one night, and the next day to go to Lancaster to hold the Assizes for that Countie also, and so to finish their Circuit. And this was the first time that ever Sir William Wild came hither on this occasion, though the other Judge had bin here before.

And whilst the Assizes were held here at Appleby aforesaid, viz: on Monday the 4th of this September, did my Cozen Phillipp Lord Wharton and his two oldest Sonnes Thomas and Goodwin, and a Grandchild of my Lord Wainmans come hither into Appleby Castle to mee, but went that night to Wharton Hall in this Countie. Also my Cozen Sir Philip Musgrave of Ednell [Edenhall] came hither to mee the same day with them, and lay in one of ye best upper chambers in Caesars Tower one night, and ye next day went away againe.

And the said Lord Wharton's three daughters that are unmarried, whom he had by his second wife, were also here with mee for a while these Assizes; for during the time of these Assizes did I lye in my owne Chamber in Appleby Castle in Westmerland.

And the 3rd day of this September about 7 a clock in the morning, being Sunday, was my Grandchild the Ladie Mary Walter, 5th Daughter and 9th Child of my Daughter Margaret, Countess Dowager of Thanet, brought to bed of her first Child which was a Sonne, in Thanet House in Aldersgate Street in London Towne, where her Husband Mr William Walter and her said Mother and youngest sister Lady Anne Tufton, then lay.

That month in the same House was this child christened by the name of William after his Father, my said Daughter standing as Deputy God-Father in his Father's stead, and Mr David Walter was ye other God-Father. And ye 21st of the same month (to my great grief and sorrow) this little William Walter my God Sonne dyed, being 3 weekes wanting 2 dayes.

And his dead bodie was opened, and towards the latter end of the same month was carryed to Church Hill neare Sarsden in Oxfordshire and buryed in the Church there, where his Father's Relacons lye burryed. And so both when this child was borne, christened and dyed and was burryed did I lye all this time in my owne chamber in Appleby Castle in Westmerland.

And the 17th day of November being Friday, about 10 a clock in the forenoon after I had layen in my Chamber in Appleby Castle in Westmerland ever since the 17th of August last, being just 3 months, did I remove with my family from thence coming through the Withdrawing Chamber and Great Chamber, into the Chappell for a while, and so through ye Hall. I took my litter at ye Hall doore in the Court, in which I rid by ye high crosse in Appleby, and through Scattergate and over Soulby Mask and through Soulby and Waitby and over Askfell into the forest of Mallerstang, and so came safe and well, I thank God, into my Castle of Pendragon there in the same Countie about 4 a clock in the afternoon, having bin accompanyed in the way by severall of the Gentry of this Country and of my Neighbours and Tenants both of Appleby, Kirby Stephen and Mallerstang etc. And my two gentlewomen and women servants rid in my Coach drawn with 6 Horses, and my Menservants on Horsback. But wee had a great storme of Raine and Wind towards the latter end of this journy. And after the said companie had taken their leave of mee here at Pendragon Castle, I came up stairs and through the great chamber into my owne chamber on the West side of it where I formerly used to lye, and where I had not bin since the 3rd day of August in 1670 (being a yeare, 3 months and some 14 days over) untill now. And where I now continued to lye till the 19th of Aprill following, being 7 months and some daies in the yeare 1672, that I removed from thence againe into my Castle of Brough in the same Countie to lye in it for a time.

In the yeare of our Lord God 1672

For on this 19th of Aprill 1672 (as aforesaid) being Friday, about 10 a clock in the fornoone after I had layen in my Chamber in Pendragon Castle in Westmerland ever since the 17th of November last, did I remove out of it, and came through the great chamber downe the staires into the Court, where at the Hall doore I went into my Horslitter in which I rid through the Gatehouse there and through the River of Eden, and over part of Ashfield and through Wharton Park and in sight of that Hall, and through Kirkby Stephen and Brough Sowerby to my Castle of Brough in the same County, my Gentlewomen and Maidservants attending me in my Coach drawn with 6 Horses and my Menservants on Horsback and a great many of my Tenants and Neighbours of Maller-stang, Kirkby Stephen, Brough and Appleby and other places in the County comeing along with me. And so we came to my said Castle of Brough about 1 a clock in the afternoon, where in the Court of it I allighted out of my litter, and came upstairs into ye Hall where all ye strangers that accompanied mee took their leaves of mee and went away to their severall Homes, and from thence I came upstairs into ye great chamber and through it to ye chamber adjoining, and came into my owne chamber in Clifford's Tower where I formerly used to lye, and where, nor in this Castle I had not bin since ye 3rd of May 1670 untill now; and now I continued to lye in it till the 15th of August following (being just a month but 4 daies) and then I removed from hence againe (as shall be hereunder written) into my Castle of Appleby in the same Countie to lye in it for a time.

And the 30th day of July in this yeare being Tuesday, whilst I lay in Brough Castle aforesaid, did my Daughter Margaret, Countess Dowager of Thanet and her youngest child the Lady Anne Tufton, and second Sonne Mr John Tufton with their servants come from their journy from Thanet House in Aldersgate Street at London, and the last night from the Inne at Greta Bridge in Yorkshire, and over Stainmoore into Brough

Castle in Westmerland, and so into my chamber in Clifford's Tower, thence to mee, where I kiss'd them with great satisfaction and joy. I having not seen my deare Daughter and Grandchild Lady Anne since the 13th of August 1669 when they with two other of my Grandchildren, namely Mr Sackville Tufton and Lady Mary Tufton went away from mee from Appleby Castle (where I then lay) back againe towards London, untill now. Nor had I seen my said Grandchild Mr John Tufton since the 14th of June in the said yeare 1669 that he and his Brother Richard (having bin there with me for a while) went back againe towards London, untill now. And they now lay in Brough Castle my Daughter and her daughter with their women in the Room at ye North West corner of ye great chamber, and her said son with their menservants in the great Roman Tower there for 7 nights together. And when they were past, on Tuesday ye 6th of ye month following in the morning, I having kiss'd them in my said chamber on taking my leave of them, they went away from thence over Stainmoore againe and so onwards on their journy towards London, whither they came safe and well (I thank God) the 14th day of ye same month, to Thanet House in Aldersgate Street there.

The 15th day of August in this yeare did I remove with my family out of the said Brough Castle into my Castle of Appleby in the same Countie, coming along in my Horslitter attended by my women servants in my Coach, and my Menservants on horsback with a great many of the Gentrey and of my Neighbours and Tenants in both places, through Warcop, Bongate and over Appleby Bridge through the Towne up into the Court of the said Appleby Castle, where I allighted and went through the Hall up into ye Chappell for a while, and then through ye great chamber and Withdrawing Chamber, I came into my owne chamber where I formerly used to lye, and where I had not bin since ye 17th of November last till now; and where I now continued to lye till the 28th of Januarie following (being 5 months and about a fortnight over) that I removed from thence into my Castle of Brougham in the same Countie to lye in it for a time.

The 28th of this August did Mr Richard Sackvill, third sone of the now Earle and Countess of Dorset come from his journy out of Scotland from his Sister Humes (who lived there) and from the Citie of Carlisle (where he lay the night before) thither into Appleby Castle in Westmerland, though I saw him not until the next day, that he came into my chamber to mee where I kiss'd him, it being the 1st time I ever saw him, or that he or any of his Parents' children were in any part of ye Landes of my Inheritance; so as he now lay in the Barons Chamber here for 3 nights

BOLEBROOKE HOUSE, Hartfield, Sussex, engraved by Letitia Byrne from a
drawing by P. Amsinck (1809)

together, on Saturday the 31st of the same month he went away from hence againe to Kendall and so onward on his journy towards London.

The same 31st of August in the evening did Sir William Wild, one of the Justices of his Majesties Court of Commin Please, and Sir Timothy Littleton one of the Barons of his Majesties Exchequer, who are now the two Judges of Assize for the Northern Circuit (as they also were the last yeare) came from their journy from Carlisle hither into Appleby Castle in Westmerland where they now lay, the first in the Barons Chamber, and the other in the Best Room in Caesars Tower for 4 nights together, in which time they held the Assizes for this Countie in the Towne Hall here, and on Wednesday the 4th of the same month they, having taken their leave of mee in my chamber, went away towards Kendall intending for Lancaster tomorrow to hold the Assizes there and so to finish their Circuit.

Also my Cozen, Sir Philip Musgrave of Eden Hall, and my Cozen Sir John Lowther of Lowther lay in this Appleby Castle during the time of these Assizes as usuall.

And the 11th of October in this yeare, being Friday, did my Daughter Margaret, Countess Dowager of Thanet with her youngest daughter and child the Ladie Anne Tufton remove out of Thanet House in Aldersgate Street at London, and go in her Coach over London Bridge into her House at Bolbrook in Sussex to lye there in it for a time, which was the first time they came to that house after they and my said daughter's second Sonne Mr John Tufton had been with mee at Brougham Castle in Westmerland but the August before; for they went from thence from mee but the 6th of that month towards London. And my said Daughter continued to lye in Bolebrooke House aforesaid till the 20th day of December following, that she removed from thence back againe to Thanet House aforesaid; but by the way she lay one night in the Inne at Croydon in Surrey which was the first time she lay in that Inne, wherein her father's dead Body did lye one night many yeares before, as he was carryed from Dorset House in London to his buryall at Withiham Church in Sussex.

And the 29th of December in this yeare being Sunday, about midnight did there fall a violent storm of thunder and lightning upon ye Island of Guernsey, which taking hold of ye Magazin, powther blew up and destroyed Castle Cornett, which was ye Garrison of that Island. By the ruins whereof were killed (to my great grief and sorrow) my deare grandchild the Lady Cecily Hatton, wife of Christopher Lord Hatton the Governor there, and with her the old Ladie Dowager Hatton his Mother, and many of his Officers soldiers and attendants, but by God's merciful guidance my said dear Grandchild's children that she left behind her, which are 3 daughters, as also their said father and some Relacons of them that were there were preserv'd alive. But ye dead bodies of my said Grandchild and her Lord's Mother were brought over into England to Portsmouth and interred in ye Abbey of Westminster the 11th of ye month following.

In the yeare of
our Lord God 1673

The 28th day of Januarie in this yeare being Tuesday, about one a clock after noon, I removed out of Appleby Castle in Westmerland with my family, after I had layen in it ever since the 15th of August before, into my Castle of Brougham in the same Countie, where I had not bin since the 17th of August 1671 till now. And now as I came from Appleby Castle I went through the Withdrawing chamber and great chamber into the Chappell for a while, where being taken with a swounding fit I was carried into ye Green Chamber, and after I was by God's blessing recovered of it I came thence againe down ye stairs through ye Hall into the Court; from whence being taken with another fit of swounding I was carryed up for a while into the Baron's Chamber. But having, also by God's blessing gotten past it, I went down again into ye Court where I took my Hors litter in which I rid through Appleby Town and over the bridge there, so through Crackenthorp, Kirbythure, Temple Sowerby and Woodside into the Court of Brougham Castle aforesaid, whither I came safe and well, I thank God, about 4 a clock that afternoon, and there I alighted and went upstairs into ye Hall, where all ye company of my Neighbours and Tenants and others that came along with me took their leaves of mee and went away; and I came upstairs through the Great Chamber and painted chamber and ye passage room, into my own chamber in ye said Brougham Castle wherein my Noble Father was borne and my Blessed Mother dyed, and where I now continued to lye till the 30th July following that I removed from thence with my family back againe to Appleby Castle aforesaid to lye in it for a time.

The 23rd of Februarie in this yeare being Sunday, about 7 a clock in the morning was my Grandchild the Lady Marye Walter brought to bed and safely delivered of her second child, which is her first daughter, in her Mother my Daughter of Thanet's House in Aldersgate Street in London. Which child was christened the 26th of that month by ye name of Mary. The Countess of Kent (whose mother was my God-daughter)

217

being one God-mother, and my said daughter of Thanet the other, and Sir William Walter ye God-father.

The 17th day of Aprill in this yeare was my deare Grandchild the Lady Anne Tufton, youngest child to my daughter Margaret, Countess Dowager of Thanet, married in St Botolph's Church in Aldersgate Street at London to Mr Samuell Grimston a Widdower, whose first wife was daughter to Sir Hennige Finch the King's Attorney General, by whom he has only one daughter now living and himself is only sonne of Sir Harbottle Grimston Master of ye Rolls, who with his Lady and many others of his relacons were present at ye marriage. As also, of my said Grandchild's Relacons, her sister, ye Lady Margaret Coventry and her children and 3 of her brothers, viz: Mr John, Mr Richard and Mr Thomas Tufton, and others; I then lying in Brougham Castle in Westmerland as I also did at the time of their removal which was ye 8th of ye month following; for then this new-marryed couple went from her Mother my said Daughter's House in Aldersgate Street aforesaid to his Father's House at ye Rolls to live there with him and his Ladie.

Eccles. 3, 8. Prov. 20.24. Pss. 26.11, 12, 13; 112.

The 13th day of June in this yeare were my greatgrandchildren my Lord Hatton's 3 little daughters tht he had by my deceased Grandchild ye Ladie Cecily Hatton, carried from Castle Cornett in ye Isle of Guernsey from their said father, now Governor of that Island, to ye sea side where they took shipp in ye Hatton Yacht and landed in England at Portsmouth the 15th of ye month, from whence they continued their journy towards London, and came well thither ye 19th of ye month to Thanet House in Aldersgate to their Grandmother, my Daughter of Thanet to live there with her, and that was the first time she ever saw those 3 Grandchildren of hers since the death of their Mother by ye unhappy accident herein above related.

Ps. 90.15, 16, 17.

The 17th day of July in this year did my Daughter the Countess Dowager of Thanet, with her daughter ye Lady Mary Walter and her Husband Mr William Walter, go from Thanet House in Aldersgate Street at London (leaving behind her there her sayd three Grandchildren, my Lord Hatton's Daughters) down to see Sir Harbottle Grimston, ye Master of the Rolls at his House called Gorhambury near St Albans in Hertfordshire, to his youngest daughter the Lady Anne Grimston, wife of ye master of ye Rolls' only Sonne, where they lay for 13 nights together, and ye 30th day of ye same month they returned from thence to Thanet House again.

And the same 30th July being Wednesday in the forenoon, after I had layen in Brougham Castle in Westmerland in ye chamber wherein my Noble father was born and my Blessed Mother dyed, for about half a yeare, viz: ever since ye 28th of January last, did I goe for a while out of it into the middle room in ye great Pagan Tower, there where my old servant Jane Bricknell dyed, and then came into my owne chamber againe, where, after a short stay I went from thence through ye little passage room and the painted chamber and great chamber and the Hall down into ye Court of that Castle, where I went into my Horslitter in which I rid (being attended by my women in my Coach drawn with 6 Horses, and my menservants on horsback) along by ye Pillar I erected in memory of my last parting there with my Blessed Mother, and through Whinfield Park and by ye Hartshorn Tree, the brother tree, and Julian Bower, and through the entry and so, out of ye Park crossing ye Rivers of Lyvennett and Eden, I went through Kirbythure, Crackenthorp, Battleburgh and over Appleby Bridge and through ye Town, into Appleby Castle, whither I came well, thank God about 3 in the afternoon, having bin accompanyed most part of ye way by many of ye chief Gentry of the County and others, and by Neighbours and Tenants hereabouts; and so after I was now alighted in the Court of this Appleby Castle I came through the Hall and upstairs to ye Chappell, and great chamber, and from thence up ye green stairs and through ye Withdrawing Room into my owne chamber where I formerly used to lye, and where I had not bin since ye 28th of January last till now; and where I now continued to lye till the 2nd of March following that I removed with my family to Pendraggon Castle to lye there in it for a time.

The 9th of August in the evening did Sir William Wilde, barronett, one of ye Justices of the King's Bench, and Sir William Ellis one of ye Justices of his Majesties Court of Common Pleas, and now ye two appointed Judges for this Northerne Circuit, come from their journy from Carlisle in Cumberland from holding the Assize there for that County, hither into this Appleby Castle in Westmerland, where they now lay, ye first in ye Baron's Chamber and ye other in ye best room in Caesar's Tower, for four nights together, and in ye time kept the Assizes in ye Moothall in Appleby Towne, which, being ended, they went away from here on Wednesday ye 13th of ye same month in ye forenoone to Kendall, and the next day to Lancaster to hold the Assizes there also, which is ye last place on this Circuit.

And my Cozen Sir John Lowther of Lowther Hall lay here most part of ye time of those Assizes as usuall, but not my Coz. Sir Philip Musgrave, though he was here on Munday ye 11th instant most of ye day and went home in ye evening.

The Kendal Diary, 1650–1675

The 21st day of Novembre in this yeare did the Dutchess of Medina with her Daughter and many persons of Quality come from their journy out of Italy (their owne Country) and landed at Dover in Kent, where His Royal Highnesse the Duke of Yorke met them, and marryed the said Dutchess' Daughter for his second wife, and they all came together to London and Whitehall and St James' the 26th of that month.[*]

And the 30th day of ye month following did ye said Dutchess of Modina, mother to the now Dutchess of Yorke, goe from her and her Husband the Duke, from St James' and Whitehall, and so out of England onwards on her journy back into Italy to her owne Home there.

---

[*] This marriage between James, Duke of York (later King James II), and Mary of Modena (an Italian Catholic) was the cause of fierce opposition in parliament.

In the yeare of
our Lorde God 1674

The 20th day of January being Tuesday, between one and 2 of the clock in the afternoon, was my Grandchild the Lady Mary Walters brought to bed of her third child, which was her second son, in Thanet House in Aldersgate Street at London, which child was christen'd the next day by ye name of John. Sir William Walter the Grandfather, and Mr William Walter ye Father, being the two Godfathers, and myself (by deputy) the Godmother.

But my said dear Grandchild, the day after his delivery, as aforesaid, was taken with the disease of ye smallpox, whereof she dyed there (to my great grief and sorrow) ye 31st of ye same month at ye age of 21 yeares and about 6 months over, and her dead Body was carryed the 5th of ye month following to Church hill near Sarsdon in Oxfordshire, and buryed the 7th of ye same, in the Vault of ye Church there, where her eldest son and her Husband's Realations lye buryed. And during all that time of her delivery, Death and Buryall (as aforesaid) did I lye in my owne Chamber in Appleby Castle in Westmerland.

And the 23rd of this Januarie dyed in Arundell House of a fitt of the [gall]Stones, Elizabeth Stuart, Countess Dowager of Arundell, and was buryed in Arundell Church or Chappell in Sussex by her Husband, Henry Howard Earl of Arundell, by whom she had eight sonnes and daughters.

And part of her jointure was ye Castle and Barony of Graystock in Cumberland.

The 20th day of March being Fryday, about 10 a clock in the fornoone after I had layen in my chamber in Appleby Castle ever since ye 30th of July last, did I remove with my family out of it, and came down through the Withdrawing Chamber, great chamber and Hall into ye Court, where I went into my Horslitter in which I rid (being attended by my women in my Coach, and my menservants on horsback, with severall of my Neighbours and Tenants) through Scattergate and over Soulby by

Mask, and through Soulby and Waitby to my Castle of Pendragon in the same Countie, whither I came safe and well, I thank God, about 3 a clock in ye afternoon; and where, after those of ye Gentry and other my Neighbours and Tenants that accompanyed me had taken their leave of mee, I came upstairs through the great chamber into my owne Chamber on ye Westside of it, where I had not bin since ye 19th of April 1672, till now. And now I continued to lye till the 24th of September following, being about half a yeare, and then removed from thence to my Castle of Brough in the same Countie to lye in it for a time.

The 29th of May did my Grandchild, Mr Thomas Tufton, 4th son and 7th child to my Daughter of Thanet and one of the Burgesses of Parliament for ye Corporation of Appleby, come from his journy from London hither into this Pendragon Castle to mee where I kiss'd him with great satisfaction, I having not seen him since ye 1st of July 1670; and that he had bin at this same Castle with me till now; and now he lay here 7 nights together, in which time he went to Appleby to see the Mayor and Aldermen, and to Ackornbank to see my Cozen Dalston, [and] his fellow Burgesses. And the 8th of the month following after I had kiss'd him, and he taken his leave of mee, he had rid away from hence onwards on his journy towards London againe, and the Southerne Parts.

The 27th July about 8 a clock in the evening was my Grandchild the Ladie Anne Grimston, youngest child to my Daughter of Thanet and second wife to her husband Mr Samuel Grimston, brought to bed in her owne chamber at ye Rolls in Chancery Lane at London of her first child, which was a Sonne who was christened the 4th of ye month following by the name of Edward.

The 31st of August being Munday, did Sir Richard Rainsford one of ye Justices of ye King's Bench, and Sir Timothy Littleton one of ye Barons of His Majesty's Exchequer, they being appointed the two Judges this yeare for the Northerne Circuit, come from the City at Carlisle in Cumberland from holding the Assizes there, and so by Brougham Castle and those wayes into my Castle of Appleby in Westmerland whither I had sent some of my servants before to entertain them, myself with ye rest remaining still at Pendragon Castle; and there at Appleby ye said Judges held ye Assizes for this Countie and lay 2 nights in my Castle there, Judge Rainsford in the Barons Chamber and Judge Littleton in ye best Room in Caesars Tower. And when they were past, the 2nd of ye month following they, with their attendants, went from thence towards Kendall where they lay that one night, and ye next day they went to Lancaster to hold ye Assizes there, also for ye night and so to finish the Circuit. And my Cozen Sir John Lowther of Lowther, and my Coz. Sir Philip Wharton of Edenille in Cumberland lay most part of ye time of these Assizes in my Castle of Appleby as usual at such times.

And the 21st of May in this yeare did my Honorable Cozen and Godson (by Deputy), Mr Robert Stanley, second Brother to the Earl of Derby, borne at Knowsley in Lancashire, come hither to Pendragon Castle to see mee, and lay here one night, and ye next day went away againe homewards to the Countess Dowager of Derby his Mother.

And the 26th day of August did my Cozen Phillip Lord Wharton's two eldest Sonnes, Thomas that was lately marryed, and Goodwin who is unmarryed, come from their Father to his house at Wharton Hall in this Countie where they lay for about a week, in which time, viz: ye 29th and 30th of the same month they came severally hither to Pendragon Castle to me for a while.

The 24th of September being Thursday, about 11 a clock in the forenoone after I had layen in my chamber at Pendragon Castle in Westmerland ever since ye 20th March last, did I remove from thence being attended by my gentlewomen in my Coach, and my menservants on horsback, and some of the Gentlemen and also my Neighbours and Tenants of Mallerstang, Appleby, Brough and other places, and so I rid in my hors litter cross ye River of Eden and through Wharton Park, Kirkby Stephen, Brough Sowerby and pt of Brough Towne into my Castle of Brough, whither I came safe and well, I thank God, about 3 a clock in the afternoon; and so up into my owne chamber in Clifford's Tower, where not in this Castle I had not been since ye 11th August 1672 untill now; and where I continued to lye till the 11th day of May following, that I removed to Appleby Castle to lye there for a time.

And the 19th day of October about 2 a clock in the morning, in her father, Lord Hatton's House at Kirkby in Northampton dyed my greatgrandchild, Miss Elizabeth Hatton, third and youngest daughter to my late deare Grandchild, the Lady Cecily Hatton deceased.

And the 27th November about 10 a clock at night in ye House at Kirkby in Northamptonshire dyed her sister Lady Mary Hatton, second daughter and child to my said dear Grandchild ye Lady Cecily Hatton, deceased.

And the 23rd December about 12 a clock at noon, dyed at ye Rolls in London my Greatgrandchild and Godson Mr Edward Grimston, first and only child to my dear Grandchild the Lady Anne Grimston, and was buryed the 28th of ye same month in the Vault of St Michael's Church at St Alban's in Hertfordshire where some of his fathers Ancestors were buryed before him, and where also was buryed my Ancestor Thomas, Lord Clifford, who was killed there in the first Battell between the 2 Houses of York and Lancaster in Henry ye 6th's times. And when (to my great greife and sorrow) these three greatgrandchildren of mine dyed as aforesaid, did I lye all ye time in my chamber in Clifford's Tower at Brough Castle.

In the Yeare of
our Lorde 1675

The 24th day of March in this yeare dyed in his House at Sarsden in Oxfordshire, Sir William Walter who was Grandfather to two of my Greatgrandchildren, for my grandchild ye Lady Mary Tufton had been married to his Sonne Mr William Walter above 4 yeares ago, leaving two children behind her who are still living, namely Miss Mary Walter who was 2 yeares old ye 23rd of February last, and Mr John Walter who was one yeare old ye 20th January last. And now at ye time of his death his sayd Sonne their father was in Italy.

The 11th day of May 1675 about 10 a clock in ye forenoon, after I had layen in my chamber in Clifford's Tower at Brough Castle in Westmerland ever since the 24th of September last, did I remove from thence with my family going by Warcopp, Bongate and over Appleby Bridge into my Castle of Appleby in the same Countie, whither I came safe and well, I thank God, about 2 a clock in the afternoon, having bin accompanied by severall of ye Gentrey and of my Neighbours and tenants who took their leaves of me then. And then I went through ye great chamber and Withdrawing Chamber into my owne chamber there, where I had not bin since ye 20th March 1673 till now, and where I now continued to lye till ye 8th of October following that I removed from thence to Brougham Castle in ye same Countie to lye in it for a time.

The 18th of June in this yeare was conferred upon my Sonne in Law James Compton, Earl of Northampton, by our now King Charles ye Second, ye Command and Trust of Constable of ye Tower of London.

The 3rd day of August did my deare daughter Margaret, Countesse Dowager of Thanet, and her Grandchild Miss Mary Hatton (the only surviving child of her deceased Mother) come from their journy from Thanet House in Aldersgate Street at London hither into this Appleby Castle in Westmerland to mee, where in my own chamber I kiss'd them with much joy, I having never seen this Grandchild of mine before, nor had I seen my daughter since ye 6th day of August in 1672 when she was with me at Brough Castle, till now. So they now lay here in the Barons Chamber 8 nights together, and when they were past, the 11th instant, they began their journy towards London againe, whither, I thank God, they came safe and well on Friday ye 20th of the same month.

And the 23rd of August being Munday, did Sir Richard Rainsford and Sir Timothy Littleton the 2 Judges of Assize for this Northerne Circuit come from holding the Assizes at Carlisle in Cumberland hither to mee to Appleby Castle in Westmerland, where they now lay, the first in the Barons Chamber, ye other in the best Roome in Caesars Tower for two nights together, in which time they held ye Assizes for this Countie in the Moothall in Appleby towne; and on Wedensday ye 25th instant they went to Kendall, and the next day to Lancaster, where they likewise held ye Assizes for ye Countie and so ended their Circuit.

The 1st day of September, about noone, did Henry Howard Earle of Norwich and Lord Marshal of England, and his eldest son ye Lord Henry Howard, and Charles Howard, Earl of Carlisle, (my Cozens), come into this Appleby Castle in Westmerland to mee for a while; so I kiss'd them, it being ye first time I saw this Lord Marshall since he was a child, or yet ever saw this son of his. And after they had dined here with severall of the Gentry of this Countie and of Cumberland, they went away from hence onwards on their journy towards London.

The 15th of this September did my dear Grandchild ye Lady Alethea Compton, youngest and only surviving child to my deceased Daughter Isabella, Countess of Northampton, come from her journy from her father's House at Castle Ashby in Northamptonshire hither into this Appleby Castle in Westmerland to mee, where I kiss'd her with much joy, I having not seen her since ye 13th of July 1670, that she was at Pendragon Castle with me, till now. And now she continued to lye here in the Barons Chamber 8 nights together, and when they were past on the 23rd instant, she began her journy towards Castle Ashby againe, whither she came safe and well, I thank God, with her Company ye 29th of the same month.

The 23rd of this September about 10 a clock at night was my Grandchild ye Lady Anne Grimston, twelfth and youngest child to my Daughter Margaret, Countesse of Thanet, deliver'd of her second child which was a daughter, in her Husband's House at Gorhambury in Hartfordshire; which child was christen'd there ye 6th of ye month following by the name of Mary; the Master of ye Rolls (ye Childs Grandfather) and my said Daughter of Thanet and ye Lady Diana Curzon being Witnesses to it.

And about that time was my Grandchild Mr Thomas Tufton, fourth son and seventh child of my said Daughter of Thanet, sworn Groome of ye Bedchamber to ye Duke of York.

The 5th day of October being Tuesday, about 10 or 11 a clock in the forenoone, after I had layen in my chamber in Appleby Castle ever since ye 11th of May last, did I remove with my family from thence, by ye waies of Crackenthorp, Kirkby Thure, Temple Sowerby and Woodsyde into my Castle of Brougham in the same Countie, where I had not bin since ye 30th day of July 1673 till now; and where I now continued to lye as usuall in the chamber wherein my Noble father was borne and my Blessed Mother dyed till the —— [blank in manuscript].

The last day of November about 7 a clock in the evening, dyed my Worthy Cozen Sir John Lowther Baronett, in his House at Lowther Hall in this Countie of Westmerland when he was about 73 yeares old; and was buryed ye 4th of ye month following in ye church there at Lowther, where many of his Ancestors lye interred. And by his death his Grandchild and heire John Lowther, my Godson, came to be Baronett, who that day was chief Mourner, attended ye Corps to ye Church, where Dr Smallwood, Parson of Graystock preach'd ye funerall sermon; there being present at ye whole Solemnitie a great many of ye Gentry of this and ye neighbouring counties, as also most of my chief servants.

THE LAST MONTHS 1676

*As we have just seen, the last entry of the 'Kendal Diary', the major part of
Lady Anne's journals to survive in an original form, is dated December 1675.
For the remainder of her life, it is necessary to turn to another source,
again an original piece which has had the good fortune to have survived.
These last few entries were dictated by Lady Anne to at least four different
scribes, one of whom was Edward Hasell, Anne's private secretary, who, she
tells us, was also the writer of the regular letters she sent to her daughter
Margaret, her son-in-law the Earl of Northampton, and to her agent in
Sussex, William Edge. This portion of the diary has remained with Hasell's
descendants for over three hundred years, and is on public view at the Hasell
home at Dalemain, near Penrith.*

*The entries here may remind the reader of the style used by Anne in the
'Knole Diary', though from some of the comments she makes, we seem to
come to know this grand old lady as perhaps never before. Right until the
very end of her long life she appears to have retained all her faculties; still we
see the interminable visits by her relatives, friends and servants, to many of
whom she gives little presents. During the last weeks she recalls, no doubt
with much pleasure, her life from the time of her birth, through her childhood,
and on through both her marriages. Here we can read comments that she
never made in her earlier notes, which makes this last part of Anne's diary so
intriguing. The only clue to her old age is the realization that she remains at
her beloved Brougham, confined to her favourite room.*

One other important factor that comes through very clearly is the strength of Anne's religious beliefs. She bemoans not being able to accompany her staff to the little church at Ninekirks, due to her confinement; instead, the parson comes to lunch at Brougham every Sunday and Wednesday and holds a short service for her in her own room. Moreover, almost every entry is followed by copious quotations from the Old Testament, particularly the Psalms, Ecclesiastes and Job, though, in the interest of brevity, most of these have been omitted.

Lady Anne's record of her last months was first transcribed by the northern historian, William Jackson, as the basis of a lecture that he gave in the 1870s. (His transcription is now preserved in the Tullie House Library in Carlisle.) Dr Williamson also gives these final entries almost verbatim in his biography of Lady Anne, published in 1922. While any abridgement in the latter is to be expected, as it is part of a far larger work, it is notable that Mr Jackson also omitted a great deal, including information which is surely of great historical interest to succeeding generations.

Apart from one short sentence which has defeated interpretation due to the ravages of time, the 'Last Months' have here been transcribed in as complete a form as they are ever likely to be.

1676

JANUARY

The 1st day. And this forenoon there came hither from her house at Seatree Park Mrs Winch, that is mother to Mr Thomas Samford of Askum [Askham], so I had her into my chamber and kist her, and she dined without with my folks in ye Painted Room, and after dinner I had her againe into my Chamber and talked with her a good while, and I gave her 4 pair of Buckskin Gloves that came from Kendall; and with her I had also Mrs Gabetis into my chamber and spoke to her a good while, and a little after they went from mee.

And this morning about 10 of the clock did some of my cheif folks, viz: Mr Thomas Gabetis my Sheriffe, Mr George Sedgwick, Mr Edward Hasell, Mr Henry Machell, and the men to the first three, ride on horsback out of this Brougham Castle to my Cozen Mr John Dalston at Millrigg, & dined there with him & his wife & children, but came back hither again about 5 of the clock at night.

And this evening about 7 a clock after I was in bed, did Allan Strickland* commit some disorders in my house of which I was acquainted next morning by Mr Thomas Gabetis my Sherriff, but he showing a great Regrett and compassion for those misdemeanors, I was moved upon his ingenious acknowledgment and Confession to pardon him.

I went not out of the house nor out of my chamber today.

Ps. 121.

The 2nd day being Sunday, yet I went not out of the house nor out of my chamber today. But my 2 gentlewomen Mrs Pate and Mrs Susan (Machell) and Mr Tho. Gabetis my Shiriff and his wife, and 3 of my Laundry maids and most of my chiefe Servants went to Ninekirkes, where Mr Grasty the Parson preached a Sermon to them and the Congregation.

And today there dined without with my folks in the Painted Room, and with the Sherriff and his wife, Mr Grasty the parson, my two

_____
* One of Lady Anne's servants.

farmers here – William Spedding and his wife, & Jeffrey Bleamire and his son, so after dinner I had them into my Room and kist the women and took the Men by the hand. And a little after Mr Grasty the parson said Common Prayers and read a Chapter and sang a Psalm as usuall to mee and them and my family, and when prayers were done they went away.

3rd Day. There dined with my folks and with Mr Tho. Gabetis my Sherriff and his wife, Mr Lancelott Machell of Crackenthorp, so after dinner I had him into my Chamber and took him by the Hand and talked with him, and I gave him a pare of Buckskin Gloves and afterwards he went away.

I went not out of the House nor out of my Chamber today.

4th Day. And this morning I saw Thomas Wright the Quaker (who lay here the last night), payd in my Chamber for 12 bushells of Malt for Beere for my house, and I took him by the hand and talked with him and a little after he went away.

And afterward I had Mr Bracken of Kirbystephen the Painter into my Chamber, and took him by the hand and talked with him, and saw him payd for drawing over 2 Coppies of the Picture of my Cozen german Francis, Earl of Bedford, and he dined without with my folks and with Mr Thom. Gabetis my Shiriff and his wife, and after dinner he went away.

And by the [London] *Gazette* this day received by the post from London I came to know that the Danes had taken Wismar from the Swedes,* and the King by his proclamation doth forbid all coffee houses or the selling of coffee publickly.

And this forenoon about 10 a clock did my Steward Mr Henry Machell ride on horsback out of this Brougham Castle toward Eden Hall in Cumberland to my Cozen Sir Philip Musgrave, but hee came back againe hither att night.

I went not out of the house nor out of my Chamber all this day.

Ps. 121.

The 5th day. And by a Letter I received this morning from my Daughter Thanet dated the 30th of December I came to know that she is much troubled with Paine in the head, but all that her Posterity are well, and that Lord Hatton was married to his second wife Mrs Yelverton the 21st day of that month, being St Thomas' Day; his first wife being my

---

* Wismar is in Mecklenburg, North Germany. At the time when Lady Anne was writing, the Swedes had already acquired Hamburg and Pomerania in their expansions under King Gustavus Adolphus.

Grandchilde who was blown up with Gunpowder in ye Isle of Guernsey.

And this afternoon did my housekeeper Richard Lowers come into my Chamber to prayers, whom I had not seen in 2 months by reason of his great sicknesse, so I took him by the hand and talked with him.

I went not out of the house nor out of my chamber today.

Ps. 23.

The 6th Day. Being Twelfth day, I remembered how this day was 54 yeares since, at night, [that] at a Mask performed in the King's Banqueting house at Whitehall & in the Privy Galleryes there, did I see King James the Scotchman, and it was the last time I ever saw him or Hee mee.

Prov. 20.24. Eccles. 3; 8.6.

And this morning, before I saw him, did Mr Thomas Gabetis my Shiriff ride away on horseback from his wife and mee and us here, out of this Brougham Castle towards Appleby where the County Court is kept in the Moot Hall therein.

And this morning after I was out of my Bed I had 7 or 8 great loose stooles downwards, which I thought did me much good, but withall weakened my Body so much that it cast me into a Swoning fitt. But God be praised I recovered soon after.

Ps. 23

And this 6th day there dined here with my folks and my Sheriffs wife, Mr Samuel Grasty our parson, & Mr James Buchanan the parson of Appleby and his 2nd Sonne, and also John Webster. So after dinner I had them into my Chamber and took them by the hand, and afterwards Mr Grasty said Prayers and read a Chapter (which he usually did upon a Wednesday) to mee and them and my family, and when prayers were done they all went away.

And this morning I set my hand to 3 good letters of Hasell's writing for mee; one to my Daughter Thanet, one to my Lord Northampton & one to Mr Wm Edge*, all in answer of letters I received from them by the last post.

I went not out of the house all this day.

Ps. 1.

The 7th Day. And today there dined here without in the painted Room with my folks and Mr Thomas Gabetis my Shiriffe and his wife, Justice Wm Musgrave of Penrith. And I had him into my Chamber and

---

* William Edge, the Receiver of Lady Anne's rents in Sussex.

took him by the hand and talked with him awhile and I gave him a pare of Gloves and then he went away.

And there allso dined here Mr Robt Willison of Penrith, the Postmaster, & after dinner I had him into my Chamber and took him by the hand and saw him payd for a Rundlet of Sack and another of White Wine, and after he went away. And a little after did Mr Hugh Wharton come hither and brought me a Letter from my Lord Wharton's eldest Son, wherein he desires if there be a new Parliament, to serve as knight for this year. And I caused Mr Hasel to write an answer wherein I gave my consent and promise of my assistance to it, and gave him 3 sh. and then he went away.

And this 7th day in the afternoon, a little after dinner did Mr Tho. Gabetis my Shiriff and his wife and servants, after I had taken my leave of them in my chamber, and after they had layen here with me during Christmas, viz: for 14 nights together, they rid away on horsback from mee and us here towards their sonnes home at Crosby Ravenside.

I went not out of the house nor out of my Chamber today.

The 8th Day. I remembered how this day was 59 years [since] my first Lord & I & our first childe the Lady Margaret went out of Great Dorset House in London towne to Knowl house in Kent to lye there for a time, and [it] was the first time I came thither after my coming but the month before from my Journey from Brougham Castle and so out of Westmerland & from the City of York, up to the said Great Dorset House to him and her, who then lay there.

Ps 55.17; 121. Prov. 20.24. Eccles. 3; 8.6.

And this forenoon I had 6 or 7 loose stools downwards which I thought did me good tho' it brought mee into a swouning fitt.

And this day in the afternoon did George Good[gion] pay mee the Kitchen stuff money and Mr Hasell received it off him in the Painted Room.

I went not out of the house nor out of my Chamber today.

The 9th day, being Sunday, yet I went not out of my Chamber all this day. Ergo, consiquently, Eccle, but my 2 gentlewomen and 3 of my Laundry maids and most of my menservants went to the Church of Ninekirks where Mr Grasty our parson preached a good Sermon to them and the Congregation. And today there dined without in the painted Room with my folks Mr Grasty the parson, and my two farmers here, namely Wm. Spedding and his wife, & Jeffrey Bleamire & his Son, and John Webster. And after dinner I had them into my Chamber and kissed her, and took them by the hand and talked with them. And afterward

The Last Months, 1676

Mr Grasty our parson said Common Prayers and read a Chapter and sang a Psalm, as usuall upon Sundays, to mee and them and my family, and when prayers was done they went away.

And this 9th day, first of all did I fix a day to receive the blessed Sacrament with my family, which I intend, God willing, shall be upon the 25th day of this month.

I went not out of the house nor out of my chamber today.

Ps. 23.

The 10th Day. And today there dined here with my folks in the Painted Room Mr Thomas Samford's wife from Askum and her 2nd Sonne, so after dinner I had them into my Chamber and kist her & took him by the hand, and I gave her a pare of Buckskin Gloves and him 5 sh. and then they went away. And there also dined without Doctor Smallwood's wife of Gra[y]stock and her Eldest Son and Daughter, and after dinner I had them into my Chamber & kist them and took him by the hand and talked a good while with them, and I gave her 2 pares of Buckskin Gloves, and each of them one pare, and then they went away. And about 5 of ye clock this evening did George Goodgion bring me 28 bookes of Devotion hee bought for mee at Penrith, and I then saw them paid for & gave them all away but six to my domestick servants.

And this morning about 9 a clock, after I had taken my leave of him in my Chamber, and after he and his man had layen here in the highest chamber in Pagan's Tower (as usually for 21 nights together during which time I kept my Christmas here) did Mr Geo. Sedgwick & his man Thos. Whaley rid on horsback out of this Brougham Castle from me and us here towards his own house near Kendall.

I went not out of the house nor out of my Chamber today.

Ps. 121.

The 11th day. And this morning I saw Wm. Spedding, one of my farmers and others payd for loading of a cartload of wood out of Whinfield Park to this Brougham Castle, and likewise for riving [cutting] of wood for firing for my house here. And he dined here in the painted Room, and after he went away. John Webster being by, he also dined here.

I went not out of the house nor out of my Chester today.

Ps. 1.

The 12th Day. I remembered how this day was 59 years (since) my first and then only childe the Lady Margaret, after shee had been in the garden of Knowl house in kent, did in the night fall desperatly sick of her long Ague of which shee was in great danger of death, she then

BROUGHAM CASTLE, Westmorland, where Lady Anne died, aged eighty-six, on Wednesday 22 March 1676, engraved by S. Noble from a drawing by F. Dayes (1804)

lying in a chamber in the tower there, which was underneath my chamber.

Prov. 20.24. Eccles. 3; 8.6.

And today there dined here in the painted Room with my folks Mrs Jane Carlton, ye Widdow, sister to Sir Wm. Carlton deceased, so after dinner I had her into my Chamber & kissed her and talked with her a while. And I gave her 5 sh. and a little after (before prayers) she went away. And Mr Grasty our parson also dined here, and after dinner he came into my chamber and said Common Prayers as usuall upon Wednesdays to mee and my family, and after prayers was ended he read the Exhortation for receiving the Sacrament which I intend, God willing, to receive ye 25th of this month with my family. And then he went away.

I went not out of the house nor out of my Chamber today.

Ps. 23.

The 13th Day. And this morning I set my hand to 3 good letters of Hasell's writing for mee, one to my Daughter Thanet, one to my Lord Northampton and one to Mr William Edge, all in answer to letters I received from them by the last post.

I went not out of this house nor out of my Chamber today.

The 14th Day. And this 14th day of this month I remembered how that day was 59 years (since) my first and only childe the Lady Margaret, now Countesse Dowager of Thanet, was removed out of the chamber in the Tower at Knowle house in Kent which was underneath mine into another chamber in the same house which looks towards the East, shee then continuing to have her Ague in great extremity.

Eccles. 3; 8.6. Prov. 20.24.

And this morning after the weekbook was payd, did Mr Henry Machell my Steward ride away on horseback out of this Brougham Castle towards Crakenthorp to see his Brother & Sister, and he lay there one night, and the next day towards evening he came back againe hither to mee.

And today there dined here with my folks in the painted Room Mr John Gilmoor my Keeper of Whinfield, and his man Wm. Labourn dined in the Hall, so after dinner I had them into my Chamber and took ye men by the hand & talked with them, and then they went away.

And there also dined without John Webster, whom after dinner I had into my Chamber and so paid him for drawing of ye Coppie of the Map of Harwood belonging to my Almshouse at Beamsley, and then he went away. And there also dined here Mrs Eliz. Atkinson, daughter of Mr

Favior of Warcop, so after dinner she came into my chamber & I kist her & gave her 2 sh. and then she went away.*

I went not out of the house nor out of my chamber today.

The 15th Day. And this morning I had Thomas Wright ye Quaker of Mallerstang (who lay here last night in the Bannister Room) into my Chamber & took him by the hand and discoursed with him a while, and saw him payd for 12 bushells of barly malt, and afterwards hee went away.

And about 4 months since was Dr Henry Compton, Bishop of Oxford, youngest brother to my Son-in-Law, the Earle of Northampton made Dean of the King's Chappell, and about a month since hee was translated to the Bishoprick of London, and now lately sworne one of his Majesty's Privy Councellors.

I went not out of the house nor out of my chamber today.

The 16th day being Sunday, which tho' it was, yet I went not to church nor out of my chamber today.

Ps. 23.

But my 2 gentlewomen rode horsback thither, and my chiefe men-servants went a foot, and three of my Laundry maids, to Ninekirks, where Mr Grasty preached to them & the Congregation.

And today there dined without with my folks in the painted Room, as usuall, Mr Grasty our parson and my 2 farmers here, namely Wm. Spedding & his wife, & Jeffrey Blamire & his Sonne, and John Webster; so after dinner I had them all into my Chamber and kissed ye woman & took them by ye hands.

And a little after, Mr Grasty said Common prayers and read a Chapter and sung a Psalm, as usuall upon Sundays, to mee & them and my family, and after prayers was ended he read the Exhortation for ye worthy receiving of the Holy Sacrament to mee & them, which I intend God willing, to receive the 25th day of this month, and then they all went away.

I went not out of the house nor out of my chamber today, tho' it was Sunday.

The 17th day being Monday, I remembered how this day was 59 years (since) I went out of Knowl house in Kent from my first and then only childe the Lady Margaret up to Great Dorset House at London to her

* According to Dr Williamson, this Mrs Atkinson was apparently the widow of Captain Atkinson, a strong supporter of Cromwell, who was executed for his part in the Kaber Rigg plot. He had been a bitter opponent of Lady Anne, but as soon as he was out of the way she, typically, took his widow and children under her wing, and allowed them to continue to live on her estates at a nominal rent.

father, my first Lord, the occasion of that journey of mine being an Award that King James would have made concerning the lands of my antient Inheritance, so I lay there with him 4 nights together, and then returned back to Knowl again to my said Daughter.

Eccles. 3; 8.6. Prov. 20.24.

And today there dined without in ye painted Room with my folks my Coz. Mr Thomas Burbeck* of Hornby and his wife and their little Daughter, and his father-in-law Mr Cattrick and his wife, and his mother. And there also dined here Mr Robt. Carlton, only son to ye Widdow Lady Carlton. So after dinner I had them all into my Chamber, and kist the women and took the men by the hand and I gave to my Coz. Mr Burbeck and his wife each of them 10 sh. and his Mother 10 sh. and his father-in-law Mr Cattrick & his wife each 10 sh. and 6 d. to the Child, and I gave Mr Charlton a pare of Buckskin Gloves, and then they all went away.

I went not out of the house nor out of my Chamber today.

Ps. 121.

The 18th day I remembered how this day was 59 years (since) I went with my first Lord, Richard Earle of Dorset, before King James, into his Inner Drawing Chamber at Whitehall where ye King earnestly desired mee to subscribe to an award which hee intended to make betwixt mee & my said Lord on the one part, & my Uncle of Cumberland & his Son Henry Lord Clifford on the other part, concerning the lands of my antient Inheritance in Craven & Westmorland. But (by God's Grace) I began to deny it, it being the first time I was ever before that King.

Eccles. 3; 8.6. Prov. 20.24.

And that same day in Knowl house in Kent, where shee then lay, had my first & then only childe the Lady Margaret a fit of her long Ague wherby shee was in great danger of death.

Ps. 23. 4,5.

And this 18th day, a little before dinner, did John Webster come hither, so I had into my Chamber and took him by the hand and saw him payd for a drawing over ye Coppy of a Mapp of the lands of Temple Sowerby, and he dined without in the Painted Room with my folks. And there also dined here Mr Websters 2 sonnes from Dalston, who brought me news that ye parson of Dalston was sadly deceased at London, so I took them by the hand & talked awhile & then they went away.

I went not out of the house nor out of my chamber today.

The 19th day I remembered how this day was 59 years and then

---

* Thomas Birkbeck lived at Hornby Hall near Brougham, and close to Ninekirks Church.

Sunday in the afternoon in the withdrawing Chamber of Queen Anne the Dane in the Court at Whitehall, did that Queen admonish mee to persist in my denyall of trusting my cause concerning my lands of Inheritance to her husband King James' award, which admonition of hers & other of my friends did much confirme mee in my purpose, so as the next day I gave that King an absolute denyall accordingly, which by God's Providence tended much to the good of mee and mine.

And today there dined here with my folks in ye Painted Room Mr Grasty our parson, so after dinner I had him into my Chamber and took him by the hand and talked with him. And a little after he said Common Prayers, as usuall upon Wednesdays, to mee and my family and when prayers was done he also read the Exhortation for worthy receiving ye blessed Sacrament of bread & wine, and when that was ended he went away.

And this afternoon, a little after dinner, did Mr James Bird the Attorney come hither to mee for a little while, as he was in his journy to London, intending shortly to go up tomorrow. So I took him by the hand & discoursed with him awhile, and gave him 10 sh. as I used to do, and then he went away from mee with reference to the prosecution of his intended Journey.

I went not out of this house nor out of my Chamber today.

Ps. 1.

The 20th day. I remembered how this day was 59 years [since] I went with my first Lord to the Court at Whitehall, where in the inner withdrawing chamber King James desired & urged mee to submitt to the Award which hee would make concerning my Lands of Inheritance, but I absolutly denyed to do so, wherein I was guided by a great Providence of God for the good of mee & mine. And that day also had my first & then only childe a dangerous fit of her long Ague in Knowl house in Kent, where shee then lay.

Ps. 23. 4, 5.

And this morning I set my hand to 3 good letters of Hasell's writing for mee, one to my Daughter Thanet, one to my Lord Northampton, and one to Mr William Edge, all in answer of letters I received from them by the last Post.

And today there dined without with my folks Mr Tho. Gabetis the Sheriff, so after dinner I had him into my chamber and took him by the hand and talked with him awhile, and a little after he went away.

And today there also dined with my folks in ye Painted Room Mr Richard Pinder the Quaker, who lives now near Newcastle, so after dinner I had him into my Chamber & took him by ye hand & talked with him.

I went not out of the house nor out of my Chamber today.

Ps. 1.

The 21st day. I remembered how this day was 59 years [since] I went out of Great Dorset House in London towne from my first Lord down to my first childe the Lady Margaret to lye there in Knowl house in Kent for a good while. I thanke God I found her alive though extreamly weak & ill with her long Ague, of which shee had been in great danger those 4 nights I was from her.

Ps. 23.

And this morning, Thomas Wright the Quaker, I saw him payd for 12 bushells of malt for my house, he having layen here the last night, and then he went away. And this forenoon did John Webster come hither to mee in my Chamber, so I took him by the hand and talked with him and gave him a quarter of Scarsole[?], and he dined without with my folks and afterwards he went away.

I went not out of this house nor out of my Chamber today.

Ps. 121.

The 22nd day. And today there dined here without with my folks in the painted Room Mr Robert Willison of Penrith, the Post master, so after dinner I had him into my Chamber & took him by the hand & talked with him, and saw him payd for a Rundlet [18½ gallons] of Sack, another of white wine and a gallon of Clarrett against my receiving ye Holy Sacrament, and then he went away.

I went not out of the house nor out of my Chamber today.

Ps. 121.

The 23rd day being Sunday I remembered how this day was 52 years [since] in the Chapell in Great Dorset House in London Town was I God-mother to him that was christened by the name of Edward Sackville, who was younger Son to my first Lord's younger brother, from whence I went down the next day from thence to Knoll House in Kent to my two daughters & their Father, to lye there.

And though it was Sunday yet I went not to church, nor out of my Chamber all this day, nor neither of my gentlewomen, but most of my chiefe menservants & 3 of my Laundry maids went to Ninekirks where our parson Mr Grasty preached there a good sermon to them & the Congregation. And today there dined here in the Painted Room with my folks Mr Grasty the parson and Wm. Spedding and his wife and Jeffrey Blamire & his son and John Webster. So after dinner I had them into my Chamber and kist the woman & took the men by the hand. And after Mr Grasty said Common Prayer and read a chapter and sung a Psalm as usuall upon Sundays to mee and them & my family, and also read ye

Exhortation for receiving ye Holy Sacrament, and a little after they all went away.

And this 23rd day I remembered how this day was 26 years [since] dyed my second Lord Philip Herbert, Earle of Pembroke & Montgomery in his lodgings near the Cockpit at Whitehall, I then lying in my owne Chamber in Appleby Castle in Westmorland, whither John Turner (whose wife then served mee) brought mee the news of it the 27th day following. And my said Husband's dead Body being unopened was wrapt in Sear Cloth and lead and so carried down and buried in the Cathedral Church at Salisbury in Wiltshire by his Brother & Father & Mother.

Job. 7.2. Prov. 20.4. Eccles. 3; 8.6.

I went not out of ye house nor out of my chamber today, though it be Sunday.

Ps. 121.

The 24th day. And this day there was none that dined here or visited me, so as I spent the time hearing some Chapters read to me and in preparing my self to receive the holy Sacrament of Bread and Wine, which I intend, God willing, to receive tomorrow with my family.

I went not out of the house nor out of my Chamber all this day.

Ps. 121.

The 25th day I remembered how this day was 52 years [since] in the withdrawing chamber at Knowl house in Kent, as wee sate at dinner, had my first Lord and I a great falling out, when but the day before I came from London from being God-mother to his Brother's youngest Son.

And this morning about 8 a clock did Mr Samuel Grasty our Parson preach a good sermon in my Chamber to me and my family, and a little after he administered the Sacrament of bread & Wine to me & them. Viz: to my 2 gentlewomen Mrs Fra. Pate, Mrs Susan Machell; Dor. Demain, Margt Dargue, Anne Chippindale & Jane Slidall, my 4 laundry maids; Isabell Jordan, my Washwoman; Mr Edw. Hasell; Mr Hen. Machell; Geo. Goodgion; Edm. Sort; Allan Strickland; Wm. Dargue; Jo. Hall; Abra. Sittin; Isaac Walker; Rich. Reynoldson, Wm. Buckle; Rich. Lowe, my housekeeper; Cuthbert Rawling; Jacob Murgatroyd; Arthur Swindin; George Loughlyye, Clerk; which I nor they received since 3rd November last. And parson Grasty dined here with my folks in the painted room and then he went away.

And there also dined in the painted room Mr Charles Crow ye parson of Warcopp, so after dinner I had him into my chamber and took him by the hand & talked with him, and I gave him 2/6 d. and then he went away.

The Last Months, 1676

I went not out of this house nor out of my Chamber today.

Ps. 121.

The 26th day. And this morning by letters I received from my daughter Thanet and by the Paquet of this week from London, I came to know that she herselfe, my said Daughter, was well, and most of her Generation & Posterity in their severall Places and Homes.

And though today I had a very ill fitt of the wind, yet I slept well in the night notwithstanding, I thank God.

I went not out of the house nor out of my Chamber all this day.

Ps. 1.

The 27th Day. I remembered how this day was 26 years did John Turner (who is since deceased, & his wife who then served mee secondly married to John Gilmore) come from his Journy from London to Appleby Castle in Westmorland, & in my owne Chamber there did first of all tell mee of the death of my second Husband, Philip Earle of Pembroke & Montgomery, & how hee dyed the 23rd of that month in his lodgings by the Cockpit at Whitehall.

And this morning I set my hand to 3 good letters of Hasell's writing for mee, one to my Daughter Thanet, one to my Lord Northampton and one to Mr William Edge, all in answer of letters I received from them by the last post.

And today there dined here with my folks besides John Webster, Mr Robert Hilton of Murton. So after dinner I had them into my Chamber and took them by ye hand and talked with them, and I gave Mr Hilton a pare of Buckskin Gloves, and I saw John Webster payd for drawing over the copies of 2 maps of Southfield, and then they went away.

I went not out of this house nor out of my Chamber today.

The 28th day. And today I had a very ill fitt of the winde, but yet never the lesse I slept well in the night, I thank God.

Ps. 23.

I went not out of the house, nor out of my Chamber all this day.

Ps. 121.

The 29th day. And yesternight late did John Bradford come from Skipton and over Cotter & Stake [Passes] afoot hither to this Brougham Castle, but I did not see him till this morning. And hee brought the newes of Mrs Sutton's death, Mother of my Almeshouse at Beamsley.

And this morning about 6 a clock, before I was out of my Bed, did I pare the topps of my Nails of my fingers and Thumbs and burnt them in the fire after I was upp.

And today there dined without with my folks in ye Painted Room Mr John Gilmoor, my Keeper of Whinfield Parke, and Mrs Saul. So after

243

dinner I had them into my Chamber and kist her & took him and his man, Wm. Labourn, who dined below in the Hall, by the hand and talked with them a good while, and I gave Mrs Saul, whose grandmother I knew well when I lived at Court, 5 sh., and then they went away.

I went not out of the house nor out of my Chamber today.

Ps. 1.

The 30th Day being Sunday, I considered how this day was 86 years & then Fryday about 7 a clock in the evening was my blessed Mother with very hard labor brought to bed of mee in hier owne chamber in Skipton Castle in Craven, where she then lay; my Brother Robert, Lord Clifford then also lying in the Castle. But my noble father than lay in Bedford House in the Strand at London, as also my Aunt of Warwick & her husband Ambrose, Earle of Warwick, who dyed the 21st of the month following. And about 6 years before my birth was my blessed Mother in the same place delivered of my eldest Brother, Francis Lord Clifford, but hee dyed before I was borne.

And this day was 27 years [since] our then King Charles (who was borne in Scotland) was beheaded on a Scaffold in the open aire near the Banqueting house at Whitehall & his dead body afterwards buried in the Chappel at Windsor in Berkshire. And when this Tragedy was performed did I lye in Baynards Castle in London and my second Lord was in his lodgings by the Cockpit at Whitehall where hee dyed about a year after.

And tho' it was Sunday yet I went not to church nor out of my Chamber today, but my 2 gentlewomen & most of my menservants went and 3 of my Laundry maids to ye church of Ninekirks where Mr Grasty ye parson preached a good sermon to them and the rest of the Congregation. And today there dined without in the painted room with my folks, Mr Grasty and my 2 farmers here, namely Wm. Spedding & his wife and Jeffrey Bleamire and his Son, and John Webster. So after dinner I had them into my Chamber and kist ye woman and took the men by the hand. And afterwards Mr Grasty said prayers & sung a Psalm as usuall upon Sundays, to mee and them and my family, and when prayers was done they all went away.

I went not out of ye house nor out of my Chamber today, though it were Sunday.

Ps. 121.

The 31st Day. I remembered how this day was 59 years when my first and then only child the lady Margaret and I then lay in Knowl house in Kent, did shee grow extreamly sick and ill of several fits of her long

Ague, so as shee was in great danger of death in all folks' opinion, but it pleased God to recover her miraculously.

Ps. 23, etc.

And this day did my familie keep as a fast for the Martyrdom of King Charles the first, though hee was beheaded the day before. The day being commanded to bee kept by Act of Parliament.

And this day, about 3 a clock in the afternoon did John Twentyman, Gardiner to the Lord Bishop of Carlisle, come from Rose Castle in Cumberland hither to this Brougham Castle to look after and order my Garden here. So hee lay in the Bannister Room 5 nights together during which time hee worked in my garden here. Upon Saturday the 5th of February in the morning hee went home again, and I sent by him a bottle of the pulp of pomcittron [apple-juice] to the Bishop of Carlisle.

I went not out of the house nor out of my chamber today.

Ps. 121.

FEBRUARY

The 1st Day. I remembered how this day was 47 years [since] dyed in her owne chamber at the Court at Whitehall the Lady Susan Vere, Countesse of Montgomery, shee who was first wife to him that was afterwards my second Lord. And when shee dyed did I & my two Daughters then lye in the Priory house in St Bartholomew in London. And her dead body was buried soon after in the Cathedral Church of Westminster by her Grandmother & her Mother the Countesse of Oxford & the Lady Bourghley. And I was first told the news of her death by Sir George Mannours, afterwards Earle of Rutland. And I was married (a second wife) to her husband about a year and 4 months after her death.

Job. 7.1.

And this morning did Wm. Johnson my Housekeeper at Appleby Castle and Henry Bonson my Herd[sman] at Southfield come hither, so I saw them both payd their board wages in my Chamber, and they dined here below in the Hall and then they went away.

And this morning I also so payed to Wm. Burbeck of Mallerstang (who lay here ye last night) for 12 bushells of malt for beer for my house and then he went away. And I also saw payd for loading of wood from

Whinfield to this Brougham Castle for firing for my house, and then they went away. And Robert Har[r]ison my Housekeeper of Brough Castle this morning came hither and he brought along with him Workmen, whom I saw payd for making a new garden and walling of it and for mending the Glass windows there, and after they had dined here they went away.

And this forenoon did John Webster come hither to mee, so I had him into my Chamber and took him by the hand and talkt with him, and he dined without with my folks in the Painted Room, and a little after dinner he went away.

I went not out of the house nor out of my Chamber all this day.

Ps. 121.

The 2nd Day. I remembered how this day was 56 years [since], about 12 of the clock in the day time, I was delivered of my little Son Thomas, Lord Buckhurst, in my owne chamber in Knowl house in Kent, where I & my eldest daughter the Lady Margaret then lay. And the same day John Conniston rid on horsback from thence to my first Lord to Great Dorset House in London towne to carry him the newes of the birth of that Son of his, who dyed in that house the 26th of July following.

Eccles. 3; 8 etc.

And today there dined here with my folks Mr Grasty our parson. So after dinner he came into my Chamber and I talkt with him and took him by the hand. And afterwards he said Common Prayers as usuall upon Wednesdays to mee and my family, and a little after he went away.

I went not out of the house, nor out of my chamber all this day.

The 3rd Day. And this morning I set my hand to 4 good letters of Hasell's writing for mee, one to my Daughter Thanet, one to my Lord Northampton, one to my Grandchilde the Lady Alethea Compton, and one to Mr William Edge; all in answer of letters I received from them by the last post.

I went not out of the house nor out of my chamber all this day.

Ps. 121.

The 4th Day. I remembered how this day was 56 years [since] my first Lord Richard, Earle of Dorset, came from Great Dorset House in London towne downe to Knowl house in Kent to mee and my eldest Daughter the Lady Margaret and his young Sonn the Lord Buckhurst, who was borne but two dayes before that, behind the first time hee ever saw that young Sonne of his who dyed there the 26th of July following.

Eccles 3; 8.6 etc.

And the 4th day of this month, about 7 a clock at night, did Robert Goodgion and Thomas Kitching my Tennants at Skipton come hither,

LADY ANNE CLIFFORD, aged fifty-six, by an unknown artist (1646)

but I did not see them till the next day, that I then had them into my Chamber & took them by the hand and talkt with them, and they lay in the Barons' Chamber for 3 nights together, and when they were past they went away back towards Skipton again.

And today there dined without with my folks in the Painted Room Mr Phillip Nanson, who is Fellow of Queen's College in Cambridge, so after dinner I had him into my Chamber and took him by the hand and talkt with him and gave him 5 sh., and then he went away.

And there also dined here with my folks Mr Thomas Langhorn of Penrith, the Shop-keeper, & so after dinner I had him into my Chamber and talkt with him a good while and then he went away. And there also dined without John Webster.

I went not out of the house nor out of my chamber all this day.

Ps. 1.

The 5th Day. I remembered how this day was 59 years [since] was my first and then only childe the Lady Margaret (now Countesse Dowager of Thanet) dangerously sick of her long Ague in Knowl house in Kent where I then lay, but her father, my First Lord, then lay in Great Dorset House in London towne.

And by a letter I received by the Post from my Cozen Sir Thomas Wharton dated at Goldesborough the 10th I came to know that a little before, his Sonn's wife was brought to bedd there of a Sonn (which is her first childe) whoe is christened by the name of Thomas.

And today I had a very ill fitt of the Wind but yet notwithstanding I slept well and soundly in the night, I thank God.

I went not out of the house nor out of my Chamber all this day.

The 6th Day being Shrove Sunday, I considered how this day was 86 years [since] the good news was brought to my father and my Aunt of Warwick and her husband, to Bedford House in the Strand, both by letter and word of mouth, that my Mother was brought a bed of mee the 30th of the month before in Skipton Castle in Craven with very hard labour.

And tho' it was Sunday today yet I went not to church nor out of my Chamber all this day. Ps. 23. Nor neither of my gentlewomen, but 3 of my Laundry maids and the 2 Yorkshire men Robert Goodgion & Tho. Kitching and most of my menservants went to Ninekirks, where Mr Grasty the parson preached to them and the Congregation.

And today there dined without with my folks in ye Painted Room, besides the 2 Craven men afore-named, Mr Grasty the parson and my 2 farmers, namely Wm. Spedding & his wife and Jeffrey Bleamire and his Son, and John Webster. And after dinner I had them into my Chamber and kist the woman and took the men by the hand. And then Mr Grasty said Common Prayres and read a Chapter (as usuall upon Wednesdayes and Sundayes) to mee and them and my family, and a little after they all went away from mee.

And this afternoon about 4 a clock did I take my leave of the 2 Craven Men, Robt. Goodgion and Tho. Kitching, and took them by the hand and talkt with them, and then about 8 a clock after they had layed in the Barons' Chamber 3 nights, they rode away on Horsback out of this Brougham Castle toward their owne homes in Craven.

I went not out of the house nor out of my chamber all this day.

Ps. 121.

The 7th Day, being Shrove Munday. And today there dined without with my folks Dorothy Wiber, the Deafe woman of my Almeshouse at Appleby, and after dinner I had her into my chamber and kist her. And I saw her payd for 5 dozen yards of Bonlace, but I was very angry with her for bringing so much and told her I would have no more of her.

And there also came along with her and dined here Dorothy Winter of Clifton, sister to John Webster, so I had her into my chamber and kist her and talked with her awhile, and a little after they both went away.

And by the letters I received by the post from my Daughter Thanet and my Lord Northampton dated the 3rd of February I came to know that there was lately a great sea-fight before Messina between the Dutch & Spanish fleet, and the French fleet, & the French were much worsted, many of their Ships being taken & Sunck.

I went not out of the house nor out of my chamber today.

Ps. 121.

The 8th Day, being Shrove Tuesday. I remembered how this day was 75 years [since] Robert Deveraux, Earle of Essex, with others of quality then goe into his house called Essex house in the Strand in a rebellious manner against Queen Elizabeth into the Citty of London, in which rebellion hee was taken and beheaded for it at the Tower in London on 25th of that month.

And today there dined without with my folks the widdow Margaret Spedding, who is sister-in-law to Wm. Spedding, one of my farmers, and after dinner I had her into my Chamber and kissed her, and talked with her a good while, and a little after she went away.

I went not out of the house nor out of my chamber today.

Ps. 121.

The 9th day being Ash Wednesday, I remembered how this day was 72 years [ago] dyed in North hall house in Hartfordshire, in her owne chamber there, my worthy Aunt Anne Russell, Countesse Dowager of

Warwick, & shee was buried a awhile after, un-opened, in the vault of Chenies church in Buckingham[shire] by her Auncestors; my mother, my self, my Cozen german the Lady Francis Bourchier, & my Uncle the Lord William Russell & his wife & their Son, who was afterwards Earle of Bedford, lying in North hall house at the time of her death & burial.

And I remembered how this day was 52 years [since] my first Lord Richard, Earle of Dorset, came into the Tower chamber in Knowl house in Kent where I then lay, and there he kiss'd mee and my two daughters, which I had by him, & that was the last time hee lay in Knowl house, for that day hee went up to Great Dorset House in London Towne & there lay the Parliament then sitting & being very full of business so as hee continued to lye there in that Great Dorset House till his death happened the 29th of March following.

And this day being Ash Wednesday, about one a clock did Mr Samuel Grasty, our parson, read Common Prayers & a Chapter as usuall upon Wednesdays to mee and my family. And afterwards, about 4 a clock, he dined here without with my folks.

And today I had a very sore fitt of the Wind, but notwithstanding I slept well after it in the night, I thank God.

Ps. 121.

And the following day in the morning did I see Mr Robert Willison of Penrith payd for a Rundlet [18½ gallons] of Sack, but I was very angry with him, because I thought it was too dear, and told him I would have no more of him, and then he slipt away from me.

I went not out of the house nor out of my chamber this day.

The 10th day I remembered how this day was 59 years did my first and then only childe the Lady Margaret (now Countesse Dowager of Thanet) remove out of the great chamber at Knowl house in Kent, called the Lord Treasurer's Chamber, into the little room within it called the Lord Treasurer's Closet, where shee continued to lye that month and the most part of the next, where shee was dangerously ill with her long Ague, soe as everyone thought shee would have dyed. And then did I lye in the same house, but her father then lay in Great Dorset House in London Towne.

And this morning I set my hand to 3 good letters of Hasell's writing for mee, one to my Daughter Thanet, one to my Lord Northampton, and one to Mr William Edge, all in answer of letters I received from them by the last post.

And this 10th day in the morning did John Webster bring the two Mapps of Flakebridge that he had drawn for mee, so I had him into my chamber and saw him payd for them, and he dined here without with my folks, and a little while after he went away.

And this afternoon about one a clock did Sir George Fletcher and his Lady and her daughter by her first husband, and Mr Flemming and his eldest daughter [come], so I had them into my Chamber and kist the women and took the men by the hand, and Sir George delivered to mee severall letters of my Auncestors which were sent me by order of my Lord Marshal, and after I had talked with them and given the women each of them Enamelled Gold Rings, they all went away.

I went not out of the house nor out of my chamber all this day.

Ps. 121.

The 11th Day. And this afternoon a little after dinner, about one a clock, after I had taken my leave of them in my chamber, did Mr Edward Hasell and his man Cuthbert rid on horseback out of this Brougham Castle towards Rose Castle in Cumberland to his Uncle & Aunt, the Bishop of Carlisle & his Lady, where he & his man lay 3 nights, and on the 14th day in the evening a little after supper they came back againe hither to mee and us here into this Brougham Castle.

I went not out of the house nor out of my chamber all this day.

The 12th day. And today there dined without with my folks in the Painted Chamber Mr Lancelot Machell of Crakenthorp, for he came from his owne house here this morning. And after dinner I had him into my Chamber and talked with him a good while and took him by the hand and he now told me that his eldest Son, Mr Hugh Machell, had by a fall from his horse badly broken his Legg about a fortnight hence. So that he came now to borrow my horslitter.

I went not out of the house nor out of my chamber all this day.

The 13th day being Sunday, tho' it was so, I went not to Church nor out of my Chamber all this day.

Ps. 121.

But my 2 gentlewomen and 3 of my Landry maids & severall of my Menservants rode on horsback to Ninekirks, where Mr Grasty the parson preached a good sermon to them and the rest [of] the Congregation. And today there dined without in the painted Room with my folks Mr Sam. Grasty our parson and my 2 farmers, namely Wm. Spedding and his Wife and Jeffrey Bleamire and his Sonne, & John Webster. So after dinner I had them into my Chamber and kist the woman & took the men by the hand. And a little after Mr Grasty said Common Prayers and read a Chapter and sung a Psalm (as usuall upon Sundays) to mee and them and my family, and after Prayers was done they all went away.

251

I went not out of ye house nor my chamber all this day tho' it was Sunday.

The 14th Day. I remembered how this day was 63 years [since] our King James' eldest daughter, the Lady Elizabeth, married in the King's Chappell at Whitehall to Prince Frederick, Elector Palatine of the Rhine & Heidelberg; her father & Mother and my selfe & my first Lord & most of the Nobility being present at her marriage.

And I remember how the 14th day of this month (or about that time) was 10 years [since] dyed my good Servant Mr Gabriell Vincent in the Roman Tower at Brough Castle, I and my familie lying then in that Castle.

Job. 7.1.

And yesternight did Arthur Swindin* wave of lying in the Musick Room where he used to lye and began to lye in the Housekeeper's chamber, Richard Lowes, that is under the Great Chamber.

And this forenoon did John Webster come hither into my Chamber, so I took him by the hand and talked with him, and he retreated from me into the drawing Room and dined with my folks.

And the 14th day, about 6 a clock in the morning, did John Hall and Abraham Fittin ride out of this Brougham Castle with my Horslitter.

And this 14th day, early in the morning, did my black spotted Bitch called Zirmue [or 'Quinne' – unclear in Manuscript] puppy in my Bed and Chamber 4 little pupies, but they were all dead.

I went not out of the house nor out of my chamber all this day.

The 15th day. And this morning did I see payed for 12 bushells of malt in my chamber to Mr Thomas Wright the Quaker of Mallerstang, who came hither last night and lay here in the Bannister Room, and a little after he went away. And this forenoon about 10 a clock did Mr Henry Machell (my Steward) ride away on Horseback out of this Brougham Castle towards Appleby Castle and lay there one night, next day towards evening he came home.

And there came hither this afternoon about one a clock, my Cozen Mrs Anne Howard, sister to my Coz. Mr Francis Howard of Corby, and her Cozen Sir Charles Howard's daughter, and two other gentlemen with them (whose names I know not). So I had them into my chamber and kist ye women and took the men by the hand and talkt with them a good while, and a little after they rode away on horsback from out of this Castle to ye said Corby Castle in Cumberland.

I went not out of the house nor out of my chamber today.

Ps. 121.

* Arthur Swindin, one of the servants at Brougham.

The Last Months, 1676

The 16th Day. And today there dined without with my folks, Mr Samuel Grasty our parson, and after dinner I had him into my Chamber and talked with him and took him by the hand. And a little after he said Common Prayers and read a Chapter (as usuall upon Wednesdays) to mee and my family, and after prayers he went away againe.

I went not out of the house nor out of my chamber all this day.

Ps. 121.

The 17th Day. I remembered how this day 59 years [ago] was my first & then only childe the Lady Margaret desperately sick & in great danger of death in Knowl house in Kent, by a fitt of her long Ague, where shee & I then lay. And then was I first told there the sad newes from Ancona in Italy which did at the time much trouble mee.*

And I remember how this day was 60 years when I & my first Lord the Earle of Dorset lay in Little Dorset House in London towne & in the afternoon in the best gallery of Great Dorset House did George Abbott, Archbishop of Canterbury, & many others come to my first Lord & mee, and did earnestly persuade mee both by fair words & threatenings to stand to the Award the four chief Judges would then make betwixt my first Lord & mee of the one Part & my Uncle of Cumberland & his son on the other part, concerning the lands of mine Inheritance. And thereupon it was agreed that I should goe to my Blessed Mother into Westmorland & begin my Journy the 21st of that month, which I did accordingly.

And the 17th day towards evening did Mr Johnson (who is brother to Mrs Anne Johnson who formerly served mee) and his man come from his owne house neare Skipton into this Brougham Castle, and he lay this night in the Barrons Chamber, and the next morning I had him into my Chamber and took him by the hand and talked with him a good while and gave him 3 pares of Buckskin Gloves, and a little after (after he had eaten something in the Painted Room) he and his man rode away on Horseback out of this Brougham Castle.

And this morning I set my hand to 4 good letters of Hasell's writing for mee, one to my Daughter Thanet, one to my Lord Northampton, one to my Cozen Sir Thomas Wharton, and one to Mr William Edge, all in answer of letters I received from them by the last post.

And this 17th day in the afternoon, about 3 a clock, did my Cozen Mr Richard Musgrave, eldest son to my Cozen Sir Phillipp Musgrave and his Lady, and their Daughter, who is their only childe Mary, come in

---

* Despite the obvious significance that this 'sad newes' had for Lady Anne, there is, however, no mention of it in her diary for February 1617.

their Coach hither from Ednall [Edenhall], so I had them onto my Chamber and kiss'd my Cozen & his wife & the child and also their gentlewoman, and I gave to my Cozens wife and daughter each of them a Gold Ring, and after they had stayed awhile they went away.

And today I had one or two ill fitts of the wind, but yet I slept well in the night, I thank God.

Ps. 12.

And this 17th day did my Servant Mr Thomas Strickland and his man Lanc: Machell ride from his owne house near Kendall, called Garnet House, towards Appleby (whither they came that night) to gather my Candlemas Rents. And he lay in the Barons' Chamber there, and his man in the Musty Chamber.

I went not out of the house nor out of my chamber all this day.

Ps. 23.

The 19th Day. I remembered how this day was 59 years [since] my first & then only Childe the Lady Margaret was desperately sick and of a fitt of her long Ague in Knowl house in Kent where shee & I lay, but her father, my first Lord, then lay at Great Dorset House in London towne.

And this morning I saw Robert Dennison, the deafe woman's Sonne, payd for leading 40 cartloads of Ling out of Whinfield park to this Brougham Castle for Brewing & Baking with, and then he went away.

And this evening did my servant Thomas Strickland and his man Lancelot Machell come about 8 a clock into this Brougham Castle, but I saw them not until ye next morning, and then I talked with them & took them by the hand, and they now lay as usuall in the Tower of League for six nights, which, being expired upon the 25th day, ye said Mr Thomas Strickland and his man Lanc. Machell rid out of this Brougham Castle to Appleby, there to receive the rest of my Candlemas Rents.

I went not out of the House nor out of my chamber today.

Ps. 121.

The 20th Day, being Sunday, I remembered how this day was 59 years had my first and then only childe the Lady Margaret a desperate fit of her long Ague in Knowl house in Kent, where shee then lay. But her father, my first Lord, then lay in Great Dorset House in London towne.

And tho' today was Sunday yet I went not to church nor out of my chamber all this day. But my 2 gentlewomen & 3 of my Laundry Maids with most of my chiefe Menservants went to this church called Nine-kirks, where he preached a good sermon (viz: Mr Grasty, our parson) to them & the rest of the Congregation (tho' one part therof seemed to Reflect upon ye Writer – so that I thought he spoke to none but mee). And today there dined here as usuall Mr Grasty, the parson, & my 2 farmers here, namely Wm. Spedding and his wife and Jeff. Bleamire & his Son, and John Webster. So after dinner I had them into my chamber, and kist her, and took ye men by the hands. And then Mr Grasty said Common Prayers & read a Chapter and likewise sung a Psalm (as usuall upon Sundays) to mee & them and my family, & prayers being done they went away.

And today I had one or 2 ill fits of the Wind, but I slept indifferent well in the night notwithstanding.

Ps. 23.4 & 5.

I thank God, but that wind put me in great danger of Death.

I went not out of the house nor out of my Chamber all this day.

Ps. 121.

The 21st day, I remembered how this day was 60 years [since] my first Lord & I did goe out of Little Dorset House in London Towne onwards on our Journy Northwards, so as that night wee lay together in the Inn at Dunstable in Bedfordshire, as wee were in our Journy towards Brougham Castle in Westmorland, to my blessed Mother, and hee to set mee as farr on my way as Litchfield in Staffordshire.

And I considered how this day was 86 years [since] dyed Ambrose, Earle of Warwick, who was husband to my blessed Mother's eldest Sister Anne Russell, Countesse of Warwick, in Bedford House in the Strand in London towne, where my noble Father, George, Earle of Cumberland, then lay, but my Blessed Mother then lay in of mee in Skipton Castle in Craven.

And this morning did John Webster come hither, so he came into my Chamber and I took him by the hand and talkt with him. And he dined here without in the Painted Room with my folks and after dinner I had him again into my chamber and spoke to him awhile, and a little after he went away.

And this day there likewise dined without Mr Samuel Grasty, our parson, who came hither this forenoon to see Arthur Swindin, who is now in a very weak condition, and so after dinner I had him into my Chamber and talked with him and Inquired of Arthur Swindin, whether hee was better; but he told mee that he was no better at all, and then hee went away from mee.

And today my Gentlewoman Mrs Frances Pate preserved for me 4 Potts and 2 Bottles of Sirrupp of Limmons.

I went not out of the House nor out of my chamber today.

Ps. 121.

The 22nd Day. I remembered how this day was 60 years [since] my first Lord & I went out of the Inne at Dunstable in Bedfordshire, & so through Stony Stratford hard by Grafton house in Northamptonshire, into the Inne at Towcester in that County, as wee were in our Journy Northwards, I towards Brougham Castle in Westmorland to my blessed Mother, & hee to set mee as farr on my way as Lichfield in Staffordshire.

And I considered how this day was 86 years was I christened in the Parish Church of Skipton in Craven by the name of Anne. Philip, Lord Wharton, my Aunt's husband, being my God-father, my noble Father then lying in Bedford House in the Strand in London towne, as hee also did when my blessed Mother was brought to bed of mee the 30th day of the month before in Skipton Castle in Craven.

And this 22nd day in ye morning, before I was out of my Bed, did I pare off ye topps of ye nails of all my fingers & toes, and when I was upp out of bed I burnt them in ye fire in ye chimney in my chamber.

And a little after in that same chamber of mine did George Goodgion clipp off all ye haires of my head, which I likewise burnt in the fire. And after supper I washed and bathed my feet and leggs in warm water, wherin beef had bin boiled and some Brann. And I had done none of this for myself, nor had George Goodgion cutt my haire for mee since the 18th of December last that he did the like in this chamber of mine in Brougham Castle.

God grant that good may betide mee & mine after it.

Ps. 23.4, 5.

And this 22nd day there came severall bits by ye post from London, which I heard read to mee next morning; and amongst ye post, one from my Daughter of Thanet dated ye 17th of this month, whereby she desired me that if there be another Parliament, I would make her Sonne John one of the Burgesses for Appleby, to which I returned an answer.

I went not out of ye House nor out of my chamber all this day.

Ps. 121.

The 23rd day I remembered how this day was 60 years [since] my first Lord & I went out of the Inne at Stony Stratford into my Cosen Thomas Elmes' house at Lilford in Northamptonshire for a while, so that day into the Inne at Warwick where wee lay that night as wee were in our Journy, I towards Brougham Castle in Westmorland to my blessed Mother, and hee to set mee as farr on my way as Litchfield in Staffordshire.

And today there dined with my folks in the Painted Room Mr Samuell Grasty, our parson, and after dinner I had him into my chamber and took him by the hand. And afterward he said Common Prayers and read a Chapter (as usuall upon Wednesdays) to mee & my family, and after prayers was done they went away.

The Last Months, 1676

And there also dined without with my folks Mr Thomas Ewbank of Ormside, ye Doctor (that married the widdow Mrs Hilton), so after dinner I had him into my chamber and took him by the hand and I gave him 6 sh. and I caused him to go into Arthur Swindin's chamber to see him, and he came up and stayd for prayers, and then he went away.

I went not out of the house nor out of my chamber today.

Ps. 121.

The 24th Day. I remembered how this day was 60 years [since] my first Lord & I, after I had been to see Warwick Castle and Church, went out of the Inne there & so out of that towne into Guy's Cliffe in that County to see it, and onwards to Killingworth Castle for a while to see it, & from thence that night wee went into the Inne at Litchfield in Staffordshire where wee lay 2 nights together because the next day was Sunday, as I was in my Journy to Brougham Castle in Westmorland to my blessed Mother.

And this morning I set my hand to 4 good letters of Hasell's writing for mee, one to my Daughter Thanet, one to my Lord Northampton, one to Mr William Edge and one to Dr Johnston, this last being in answer of one from him with which hee sent by my Lord Marshall's directions severall of my Ancestors letters I received from them by the last post.

And this 24th day in the morning I had a most extream fitt of the wind, and so as it had like to have been a Swouning Fitt, tho' it did not prove so, God be thanked.

And this morning John Webster came hither and I had him into my chamber and talked with him & took him by the hand, & he dined here with my folks, and after dinner he went away.

And there also dined without with my folks young Mr Blenkinsop of Brough, so after dinner I had him into my chamber & talked with him & gave him 10 sh. and hee now told mee that his youngest sister who was lame was lately deceased, & then he went away.

And Henry Ram, my Tennant of Flakebridge, also dined here and after dinner hee came into my chamber and I took him by the hand and talked with him a while after he went away.

I went not out of the House nor out of my chamber all this day.

Ps. 121.

The 25th day. I remembered how this day was 67 years, and then Saturday, I was married to my first Lord Richard Sackville, then but Lord Buckhurst, in my Mother's Chamber in Austin Fryers in London, where shee & I then lay. But that Lord of mine came to bee Earle of Dorset within two dayes after by the death of his father, Robert Sackville, Earle of Dorset.

And I remembered how this day was 60 years [since], & then Sunday, my first Lord & I went forenoon & afternoon into the Church at Litchfield, to the Sermon & Service there, and afterwards into other of the most remarkable places in that towne & that night wee lay againe in the Inne there, from whence I continued my Journy the next day towards Brougham Castle in Westmorland to my blessed Mother.

And this 25th day in the forenoon, about 9 a clock, after I had taken my leave of him, did Mr Thomas Strickland, one of my Chief Officers, and his man, Lancelot Machell, ride on horseback out of this Brougham Castle towards Appleby Castle to receive there the rest of my Candlemas Rents, and they lay there for 3 nights, and upon the 28th day, being Monday, a little after Supper they came back here to mee and us here.

I went not out of the House nor out of my chamber all this day.

The 26th day, I remembered how this day was 60 years [since] I & my Lord went out of the Inne at Litchfield, where wee had layen two nights together, into Sir George Curzon's house at Croxall in Darbyshire, & that was the first & last time that I was ever in that house, from whence wee went to Burton upon Trent in Darbyshire where my first Lord & I then parted, he returning back to Litchfield where hee was to make stay for 4 or 5 dayes there, about a great foot race that was then there. But I proceeded on my Journy towards Brougham Castle in Westmorland to my blessed Mother and came that night to Darby & lay in the Inne there that night, which was the first & last time that I ever lay in that towne.

I went not out of the house nor out of my chamber today.

Ps. 121.

The 27th day. I remembered how this day was 60 years did I go out of the Inne at Darby into two Houses at Hardwick, now both belonging to the Earl of Devonshire, and so from thence into the Inne at Chesterfield in that County where I lay there that one night.

And tho' today was Sunday yet I went not to the Church nor out of my Chamber all this day.

Ps. 23

But my 2 gentlewomen went & 2 of my Laundry maids and most of my menservants rode on Horseback to Ninekirks, where Mr Grasty the parson preached a very good sermon to them & the Congregation.

I went not out of the House nor out of my chamber all this day, tho' it be Sunday.

Ps. 121

The 28th Day. I remembered how this day was 60 years [since] I went out of the Inne at Chesterfield in Darbyshire into the Earle of Shrousberie's house called Sheffield in Yorkshire for a while to see it, & that evening I went into the Inne at Rotherham in that County where I lay that one night as I was in my Journy towards Brougham Castle in Westmorland to see my blessed Mother. And that was the first time I came into Yorkeshire after I was married and (became) Countesse of Dorset.

And today here in the Painted Room with my folks there dined Mr Christopher Dalston of Accorn Bank, eldest Sonne to my Cozen Mr John Dalston, and his wife. So after dinner I had them into my chamber and kist his wife and took him by the hand, and likewise I talked with them a good while, and I gave his wife a pare of Buckskin Gloves, and then they went away.

And there also dined here with my folks John Webster, who came hither this morning, att which time I had him into my chamber and talked with him and took him by the hand, and after dinner he went away.

And this evening about 5 a clock did John Twentyman (who is Gardiner to the Ld Bishop of Carlisle) come hither and he lay in the Bannister Room.

I went not out of the House nor out of my chamber today.

Ps. 121.

The 29th Day. I remembered how this day was 60 years [since] I went out of the Inne at Rotherham in Yorkeshire into a poor parson's house at Peniston in that County, where I lay there that one night, as I was in my Journy towards Brougham Castle in Westmorland to see my blessed Mother.

And today there dined here with my folks Margaret Waugh of Appleby, that formerly served mee, so I had her into my chamber after dinner and kissed her and talked with her a good while, this being the first time I saw her since I came to Brougham Castle, and a little while after she went away. And there also dined without with my folks young Wm. Mid[d]leton, Roger Mid[d]leton's brother, that once served mee, and after dinner I had him into my Chamber & took him by the hand, but I gave him nothing, and then he went away. He came hither yesternight and lay in the Bannister Room.

And this afternoon did Thomas Strickland pay to Mr Edward Hasell for my use £305 5 sh. of my Westmorland rents due at Candlemas last, for which I now gave Strickland an acquittance under my hand & saw ye money put into ye trunk in my chamber.

I went not out of the house nor out of my chamber today.

Ps. 121.

MARCH

The 1st Day I remembered how this day was 60 years [since] I went out of the poor Parson's house at Peniston in Yorkshire, over Peniston Moor (where never any coach went before mine), into the Inne at Manchester in Lancashire where I lay that one night as I was on my Journy towards Brougham Castle in Westmorland to see my Blessed Mother.

And today there dined here with my folks John Webster, who came into my chamber before dinner. And I took him by the hand and talked with him, and after dinner he came again into my chamber and stayd till Mr Grasty had said Prayers, and then he went away.

And there allso dined here Mr John Gilmoor who lives at Julian Bower, and his man Wm. Labourn dined below in ye Hall, and after dinner I had them both into my Chamber and talkt with them and took them by the hand, and after Prayers they went away.

And today there dined here also Mr Samuel Grasty, our parson, and after dinner he came into my chamber and said Common Prayers (as usuall upon Wednesdays) and read a Chapter to mee and them and my family, and when Prayers was ended he went away.

I went not out of the house nor out of my chamber today.

Ps. 121.

The 2nd day I remembered how this day was 60 years [since] I went out of the Inne at Manchester in Lancashire into the poor cottage at Chorley where I lay in a poor ale-house there that one night (which was within 3 miles of Latham house, but I did not see it by reason of the mist) as I was in my Journy towards Brougham Castle in Westmorland to see my blessed Mother.

And this morning I set my hand to 3 good letters of Hasell's writing for mee, one to my Daughter Thanet, one to my Lord Northampton, and one to Mr William Edge, all in answer of letters I received from them by the last post.

And today there dined without with my folks in the Painted Room Mrs Willison of Penrith (whose husband is gone into Scotland), and after dinner I had her into my chamber and kissed her and took her by the hand, but I told her I would have no more wine off her husband because he used me so badly, and then she went away.

I had a very ill fitt of the wind today, and yet nevertheless I slept well in ye night notwithstanding, I thank God.

Ps. 23. 4, 5.

The Last Months, 1676

I went not out of the House nor out of my Chamber all this day.

The 3rd Day I remembered how this day was 60 years [since] I went out of the poor cottage at Chorley (though it was Sunday, by reason the lodgings were so bad) into the inne at Preston in Andersey in Lancashire where I lay that one night as I was in my Journy towards Brougham Castle in Westmorland to see my blessed Mother.

And this day, both in the forenoon and afternoon did Mrs Frances Pate preserve for me in her owne chamber a good many of Apples and Lemmans.

And today I had a very ill fitt of ye wind, but yet nevertheless I slept well in the night, I thank God.

Ps. 23. 4, 5.

I went not out of the house nor out of my chamber all this day.

The 4th day I remembered how this day was 60 years [since] I went out of the Inne at Preston in Lancashire into Lancaster towne in that County, where I lay in a poor Inne there that one night and where I went up upon the leads of the remaining part of that old Castle, as I was in my Journy towards Brougham Castle in Westmorland to see my blessed Mother.

And this morning I saw payd severall persons for graving and working in my Garden here at Brougham Castle. And afterwards I saw Mr Willison of Penrith payd for a Rundlet of Sack and White Wine, and he dined here with my folks in the painted Room, and then he went away.

And today there allso dined without with my folks in the painted Room Mr Robert Hillton of Murton, and after dinner I had him into my chamber and took him by the hand and gave him 3 yards of Ducap* and a Pot of Alchermy to carry to his wife, and then he went away.

And tho' I had a very ill fitt of the wind today yet I slept well at night, I thank God.

Ps. 23.

I went not out of the house nor out of my chamber today.

Ps. 23.

The 5th day, being Sunday, I remembered how this night was 52 years [ago] was the last night that ever I lay in Great Dorset House in London towne, for the next day I went from thence from my first Lord downe to Knowl house in Kent to my two Daughters, and I never lay in Great Dorset House after, for my first Lord dyed the 28th day of that month in the lead chamber in Great Dorset House.

---

* A material suitable for upholstery work.

And I remembered how this day was 60 years [since] I went out of the poor Inne in Lancaster towne and so out of that County into the Inne at Kendall in Westmorland, where I lay that one night, as I was in my Journy to Brougham Castle to see my blessed Mother.

And I remembered how this 5th day of March is just 5 months since I and my family removed out of Appleby Castle hither to Brougham Castle.

Rev. 9. 5, 10.

And today there dined without with my folks in the painted Room Mr Samuel Grasty, our parson, and my 2 farmers here, namely William Spedding and his wife and Jefferie Blamire and his Sonne, and John Webster. So after dinner I had them all into my chamber and kist the woman and took them by the hand, and Mr Grasty was payd his 20 sh. for saying Prayers to me and my family for a month last past, and after he said Common Prayer and read a Chapter & sung a Psalm (as usuall upon Sundays) to mee & them aforesaid, and when Prayers was done they all went away.

I went not out of ye house nor out of my chamber for all this Sunday, tho' it was so.

The 6th day I remembered how this day was 67 years [since] my blessed Mother with many in our company brought mee from her house in Austin Fryers to the Court of little Dorset House in Salisbury Court in London towne to lye there with my first Lord, which was the first time I ever lay in that new-built house, I being but married to my first Lord the 25th of the month before.

And I remembered how this day was 60 years (since) I went out of the Inne at Kendall to Brougham Castle in Westmorland to my blessed Mother to see her, and that was the first time that I was in Brougham Castle after I was Countesse of Dorset, or in a good while before.

And this morning I saw John Pattison of Moorhouse payd for a Stak of Hay for my stables, and then he went away.

And today there dined here with my folks John Webster, so after dinner I had him into my chamber and took him by the hand and talked with him, and a little after he went away from mee.

And this evening, about 4 a clock, did Thomas Wright the Quaker of Mallerstang come hither, so he lay in the Bannister Room, and the next morning I had him into my chamber and took him by the hand and saw him payd for 12 bushells of malt for my house, and then he went away.

I went not out of the house nor out of my chamber all this day.

The 7th Day. And this 7th day in the morning, about nine of the clock, dyed Arthur Swindin, my Under Butler, in the chamber under the great chamber at this Brougham Castle, who has served mee about 14 or 15 years. And the next day, about 2 of the clock in the afternoon, his dead body was buried in Nine Church (this Parish Church), where Parson Grasty preached his funerall sermon, and most of my servants and others attended the Corps at the funerall.

And today there dined without with my folks in the Painted Room Mr Thomas Gabetis, my Sheriff, and Mr John Thwaite of Appleby, and after dinner I had them both into my chamber and took them by the hand and talked with them a good while, and afterward they both went away.

And there also dined here in the Painted Chamber with my folks John Webster, so I had him into my chamber after dinner and before dinner and took him by ye hand and talked with him, and then he went away.

I went not out of the House nor out of my chamber all this day.

The 8th day. And today I had a very ill fitt of wind after dinner, but nevertheless I did sleep indifferent well in the night, I thank God.

Ps. 23. 4, 5.

I went not out of the House nor out of my chamber all this day.

The 9th Day. And this morning I set my hand to 4 good letters of Hasell's writing for mee, one to my Daughter Thanet, one to my Lord Northampton, one to Mr William Edge and one to Mrs Elizabeth Gilmore, all in answer of letters I received from them by the last post.

And today there dined with my folks in the painted Room my Cozen Mr John Dalston of Accorn Bank. So after dinner I had him into my chamber and took him by the hand and talked with him, and then he went away.

And there also dined with my folks Mr John Gilmoor, my Keeper of Whinfield Park, and his man William Labourn dined below in the Hall, and after dinner (after my Cozen was gone from mee) I had them both into my chamber and took them by the hand and talked with them, and then they went away.

And though today I had an Extream ill fitt of the wind, yet, notwithstanding, I slept pretty well in the night, I thank God.

Ps. 23. 4, 5.

I went not out of the house nor out of my chamber all this day.

The 10th Day. And this morning I saw not only A. Strickland payd for the weekbook in my chamber, but I also saw G. Goodgion payd for 249 yards of Linnen cloth that he bought for mee at Penrith, designed for 20 pares of Sheets and som Pillowveres [pillow-cases] for the use of my house. And after dinner I gave away severall old Sheets which were divided amongst my servants.

And this afternoon did Margaret Montgomery of Penrith, the Seamstress,

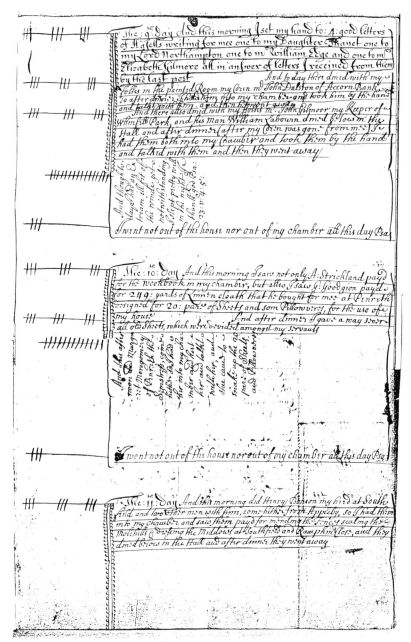

A PAGE FROM THE MANUSCRIPT OF THE 'LAST MONTHS' DIARY, showing the
entries for 9, 10 and 11 March 1676

come hither so I had her into my chamber and kist her and talked with her, and shee came to make up the 20 pares of Sheets and Pillowveres.

I went not out of the house nor out of my chamber all this day.

The 11th day. And this morning did Henry Bonson, my herd at Southfield, and two other men with him, come hither from Appleby, so I had them into my chamber and saw them payd for mending the Fences, scaling the Molehills & dressing the Middows at Southfield and Rampkin Close; and they dined below in the Hall, and after dinner they went away.

And today I had a very Extream fitt of ye wind, but yet I slept well in the night, I thank God, notwithstanding.

Ps. 23.

I went not out of the house nor out of my chamber today.

Ps. 121.

The 12th day, being Sunday. And though it was so, yet I went not to church nor out of my chamber all this day. But one of my gentlewomen and one of my Laundry maids and most of my chiefe Menservants went to Ninekirks, where Mr Grasty the parson preached a good sermon to them & ye Congregation. And today there dined without my folks in the Painted Room Mr Sam. Grasty, our parson, and my two farmers here, namely Wm. Spedding and his wife and Jeffery Blamire and his Son, and John Webster. So after dinner I had them into my chamber and kist the woman and took them by the hand. And a little after Mr Grasty said Common Prayers and read a Chapter and sung a Psalm in my chamber to mee and my family (as usually is done upon Sundays), and after prayers they all went away.

And tho' this day I had an Extream ill fit of the wind in the afternoon, so that I was in great danger (and yet in no danger) of Death, and yet I slept well in ye night I thank God, notwithstanding.

Ps. 23.4.

I went not out of the house nor out of my chamber all this day, tho' it was Sunday.

The 13th day. I remembered how this day was 60 years [since] I went from my blessed Mother out of Brougham Castle in Westmorland to Naworth Castle in Cumberland where I lay there in it for two nights with the Lord William Howard (my first Lord's Uncle) and his wife the Lady Elizabeth Dacres (my father's Cozen german) and with many of their Sonns and their Sonns' wives, and their daughters & their children and Grandchildren, which was the first time I came into Cumberland since I was first married and Countesse of Dorset.

And today there dined without with my folks in the Painted Room Sir Christopher Clapham.* And after dinner I had him into my chamber and discoursed with him a good while, and then he went away, and I had not seen him (since) a long time before. And the said Sir Christopher brought mee a letter from my Grandchild, Lady Alethea, to which I returned an answer.

And there also came along with him and dined here Mr James Buchanan, ye parson of Appleby, so after dinner I had him into my chamber and took him by the hand and talked with him, and then he went away.

And there also dined without with my folks John Webster and his mother, Isabell Webster, and after dinner I had them both into my chamber & kissed her and took him by the hand, and a little after they went away.

I went not out of the house nor out of my chamber today.

Ps. 121.

The 14th day I remembered how this day was 15 years [since] my youngest Daughter, Isabella, Countesse of Northampton, since deceased, was delivered of her youngest and only surviving childe of six, and was her third Daughter, in her Lord's House in Lincoln Inn fields, which childe was afterwards christened by the name of Alethea, I then lying in Appleby Castle in Westmorland, whose life and fortune God preserved.

And this morning I set my hand to a good letter of Hasell's writing for mee to my deare Grandchilde, the Lady Alethea Compton, in answer to a letter Sir Christopher Clapham brought mee yesterday from her.

And this forenoon about 10 a clock did John Webster come hither, so I had him into my chamber and talked with him and took him by the hand, and he dined without with my folks in ye Painted Room, and a little after he went away.

I went not out of the house nor out of my chamber today.

Ps. 121.

The 15th day I remembered how this day was 60 years [since] in the morning I went out of Naworth Castle in Cumberland from the Lord William Howard and his wife into the Citty of Carlisle in the same County, where I went into the Castle there and into the chamber in that Castle wherein was borne into the world the Lady Anne Dacres, shee

---

* Christopher Clapham had been steward of Lady Anne's Westmorland estates for many years and had also served as MP for Appleby. By 1676 he had retired and had received a knighthood.

that was afterwards Countesse Dowager of Arrundell, and I went into the Cathedrall church there wherein was buried my great grandfather, William, Lord Dacres. And from thence I went the same day into Brougham Castle in Westmorland, where I continued to lye with my blessed Mother till the 2nd of the month following, that I went away from her, and never saw her after.

And today there dined without with my folks in the Painted Room Mr Samuel Grasty, our parson, so after dinner I had him into my chamber and talked with him, and afterward he said Common Prayer and read a Chapter to me and my family (as usuall upon Wednesdays), and when Prayers was ended he went away.

And today I had a very ill fit of ye wind.

Ps. 23. 4.

I went not out of the house nor out of my chamber all this day.

The 16th Day. And today there dined without with my folks in the Painted Room Mr Richard Jackson, the Scoolmaster of Appleby, so after dinner I had him into my Chamber and took him by the hand and talked with him a good while, and then he went away.

And there also dined here Mr Leonard Smith of Appleby, and likewise John Atkinson, the Taylor, so after dinner I had them into my Chamber and talked with them a good while and took them by the hand, and a little after they went away.

And John Webster also dined without with them and my folks, and after dinner he came into my Chamber and I took him by the hand and spoke to him, and then he went away.

And this afternoon, a little after dinner, did Mr James Bird, the Attorney, come hither, he being but lately come from his Jorney from London, so I had him into my Chamber and took him by the hand & talked with him, and I gave him 10 sh. as I used to do, and then he went away.

I went not out of the House nor out of my chamber today.

The 17th Day. And today no body dined here but my owne folks, so that there is none to be superadded.

And today I had a very ill fitt of the wind, but yet I slept in the night indifferently well, I thank God.

Ps. 23.

I went not out of the House nor out of my Chamber all this day.

The 18th Day. And yester night did Thomas Wright the Quaker that was att Mallerstang come hither, and he lay this night in the Bannister Room, and this morning I had him into my Chamber and took him by the hand and saw him payd for 12 bushells of malt for a Brewing of Beer for my House att this Brougham Castle. And a little after he went from me and us here towards his owne home.

I went not out of this house nor out of my chamber today.

The 19th Day, being Sunday, Palm Sunday. And this Sunday morning I had a very violent fitt of the wind, so that it caused me to fall into a Swouning Fit for about halfe an hour together, so as I thought I should have dyed, but it pleased God I recovered and was better afterward.

And today there dined without with my folks in the Painted Room Mr Grasty, oure parson, and my 2 farmers here, namly Wm. Spedding and his wife and Jeffrey Blamire and his Sonne, and John Webster. So after dinner they came into my chamber and I kist the woman & took the men by the hand. And a little after Mr Grasty said Common Prayer and read a Chapter and sung a Psalm as usuall upon Sundays to me and them and my family, and after prayers they all went away.

I went not out of the house nor out of my chamber today.

Ps. 1.

The 20th Day. I remembered how this day was 60 years [since] I and my blessed Mother in Brougham Castle in Westmorland, where wee then lay, give in our answer in writing that we would not stand to the Award the then four cheif Judges meant to make concerning the lands of mine Inheritance, which did spin out a great deal of trouble to us, yet God turned it for the best.

Deut. 23.5.

And this morning John Webster came hither, so I had him into my chamber and took him by the hand and spoke to him, and he dined without with my folks and then he went away.

I went not out of the house nor out of my chamber today.

The 21st Day. I went not out of the house nor out of my chamber all this day.

Ps. 121.

The 22nd Day.

Epilogue

The final entry of Lady Anne's diary is completed on her behalf, perhaps by Edward Hasell:

> On Wednesday the 22nd, about 6 a clock in the afternoon, after she had endured all her pains with a most Christian fortitude, always answering those that asked her how she did with – 'I thank God I am very well' – which were her last words directed to mortals, she, with much cheerfulness, in her own chamber in Brougham Castle, wherein her noble father was born and her blessed mother died, yielded up her precious soul into the hands of her merciful Redeemer.

Her body, in accordance with the instructions in her will, was wrapped in cear cloth and encased in lead, with a brass inscription on her breast. On the 14 April 1676 her horses, which had drawn her coach so many times on her journeys from castle to castle, drew her on her last journey to St Lawrence Church in Appleby, where she was laid in the vault she had planned for herself, adjacent to her mother's and built soon after her mother's death some sixty years before. It is recorded that a vast retinue of local gentry, friends and tenants attended the hearse on its journey from Brougham, and that the chief mourner was her favourite grandchild, John Tufton. Her cousin, Sir Philip Musgrave, and her old friend, John Dalston, and their sons, were also present.

The funeral sermon was preached by another old friend, Bishop Edward Rainbowe of Carlisle. His text was taken from Proverbs 14.1: 'Every wise woman buildeth her house.'

The Bishop expanded his theme to no less than eighteen points covering Anne's long life, including 'Her Birth', 'Her Buildings', 'Her Humility' and 'Her Religion'. Among his concluding words the following extract seems to convey exactly the prevailing opinions of the time concerning this great lady:

> A little before her death, patience and meekness and low thoughts of herself, which had been her practice, were now her argument.

Discoursing frequently with one of her nearest attendants, and seeing her and others passionately concerned and busie about her, who deserved less; expostulating why any of these outward things should trouble her, who deserved so little and had been blessed with so much.

Lady Anne's tomb is plain, bearing no effigy like that in marble she created for her mother. But on the wall behind is a remarkable display of the coats of arms of her ancestors, a final summary of the inheritance of this lady, who may not have been the most famous, but was certainly one of the most colourful of her times.

I cannot end without recounting a delightful story which so well illustrates how much the spirit and the memory of Lady Anne still lingers in the minds of Westmorland folk to this day.

Not long after the Second World War Lord Hothfield offered to instal electricity for the first time in the almshouses in Appleby which Lady Anne had founded some three hundred years before. His proposal was politely declined, the reason being given that, 'Lady Anne would not have liked it.'

THE DIVIDED INHERITANCE

The Castles and Manors of Westmorland together with the Sheriffwick of Westmorland

INHERITED FROM LADY ANNE BY:

MARGARET SACKVILLE = JOHN TUFTON, 2nd Earl of Thanet
(1614–76)　　　　　　　　(1609–64)

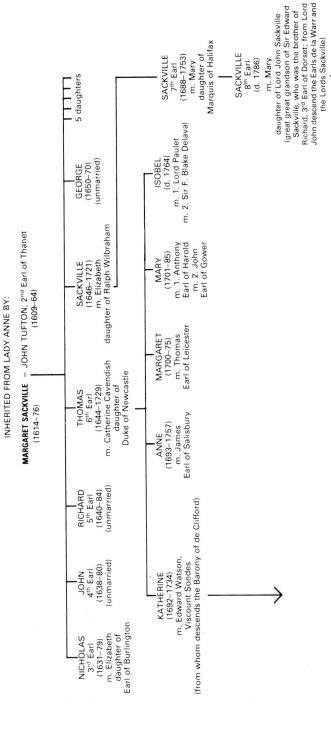

NICHOLAS
3rd Earl
(1631–79)
m. Elizabeth
daughter of
Earl of Burlington

JOHN
4th Earl
(1638–80)
(unmarried)

RICHARD
5th Earl
(1640–84)
(unmarried)

THOMAS
6th Earl
(1644–1729)
m. Catherine Cavendish
daughter of
Duke of Newcastle

SACKVILLE
(1646–1721)
m. Elizabeth
daughter of Ralph Wilbraham

GEORGE
(1650–70)
(unmarried)

5 daughters

KATHERINE
(1692–1734)
m. Edward Watson,
Viscount Sondes
(from whom descends the Barony of de Clifford)

ANNE
(1693–1757)
m. James
Earl of Salisbury

MARGARET
(1700–75)
m. Thomas
Earl of Leicester

MARY
(1701–85)
m. 1. Anthony
Earl of Harold
m. 2. John
Earl of Gower

ISOBEL
(d. 1764)
m. 1. Lord Paulet
m. 2. Sir F. Blake Delaval

SACKVILLE
7th Earl
(1688–1753)
m. Mary
daughter of
Marquis of Halifax

SACKVILLE
8th Earl
(d. 1786)

m. Mary
daughter of Lord John Sackville
(great great grandson of Sir Edward
Sackville, who was the brother of
Richard, 3rd Earl of Dorset; from Lord
John descend the Earls de la Warr and
the Lords Sackville)

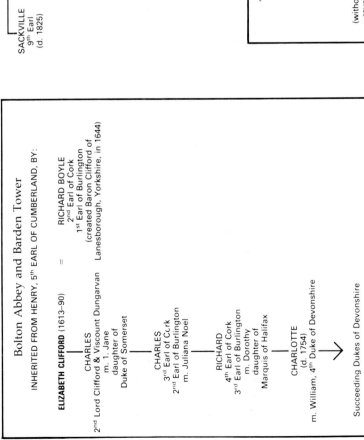

Bolton Abbey and Barden Tower

INHERITED FROM HENRY, 5ᵗʰ EARL OF CUMBERLAND, BY:

ELIZABETH CLIFFORD (1613–90) = RICHARD BOYLE
2ⁿᵈ Earl of Cork
1ˢᵗ Earl of Burlington
(created Baron Clifford of
Lanesborough, Yorkshire, in 1644)

CHARLES
2ⁿᵈ Lord Clifford & Viscount Dungarvan
m. 1. Jane
daughter of
Duke of Somerset

CHARLES
3ʳᵈ Earl of C¢rk
2ⁿᵈ Earl of Burlington
m. Juliana Noel

RICHARD
4ᵗʰ Earl of Cork
3ʳᵈ Earl of Burlington
m. Dorothy
daughter of
Marquis of Halifax

CHARLOTTE
(d. 1754)
m. William, 4ᵗʰ Duke of Devonshire

Succeeding Dukes of Devonshire

SACKVILLE
9ᵗʰ Earl
(d. 1825)

CHARLES
10ᵗʰ Earl
(d. 1832)

HENRY
11ᵗʰ and last Earl of Thanet, and
last Sheriff of Westmorland by heredity
(1775–1849)
by Julie Durieux

Sir RICHARD TUFTON
1ˢᵗ Baronet
(d. 1871)
m. Adelaide Lacour

HENRY JAMES
1ˢᵗ Baron Hothfield
(1844–1926)
m. Alice Clitherow

Succeeding Lords Hothfield

The Honour of Skipton and its Castle

INHERITED FROM LADY ANNE BY:

ISABELLA SACKVILLE = JAMES
(1622–61)   3ʳᵈ Earl of Northampton

ALETHEA
m. Sir Edward Hungerford
(1661–78)

(without issue – on her death, Althea's share of the inheritance
reverted to the Earls of Thanet; the Earls, and subsequently
Marquises, of Northampton descend from James' second
marriage, to Mary, daughter of Viscount Campden)

Appendix 1

THE KNOLE CATALOGUE*

A CATALOGUE of the Household and Family of the Right Honourable
RICHARD, EARL of DORSET in the year of our Lord 1613 and so continued
until the year 1624, at KNOLE

AT MY LORD'S TABLE

My Lord

My Lady Margaret

Mr Sackville

John Musgrave

My Lady

My Lady Isabella

Mr Frost

Thomas Garret

AT THE PARLOUR TABLE

Mrs Field

Mrs Grimsditch

Mrs Fletcher

Mr Dupper, Chaplain

Mr Matthew Caldicott

Mr Edward Legge, Steward

Mr Peter Basket, Gentleman of the
  Horse

Mr Marsh, Attendant on my Lady

Mr Wooldridge

Mr Cheyney

Mr Duck, Page

Mr Josiah Cooper, Page

Mr John Belgrave, Page

Mr Billingsley

Mr Graverner, Gentleman Usher

Mr Marshall, Auditor

Mr Edwards, Secretary

Mr Drake, Attendant

Mrs Willoughby

Mrs Stewkley

Mrs Wood

AT THE CLERKS' TABLE IN THE HALL

Edward Fulks & John Edwards, Clerks
  of the Kitchen

Edward Care, Master Cook

William Smith, Yeoman of the Buttery

Henry Keble, Yeoman of the Pantry

John Mitchell, Pastryman

Thomas Vinson, Cook

John Elnor, Cook

Ralph Hussie, Cook

John Avery, Usher of the Hall

---

* Taken from the original document, which was completed in the 1620s and is hanging
still, framed under glass, at Knole House in Kent.

Appendix 1: The Knole Catalogue

Robert Elnor, Slaughterman
Ben Staples, Groom of the Great
  Chamber
Thomas Petley, Brewer
William Turner, Baker
Francis Steeling, Gardener

Richard Wickling, Gardener
Thomas Clements, Under Brewer
Samuel Vans, Caterer
Edward Small, Groom of the Wardrobe
Samuel Southern, Under Baker
Lowry, a French Boy

THE NURSERY

Nurse Carpenter
Jane Sisley

Widow Ben
Dorothy Pickenden

AT THE LONG TABLE IN THE HALL

Robert Care, Attendant on my Lord
Mr Gray, Attendant Likewise
Mr Roger Cook, Attendant on Lady
  Margaret
Mr Adam Bradford, Barber
Mr John Guy, Groom of my Lord's
  Bedchamber
Walter Comestone, Attendant on my
  Lady
Edward Lane, Scrivener
Mr Thomas Poor, Yeoman of the
  Wardrobe
Mr Thomas Leonard, Master
  Huntsman
Mr Woodgate, Yeoman of the Great
  Chamber
John Hall, Falconer
James Flennel, Yeoman of the Granary
Rawlinson, Armourer
Moses Shonk, Coachman
Anthony Ashley, Groom of the Great
  Horse
Griffin Edwards, Groom of my Lady's
  Horse
Francis Turner, Groom of the Great
  Horse
William Grynes, Groom of the Great
  Horse
Acton Curvett, Chief Footman
James Loveall, Footman

Sampson Ashley, Footman
William Petley, Footman
Nicholas James, Footman
Paschal Beard, Footman
Elias Thomas, Footman
Henry Spencer, Farrier
Edward Goodsall
John Sant, the Steward's Man
Ralph Wise, Groom of the Stables
Thomas Petley, Under Farrier
John Stephens, the Chaplain's man
John Haite, Groom of the Stranger's
  Horse
Thomas Giles, Groom of the Stables
Richard Thomas, Groom of the Hall
Christopher Wood, Groom of the
  Pantry
George Owen, Huntsman
George Vigeon, Huntsman
Thomas Grittan, Groom of the Buttery
Solomon, the Bird-Catcher
Richard Thornton, the Coachman's
  Man
Richard Pickendon, Postilion
William Roberts, Groom
The Armourer's Man
Ralph Wise, his Servant
John Swift, Porter's Man
John Atkins
Clement Doory

The Diaries of Lady Anne Clifford

THE LAUNDRY MAIDS' TABLE

Mrs Judith Simpton
Mrs Grace Simpton
Penelope Tutty, Lady Margaret's Maid
Anne Mills, Dairy-Maid
Prudence Butcher
Anne Howse

Faith Husband
Elinor Thompson
Goodwife Burton
Grace Robinson, a Blackamoor
Goodwife Small
William Lewis, a Porter

KITCHEN AND SCULLERY

Diggory Dyer
Marfidy Snipt
John Watson

Thomas Harman
Thomas Johnson
John Morockoe, a Blackamoor

Appendix 2

SOME PLACES TO VISIT

Appleby Castle, Cumbria (Ferguson Industrial Holdings plc)
  Open from Easter to September (gardens and keep, 10 a.m. to 5 p.m.; Great
  Hall, 10 a.m. to 5 p.m., closed Monday and Saturday).

Barden Tower, North Yorkshire (Devonshire Estates)
  Apply at café to view the chapel.

Bolebrooke House, Sussex (Privately owned)
  Viewing only possible from outside.

Brough Castle, Cumbria (English Heritage)
  Open throughout the year, except at Christmas (from October to March,
  9.30 a.m. to 4.30 p.m.; from April to September, 9.30 a.m. to 6.30 p.m.).
  Closed two days a week – please check with the curator beforehand
  (tel. 093 04219).

Brougham Castle, Cumbria (English Heritage)
  Open throughout the year, except at Christmas (from mid-October to
  mid-March, 9.30 a.m. to 4.30 p.m.; from mid-March to mid-October,
  9.30 a.m. to 6.30 p.m.).

Castle Ashby, Northamptonshire (Marquess of Northampton)
  Opening limited – apply to the Estates Office in advance.

Knole House, Kent (National Trust)
  Open from April to October (Wednesday to Saturday, 11 a.m. to 5 p.m.;
  Sunday, 2 p.m. to 5 p.m.; bank holidays, including Easter Monday, 11 a.m.
  to 5 p.m.).

Pendragon Castle, Cumbria
  Now a ruin situated on farmland.

Sackville College, East Grinstead, Sussex
  Open from May to September (2 a.m. to 5 p.m.).

St Anne's Almshouses, Appleby, Cumbria
  Apply to the warden to view the courtyard.

Skipton Castle, North Yorkshire (H. Fattorini, Esq)
  Open throughout the year, except Christmas Day (Summer: Monday to
  Saturday, 10 a.m. to 6 p.m., Sunday, 2 p.m. to 6 p.m.; Winter: Monday to
  Saturday, 10 a.m. to 4 p.m., Sunday, 2 p.m. to 4 p.m.).

The Diaries of Lady Anne Clifford

Wilton House, Wiltshire (Earl of Pembroke)
Open from mid-April to mid-October (Tuesday to Saturday, 11 a.m. to 6 p.m.; Sunday, 1 p.m. to 6 p.m.).

Regrettably, Hothfield House, Londesborough, and Thanet House have not survived.

While every care has been taken to ensure that the above details are correct, the author cannot guarantee that opening times will not vary in the future.

Bibliography

MANUSCRIPT SOURCES

British Library, Harleian MS. 6177
Cumbria Record Office, Kendal, Hothfield Manuscripts (WD/HOTH)
The Dalemain Collection (Mr R.B. Hasell McCosh), Dalemain, nr. Penrith
Kent County Record Office, Maidstone, Sackville Collection (U269 F48/1–3)

OTHER SOURCES

Clifford Association Archives
Cumbria Record Offices, Carlisle and Kendal
Jackson Library, Carlisle
Northamptonshire County Record Office, Northampton
Public Record Office, Chancery Lane, London
Trinity College Library, Dublin

FURTHER READING

Archaeologia Cantiana
Clifford, Arthur, *Collectanea Cliffordiana*, Paris, 1817 (reprinted, Skipton Castle, 1980)
Clifford, Hugh, *The House of Clifford*, Phillimore & Co., Chichester, 1987
Holmes, Martin, *Proud Northern Lady*, Phillimore & Co., Chichester, 1973
Nicholson, J. and Burn, R. *The History of Cumberland and Westmorland*, 1777
Phillips, Charles J., *History of the Sackville Family*
Roxburghe Club Journal
Sackville-West, Vita, ed., *The Diary of the Lady Anne Clifford*, Heinemann, 1923
——, *Knole and the Sackvilles*, 1923
Surtees Society Journal
Transactions of the Cumberland and Westmorland Antiquarian and Archaeological Society

The Diaries of Lady Anne Clifford

Whitaker, T.D., *The History of Craven*, 1805

Williamson, G.C., *George Clifford, Third Earl of Cumberland*, Cambridge University Press, 1920

——, *Lady Anne Clifford*, Titus Wilson, Kendal, 1922

Yorkshire Archaeological Society Journal

Index

In the case of persons with the same surname, titles as given in the text are included in alphabetical order, e.g. Dr John, John, Lord John, Mr John, Sir John. Numbers in *italics* refer to illustrations.

Abbreviations:
AC: Anne Clifford
gr: grandchild
gt-gr: great-grandchild
n: note

Abbott, George, Archbishop of Canterbury 29, 253
Abergavenny, Lady 35n
Achin (servant) 48
Adams, Judge 130
Alexander, Henry 24
Amherst, Dr Jeffrey 48+n
Amherst, Mr (serjeant-at-law) 35, 36, 82
Anne of Denmark, wife of James I 23, 24, 27, 44, 45, 57n, 64, 66, 240; death and funeral 69, 70, 74–5
Appleby Almshouses *see* St Anne's Almshouses
Appleby Castle 3, 4, 96, 97, 100, 110, *111*, 112, 118–19, 125, 142; Caesar's Tower 110, 118–19, *120*, 142
Appleby Church *see* St Lawrence's Church, Appleby
Arundel, Elizabeth Stuart, Countess Dowager of 221
Arundel, Lady 28, 29, 43, 44, 64, 66
Arundel, Lord 44, 47, 66
Arundell, Mrs 59
Aske's Rebellion 110n
Asken, Mr 49
Atkins, Judge 127, 133
Atkinson, Captain 238n
Atkinson, John 267
Atkinson, Mrs Elizabeth 237, 238n
Atkinson, Robert 174

Austin Friars *see* St Austin (Augustine) Friars

Baker (servant) 42n
Baker, Cicely, Countess Dowager of Dorset 15
Baker, Mrs Sibilla 140
Balliol, King Edward 6, 139
Bannockburn, Battle of 6
Barden Tower 3, 9, 100, 101, 106, 115n, 140, 142, *186*
Barnwelt (traitor) 73n
Basket (*or* Baskett), Peter 31+n, 32, 37, 42, 50, 51, 80
Baston, K. 37
Bath, Countess of 22, 24, 25, 26, 97
Bath, Earl of 91
Bathurst, Mrs 32, 38
Baynard's Castle 92, 95, 96
Beamsley Almshouses 121, 182, 237, 243
Beauchamp, Lady (Frances Devereux) 33n, 49n, 51, 56, 59n, 66n, 67, 71, 72, 73, 74, 75, 76n, 80n
Beauchamp, Lord 49n
Beauchamp, Maud 7
B(e)aumont, Mary, Countess Dowager of Northampton 121
Bedding, Thomas 29
Bedford, Countess of 23, 26, 27, 38, 44, 47, 56, 71, 78, 132

Bedford, 2nd Earl of 24, 91
Bedford, 3rd Earl of 91
Bedford, Francis, 4th Earl of 23, 92, 232
Belcamp, Jan van 97
Bellasis, Mr 32
Bernard, Judge Sir Robert 147, 151
Billingsley, Mrs Bridget 182
Billingsley, Sir Thomas 175, 181
Bird, Mr James 240, 267
Blamire (or Bleamire), Jeffrey (farmer) 232–68 passim
Blenkinsop, Mr 257
Blentre, Mr 41
Blunt, Lady 23
Bohemia, Elector Frederick of 80n
Bohun, Humphrey de, 4th Earl of Hereford 6
Bolebrooke (or Bollbroke) House 87, 92, 177, 215
Bolton Abbey 3, 115n
Bongate Church 138
Bonson, Henry 245, 265
Books of Record xii, xiii, 139n
'boon hen' 102
Booth, Sir George 142n
Boroughbridge, Battle of 9
Boswell, Sir Ralph 67, 81
Bosworth, Battle of 9
Bourchier, Frances (cousin of AC) 23, 25+n, 27, 91, 250
Boyle, Charles, Lord Dungarvan 130, 148, 160
Boyle, Elizabeth (née Clifford), Countess of Cork 108, 115+n, 130, 160, 161+n, 171, 184, 185
Boyle, Lady Anne 184
Boyle, Richard, Earl of Cork 108, 115, 130, 147–8, 160, 161+n, 184
Bracken, Mr (painter) 232
Bradford, Adam (barber) 51n, 57
Bradford, John 243
Brakely, Viscount 41n
Brandon, Lady Eleanor (later Clifford) 10
Bricknell, Jane 208, 219
Bridges, Mrs Elizabeth 22, 23
Bridgewater, Lady 67
Bromedish (servant) 82
Bromflete, Henry, Lord Bromflete and Baron Vesci 8

Bromley, Baron 39
Brough Castle 3, 4, 141, 145, 146, 152, 158, 178; Clifford's Tower 152, 200; fire at 180; Roman Tower, 152
Brough Mill 150
Brougham Castle 3, 4, 7, 110, 120, 142, 157, 236, and passim in 'Kendal Diary'
Brougham Chapel 97, 138, 155
Brougham Manor 152
Bruce, Lord 66
Brunstall, Michael 81
Buchanan, Mr James, Parson of Appleby 233, 266
Bucher, Prudence 40
Buchin, Kate 54
Buckhurst, Thomas, Lord (infant son of AC) 246
Buckingham, Earl of 45, 49n
Buckle, William 242
Burbeck (or Birkbeck), Mr Thomas 239+n
Burbeck, William 245
Burghley (or Burleigh or Bourghley), Lady 45, 245
Burghley (or Burleigh), Lord William Cecil of 22+n
Burley Breaks (game) 54+n
Burridge, Mr 37
Burtie, Mr H. 49n
Burton, Kate 60, 64, 78, 79
Burton, Sir Edward 79
Butcher, Lord x
Buxton, Kath. 37
Byfield, Mr 171

Caerlaverock, siege of 6
Caesar's Tower see Appleby Castle
Caldicott, Matthew 33+n, 35, 40, 52, 54, 57, 60, 61, 65, 66
Calvert, Sir George 68
Canterbury, Archbishop of 29
Care, Mrs 82
Carew, Lady 72
Carew, Lord 75
Carey, Mrs Mary 23, 25, 26
Carey, Lady 44
Carey, Victoria (Lady Vurdale) 200
Carlisle, Earl and Countess of 182
Carlisle Castle 266
Carlston, Thomas 132

Index

Carlton, Lady 239
Carlton, Mrs Jane 237
Carlton, Robert 239
Carlton, Sir William, 237
Carr, Colonel 202
Carr (or Ker), Lady Frances and Lord Robert see Somerset
Castle Ashby 117, 118, 122
Castle Cornett, Guernsey 215
Cattrick, Mr and Mrs 239
Cavendish, Lady Elizabeth 37n, 72
Cavendish, Lord 66
Cecil, Frances, Countess Dowager of Thanet 118
Cecil, Lady 24n
Cecil, Sir Robert 22, 23
Cecil, William, Lord Roos 28, 29, 53, 68n
Challoner, Dr 24
Challum, Sir Thomas 73
Chambers, Mr (steward) 27
Chantrell, Mr 78
Charles I, King 97; as Prince of Wales 41n, 106, 198; execution of 244, 245
Charles II, King 102, 112, 144, 150, 157, 176, 198, 201, 206
Chaworth, Sir George 47
Chenies Church 89, 250
Cheyney, 'Cousin' 41
Cheynie House 87
Chichester, Sir Arthur 31n
Chippindale, Anne 242
Cholmely, Sir Henry 144
Chorley 260, 261
Chronicles of Lanercost 6
Civil War 92, 95, 100, 101, 106
Clanricarde, Lord 54
Clapham, Christopher (later Sir) 144, 266+n
Clapham, Richard 127
Clapham, Sheffield 182
Clarendon, Edward Hyde, Earl of 85
Clebom, Mr 42
Clement X, Pope 201
Clerkenwell 73, 96
Clifford Anne, Countess of Dorset, Pembroke and Montgomery ii, 98–9, 247; appearance 1–2; at Elizabeth I's funeral 1; birth 1, 244, 248; births of children 15, 246; builds her tomb 133; character x, xi,

xii–xiii, xiv, 89, 102, 269–70; christening 256; death and burial 269–70; deaths of sons 85; inheritance disputes x–xi, 2–4, 14, 37, 38, 45, 49, 52, 54, 56, 59, 62, 67n, 69, 76+n, 88, 91, 92, 95, 253, 268; love of books 48n, 91; love of country life 102, 112; marriages: x, with first husband, Richard Sackville 15, 85, 87, 88, 257, with second husband, Philip Herbert 88–91, 94, 96, 100, 105; parting from her mother 18, 31; relations with tenants see tenants; religious devotion: 32, 229–30, 235, 242, Roman Catholicism 102; will 269
Clifford, Dorothy 191n
Clifford, early ancestors of AC 5–9
Clifford, Francis, 4th Earl of Cumberland ('Uncle Cumberland') 2, 4, 10, 18, 28+n, 33, 37, 46, 47, 51n, 52, 56, 62, 73, 74, 92, 94, 142
Clifford, George (cousin of AC) 30, 57, 64, 72
Clifford, George, 3rd Earl of Cumberland (father of AC) 1, 2, 10, 12, 21n, 22, 24, 26, 97, 98–9, 108, 244, 256; death of 14; voyages of 11, 65+n, 81
Clifford, Henry, 1st Earl of Cumberland (gt-grandfather of AC) 9–10, 178, 184
Clifford, Henry, 2nd Earl of Cumberland (grandfather of AC) 10
Clifford, Henry, 5th Earl of Cumberland ('Cousin Clifford') 24, 40, 41, 47, 51n, 56, 62, 64, 67n, 69, 72, 73, 74, 75, 78, 94, 95, 100, 108; his wife 78
Clifford, Lady Elizabeth see under Boyle
Clifford, Lord Francis (brother of AC) 1, 97, 98–9, 244
Clifford, Lord Henry, 'The Shepherd Lord' x, 9, 14, 95, 191n
Clifford, Lord John, 'The Butcher' 8
Clifford, Lord Robert (ancestor of AC) 6–7, 91, 139, 154
Clifford, Lord Robert (brother of AC) 1, 80, 97, 98–9, 164, 244
Clifford, Thomas, Lord Clifford of Chudleigh 102, 222
Clifford Castle 5
Clifford's Tower see Brough Castle
Cobham, Lord 66n
Cocke, Reynold 169

coffee, ban on 232
Coleby, Mr John 181, 185
Compton, Alethea (gr of AC) 150, 152, 202, 203, 226, 246, 266
Compton, Anne (gr of AC) 125, 146–7, 148–9
Compton, Dr Henry, Bishop of Oxford, subsequently Bishop of London 238
Compton, Isabella (daughter of AC) see Sackville, Lady Isabella
Compton, Isabella (gr of AC) 130–1, 136
Compton, James, Earl of Northampton (son-in-law of AC) 96, 118, 121, 142, 198, 199, 225, 240–60 passim
Compton, James (gr of AC) 140, 143, 152, 158
Compton, Lady Cecily ('Sister Compton') 35n, 43, 49n, 50, 51, 56+n, 67, 72, 74, 79+n
Compton, Lord 36n
Compton, Mr Henry (brother of earl) 133–5
Compton, Sir Charles 121
Compton, Sir Henry ('Brother Compton') 35+n, 60, 61, 67, 72, 74, 78
Compton, William (gr of AC) 116–18, 146–7, 152
Compton Church 131
Coniston (or Couniston), Ralph 37, 68, 82
Coniston, Wat 68, 70, 81
Conniston, John 246
Cook, John 51
Coolinge, Peter 75
Corby Castle 137, 252
Cork, Earl and Countess of see Boyle
Cornwallis, Mr Thomas 65
Cotton (prisoner in Tower) 73
Coventry (servant) 40, 61
Coventry, Anne (gt-gr of AC) 130
Coventry, Henry (gt-gr of AC) 187
Coventry, John (gt-gr of AC) 123
Coventry, Lady Margaret (Tufton, gr of AC) 123, 130, 135, 142, 151
Coventry, Lord Thomas (father of George) 118, 154
Coventry, Margaret, II (gt-gr of AC) 135
Coventry, Mr George (husband of Margaret, née Tufton) 118
Coventry, Thomas (gt-gr of AC) 142, 143
Coventry, William (gt-gr of AC) 151

Craven estates 3, 6, 101; see also Anne Clifford, inheritance disputes
Crewe, Sir Randal 45n, 47
Cromwell, Oliver 6, 101, 102, 112n, 162
Crook, Mr Charles, Parson of Warcop 242
Cumberland, Earls of see under Clifford
Cumberland estates 265
Cundy, Agnes de 5
Curvett, Acton 39n
Curzon, Lady Diana 206, 266
Curzon, Mary, Countess of Dorset 96
Curzon, Sir George 158

Dacre, Lady Anne (later Clifford) (grandmother of AC) 10, 266–7
Dacre, William, Lord Dacre of Greystoke (gt-grandfather of AC) 10, 267
Dacres, Lady Elizabeth 265
Dacres, Lord and Lady 79, 206
Dallison, Sir Maximilian and Lady 78–9
Dalston, 'Cousin' 222
Dalston, Mr Christopher 259
Dalston, Mr John 191, 203, 231, 263, 269
Damse, Marquis 52n
Daniel, Samuel 2, 61n, 97
Darby, John 132
Darcy, Lord and Lady 206
Dargue, Margaret 242
Dargue, William 242
Davis, Mr 53, 59, 64, 68, 69, 73, 75n, 81
Davy, Mr 35
Dawson, Richard 54
Demian, Dor. 242
Dennison, Robert 254
Dent, John and Richard 74
Denzill, Ambassador 187
Derby, Lady 23, 44, 45, 51, 97
Devereux, Robert, 3rd Earl of Essex 22, 33, 44n, 61, 249
Devonshhire, Lady 78
Digby, Sir John 31n, 47
Dombvill (or Dumbell), Mr 37, 41
Donne, Dr John 60+n
Donne, old Lady 67
Donne, young Lady 67
Dormer, Mr 26
Dorset, Anne, wife of 2nd Earl of 50+n
Dorset, Anne Spencer, Countess Dowager of 15

Index

Dorset, Cicely Baker, Countess Dowager of 15
Dorset, 2nd Earl of 15
Dorset, 3rd Earl of *see* Sackville, Richard
Dorset House, Great 15, 65, 114, 241, 250, 261
Dorset House, Little 15
Douglas, Sir Robert 47
Drax, Mr Henry 176
Dudley, Lady 75
Dudley, Margaret 75
Dudley, Mr John 30, 31, 39
Dudley, Mrs Mary (later Lady Hume) 71
Dumbell (*or* Dombvill), Mr 37, 41
Dunbarr, Viscount 190
Dungarvan, Lord *see* Boyle, Charles
Durin, William 40
Dutch Wars 207n
Dutton, Mr 26

Earke, Erasmus 128
Earle, Serjeant 127
Edenhall 254
Edge, Mr William 165, 205, 233–63 *passim*
Edmondes, Sir Thomas 72
Edward IV, King 8
Edwards (servant) 40
Effingham, Lady 42, 71
Egerton, Lord Chancellor 51n
Elizabeth, Princess (daughter of James I) 24, 26n, 27, 252
Elizabeth I, Queen 1, 21, 249
Elizabeth, Queen of Bohemia 150, 156
Ellis, Judge Sir William 219
Elme, Thomas 256
Erskine, Sir Thomas 22
Erwin, Lady Anne 69
Erwin, Sir William 69
Essex, Earl of *see* Devereux
Essex House 44
Evans, Dr 188
Evers, Serjeant 127
Ewbank, Mr Thomas 257
Ewyas, Robert 5
Ewyas, Sibilla 5
Exeter, Countess of 40n, 53, 68+n

Fanshaw, Lord 202
Favior, Mr 237–8

Fennett, Ensign Robert 142
Fenwick, Mr 178
Fielding, Lady 43
'Fire Dog' 80
Finch, Lady 22, 25
Finch, Sir Hennige 218
Finch, Sir Moyle 25, 27
Fisher, Henry xii, 15
Fittin, Abraham 252
Fitz-Geoffrey, Isobel 4
Fitz-Osbern, William, Earl of Hereford 5
Fitz, Walter, Maud 5
Fitz-Warren, Lord 23
Flakebridge (map-maker) 250
Flemming, Mr 251
Fletcher, Mary 191n
Fletcher, Sir George and Lady 251
Fletcher, Sir Richard 191n
Flocknall, Mr 21
Flodden, Battle of 9
Frederick, Prince, Elector Palatine 252
Furnivall, Serjeant 127

Gabetis, Mr Thomas 113, 132, 209, 231–63 *passim*
Gabetis, Mrs 231–63 *passim*
Gage, Sir Edward 67
Garnet House 254
Gaveston, Piers 6
George, Sir Edward 56, 80
Gifford (servant) 79n
Giles, Tom (groom) 48, 50
Gillmore, Mr John 188–9, 237, 243, 260, 263
Gillmore, Mrs Elizabeth 188–9, 263
glecko (game) 29+n, 43, 61, 80
Glenham, Lady Anne 56+n
Glenham, Sir Henry 56+n
Glenham, Sir Thomas 76n
Glenham, Thomas 30, 31, 40, 52, 53, 54, 61, 67
Gloucester, Henry, Duke of 144
Goatley, John 166
Godding, son of Humphrey 32
Goodgion, George 188–9, 234, 235, 242, 256, 263
Goodgion, Robert 246, 248, 249
Goodwin, Mrs 26n
Gotchley, John 162

Grantham, Lady 29, 33, 49
Grantham, Sir Thomas 29n
Grasty, Mr Samuel, Parson of Ninekirks 231–68 *passim*
Gray, Lady Elizabeth 29, 43
Graystock 221
'Great Books', the xii, xiii
Great Fire of London 102, 188
Great Picture, The, 97, 98–9
Griffin, Mr 23
Grimston, Anne *see under* Tufton
Grimston, Edward (gt-gr of AC) 222, 223
Grimston, Mary (gt-gr of AC) 226
Grimston, Mr Samuel 218
Gromston, Sir Harbottle 218
Graverner (*or* Grosvenor) (usher) 33+n, 40
Grye, Lady Elizabeth 72
Guernsey, accident on 215, 233
Gustavus Adolphus, King of Sweden 232n

Hailes (*or* Hales), Judge Matthew 127, 130, 133
Hall, 'Cousin' 81
Hall, John 189, 242, 252
Hammers, Mr and Mrs 73
Hammon (*or* Hamon) (servant) 36, 72
Hampton Court 25
Hanns, Mrs 43
Harborton, Mr Justice 109
Harrington, Lady 24, 27
Harrison, Major-General Thomas 112+n
Harrison, Robert (housekeeper) 246
Hart, Sir Percival 59, 60, 62
Hartley, Mrs 60
Hartshorn Tree, legend of 6–7, 139
Harwood, map of 237
Hasell, Edward (AC's secretary) xiii, 229, 231–69 *passim*
Hasell McCosh family xiii
Hatfield, Henry 140
Hatton, Anne (gt-gr of AC) 191–2, 218
Hatton, Cecily *see under* Tufton
Hatton, Dowager Lady 24n, 202, 215–16; daughter of, 50n
Hatton, Elizabeth (gt-gr of AC) 218, 223
Hatton, Lord Christopher 192
Hatton, Margaret *or* Mary (gt-gr of AC) 202, 218, 223
Hatton, Mr Christopher (later Lord II) 188, 191–2, 205, 206, 232

Hatton, Sir William 76n
Hay, James, Viscount Doncaster 47, 51n, 60, 64, 74, 82+n
Hay, Lady Lucy (Percy) 60, 64+n
Heardson, Mr 56
Hennige, Sir Thomas 147
Henrietta Maria, Queen (wife of Charles I) 149, 198
Henrietta Maria, Princess (sister of Charles II) 149, 159
Henry of Bourbon 198
Henry II, King 5, 6
Henry III, King 4, 5
Henry VII, King 9
Henry VIII, King 9–10
Henry, Prince (son of James I) 23, 24n, 26, 41n, 44, 57n, 66
Herbert, George (poet) 91
Herbert, Henry, 2nd Earl of Pembroke 47, 56, 61n, 105
Herbert, Lady Mary (Sidney), wife of 2nd Earl 44, 56, 61n, 66–7, 75, 105
Herbert, Mr James (son of 4th Earl) 199
Herbert, Philip, 4th Earl of Pembroke and Montgomery (second husband of AC) x, xii, *90*, 94, 96, 100; character and death 105
Herbert, Sir William 33
Herbert, William, 3rd Earl of Pembroke (brother of Philip) 89
Hertford, Lady 73
Hertford, Lord 49n, 73, 75
Hicklin, Mr 27
Hilton, Mr Robert 243, 261
Hilton, Mrs 257
Hilton, Thomas 42, 81
Hinde, Mr 176
Hobart, Lord 38, 52
Hodgson, Mr 31, 56, 57
Hollis, Lord 187
Holmes, Martin: *Proud Northern Lady* xiv
Hookfield (servant) 42n
Horn, Nan 73
Hornby Hall 239n
Horseley 32, 33n, 35
Hortitius (cook) 51
Hothfield, Lord 96, 270
Hothfield House 96, *134*, 135
Hothfield papers xii, 15

Hough's Mill 147
Howard, Charles, Earl of Carlisle 31, 62, 178, 226
Howard, Henry, Earl of Arundel 221
Howard, Henry, Earl of Norfolk 226
Howard, Lady, Countess of Suffolk 43, 68n, 81n
Howard, Lord William 29, 37, 40, 54, 74, 76n
Howard, Mr Francis 252
Howard, Mrs Anne 252
Howard, Sir Charles 252
Howard, Sir Thomas 57
Howard, Sir William 37
Howard, Thomas, Earl of Suffolk 21n, 22, 76n, 81+n, 81n
Howard, William (son of Lord William) 30, 39, 265
Howbridge, Mrs 26n
Hubbard, Lord 38
Hume, Lady 38, 71
Hume, Lord 71
Humphrie, Mrs 26
Hunsden, Lord 71, 72
Hutchins, Mary 71
Hutton, Julia 191n
Hutton, Sir Richard 191n
Hyde, Anne, Duchess of York 208
Hyde, Edward, Earl of Clarendon 85

In Praise of a Solitary Life 70

Jackson, Mr Richard 267
Jackson, William 230
James I and VI, King 4, 18, 21, 22, 24, 41, 44, 47, 49, 57n, 64, 66, 68n, 69+n, 71, 76, 87, 106, 233, 239, 240; coronation 25
James II, King (as Duke of York) 144, 176, 201, 208, 220n
James, Mr 36
Jenkins, Jack 27
Joeniers, Baron de 48
John, King 4
Johnson, Dr 257
Johnson, Mr 253
Johnson, Mr Thomas 132
Johnson, Mrs Anne 253
Johnson, William (housekeeper) 245
Jones, Inigo 91

Jones, Richard 35, 65
Jordan, Isabell 242
Josiah (servant) 51, 57
Judith (servant) 30, 51, 53, 82

Kaber Rigg plot 238n
Katherine, Queen (wife of Charles II) 157, 177, 193
Keeper, the Lord 51, 52, 55, 59n
Kendal (*or* Kendall) (servant) 36, 38
'Kendal Diary', manuscript of xii–xiii, 97
Keniston, Mr 70
Kent, Countess of 217–18
Kent, Earl of 23
Ker (*or* Carr), Lady Frances and Lord Robert *see* Somerset
Kidd, Mr 39
Kildare, Lady 24
Killaway, Mr 188
Killigrew, Sir Peter 206
Killingworth Castle 257
Kingston, Thomas 188
Kinloss, Lady 72
Kinson, Mrs 26
Kirkby Thore Church 97
Kitching, Thomas 246, 248, 249
Knightley, Lady Elizabeth 23–4
Knightley, Sir Richard 23
'Knole Diary', manuscript of xi–xii, xiv, 15
Knole House 58, 67, 85, 250 and *passim* in 'Knole Diary'
Knolles, Lady 38
Knolles (*or* Knollys), Lord 38n, 41n
Knolles, Richard: *The Generall Historie of the Turks* 54n

Labourn, William 237, 243, 260, 263
Lake, Lady (Arthur) 72, 73
Lake, Lady Lettice 68+n
Lake, Mrs Ann (Lady Rous) 28
Lake, Sir Arthur 68n, 76n
Lake, Sir Thomas 68+n, 76n
Lancaster 261
Lancilwell 26
Langhorn, Mr Thomas 248
Langley, Edward xiii
Larkin (servant) 66
Laurie, Jack 36
Law, Lady 78n

Layfield, Dr 37, 51
Legge (*or* Legg), Edward 32+n, 33, 49, 50, 67, 69, 80
Leicester, Robert, Earl of: *Commonwealth* 81+n
Lennard, Mr Pembroke 79
Leybourne, Idonea de *see* Viteripont
Leybourne, Sir Roger de 4
Lichfield 258
Lincoln, Lady 74
Lindsay (servant) 52
Linsey, Mrs 65
Lisle, Lady 60, 62
Lisle, Lord 60, 61
Littleton, Judge Sir Timothy 204–5, 209, 215, 222, 226
Littleton, Sir Charles 188
Llewelyn, Margaret 5
London, Bishop of 57, 71
Long Parliament 144
Longueville, Lady Susanna 74
Longworth, Mr 75n
Loughlyye, George 242
Lowe, Richard 242
Lowers (*or* Lowes), Richard (housekeeper) 233, 252
Lowther, Lady 60, 197
Lowther, Mr John 188
Lowther, Sir Hugh 191n
Lowther, Sir John 144, 177, 187, 188, 191+n, 196, 197, 215, 219, 223, 227
Lune, Mr 54

Machell, Mr Henry 231, 232, 237, 242, 252
Machell, Mr Hugh 251
Machell, Mr Lancelot 232, 251, 254, 258
Machell, Mrs Susan 231, 242
Mad Lover, The (play) 44
Mainwaring, Captain 53n
Mallerstang Church 97, 168, 169, 202
Manners, Sir George and Lady Katherine *see* Rutland
manuscripts of AC's diaries xi, xii, xiv, 15, 230, 264
Marsh, Edward (later Sir Edward) 33, 35, 37, 38, 39–40, 41, 49+n, 53, 59, 61, 69
Marsh, Mr Christopher 114, 127
Marshall, Mr 42
Mary (servant) 53, 76, 79, 80

Mary, 'Cousin' 71, 76, 78
Mary of Medina 220+n
Mary, Princess of Orange 144
Mary, Queen (wife of Charles I) 106
Mary, Queen Dowager 149, 159, 176, 177
Mary, Queen of Scots 11
Matthew (servant) *see* Caldicott
Matthews, Mrs 42
Maubton, Secretary 78n
Maynard, Serjeant 127
Medina, Duchess of 220
Medina, Mary of 220+n
Mene, Mr 25
Messina, Battle of 249
Metcalf, Mr Thomas 168
Middleton, Roger 259
Middleton, William 259
Minerill, Mr 25
Molyneux, Mr Roger 197
Monck, General George 144+n
Montagu(e), Lord Chief Justice 41n, 45n, 47
Montgomery, Lady 40n, 44, 45
Montgomery, Lord 47, 60
Montgomery, Margaret 263–4
Montaigne, Michel de: *Essays* 41; *Plays* 48
Mordant, Mr John 156, 157
Mordaunt, Lord 36n
Monmouth estates 5–6
Morpeth, Edward, Lord and Lady 200
Mountjoy, Lord, Earl of Devonshire 21n, 22
Murgatroyd (tenant) 102
Murgatroyd, Jacob 242
Murray, George 25
Musgrave, Christopher 177
Musgrave, Justice William 233
Musgrave, Mary 253–4
Musgrave, Mr Richard 202, 253–4
Musgrave, Sir Philip 177, 187, 190+n, 191, 203, 210, 215, 219, 232, 253, 269
Musgrave, Sir Richard 191n

Nanson, Mr Phillip 248
Naworth Castle 265, 266
Needham, Lady 23
Neville, Bess 67
Neville, Lady Cecily ('Cousin Cecily') 35, 37, 38, 41
Neville, Lady Mary 61n, 65
Neville, Lord John 7

Index

Neville, Lord Ralph 7
Neville, Mary 28
Neville, Moll 48, 60, 61, 64, 70n, 71, 75n, 76
Neville, Sir Henry 36, 61+n, 80
Newdigate (or Nudigate), Judge Richard 122, 138
Newton, Lady 22
Newton, Mrs 29
Nichols, Elizabeth 164
Nichols, Judge 39
Ninekirks Church 141, 155, 156, 157, 244, 251
Norris, Lord 61
North, Lord 71
North, Sir John 74
North Hall 100
Northampton, Countess of see Sackville, Isabella
Northampton, Earl of see Compton, James
Northumberland, Countess of 24, 44
Northumberland, Henry Percy, Earl of 73+n

Oldworth, 'Cousin' 78n
Óliver, Sir John 31n
Orberton, Mr 48
Orfuir, Mr 73
Orkney, Master of 25
Orleans and Anjou, Duke of 149
Ossery, Earl of 207
Otley, Mr 206
Otway, Mr 160
Ovid: Metamorphoses 76
Oxford, Countess of 245
Oxford, 17th Earl of 89

Page, Mr 68
Paget, Lord 61
Palmer, Sir Francis 26
Parker, Judge (later Baron) John 115, 119, 124, 128, 135, 138, 141
Parker, Sir Thomas 65
Pate, Mrs Frances 231, 242, 255, 261
Pattison, John 262
Paulett, Mrs Jane 182
Pembroke, Earls of see Herbert
Pendragon Castle 3, 4, 146, 153, 154, 158 and passim in 'Kendal Diary'
Pennis (servant) 80n

Penniston(e), Lady 75, 79+n, 81n
Penniston(e), Sir Thomas 79
Percy, Elizabeth 7
Percy, Lady Lucy 64+n
Petley (servant) 50
Petty, Thomas 33
Pickering, Sir Christopher 37
Pilgrimage of Grace 110n
Pinder, Mr Richard (Quaker) 240
plague 25, 26, 27, 177
Pond, William 27
Pons, Richard 5
Pons, Walter (became de Clifford) 5
Pons, William 5
Pontoise, siege of 8
Poston, Katherine 182
Preston, 261
Puleston, Judge 119, 120
Punn, William 41, 42, 47, 55

Rainbowe, Edward, Bishop of Carlisle 245, 251, 269
Rainsford, Judge Sir Richard 177, 182–3, 187, 190, 222, 226
Raleigh, Lady 28, 72
Raleigh, Sir Walter 28n
Raleigh, Wat. 36n
Ramsbury (or Ramsburie) House 92, 164
Ram, Henry 257
Ran (or Rann), Mr 50, 51, 52, 54, 60, 61, 70, 81
Raynham Church 171, 176, 178, 207
Rawling, Cuthbert 242
Reynolds, Mrs 72
Reynoldson, Richard 242
Richard III, King 9
Rich, Lady 24n 26, 28, 38, 44, 52n, 59, 60, 64, 65n, 70
Rich, Lady Harriet 71
Rich, Lord 71
Rich, Mr Charles 71, 72
Rich, Mr Nathaniel 71
Rich, Sir Henry 52n, 70, 72
Rich, Sir Robert 28n
Rilyston, Judge 115
Rivers (servant) 32, 33, 37, 39, 40, 47–8, 49
Rivers, Sir George 59
Rockingham Castle 23
Rodes, Lady 197

Rodes, Mrs Jane 197
Rodes, Sir Francis 197
Rolls, Elizabeth 135
Roman Tower *see* Brough Castle
Roos, Lord *see* Cecil, William
Rose, Mr 50
Roses, Wars of 6, 8
Ross (*or* Rosse), Lady 68+n, 76n
Roxburrow, Lady 55
Rupert, Prince 151, 176, 201
Russell, Francis, 4th earl of Bedford (cousin of AC) 27, 29, 30, 56, 57, 64, *77*, 88, 94, 95
Russell, Francis (son of earl) 67
Russell, Lady ('Aunt Russell') 27
Russell, Lady Margaret (mother of AC) 1, 3, 10, *13*, 14, 21, 22, 32, 33, 66n, 91, 97, *98–9*, 164, 249, 262; birth of AC 244, 248; death and burial 35n, 36+n, 39; last meeting with AC 18, 31+n; memorial 219
Russell, Lord, of Thorney 22, 23, 24, 25, 26n, 27, 30, 67, 80
Russell, Lord William 250
Russell, Mr Edward 194, 195
Russell, Mr William 182, 194, 195
Ruthven, Lady 44, 45, 57, 64
Rutland, Edmund, Earl of 8
Rutland, Katherine Manners, Countess of 42, 61, 78
Rutland, Sir George Manners, Earl of 29, 78, 245
Ruvy, John 54
Ryder, Mrs 55

Sackville, 'Cousin' 73, 80
Sackville, Edward 241
Sackville, Lady ('Sister Sackville') 28, 41, 51, 59n, 64, 67, 72, 79+n, 80n
Sackville, Lady Cecily *see* Compton, Lady Cecily
Sackville, Lady Isabella (younger daughter of AC) 85, *86*, 91, 94, 95, 142; births of children 116–18, 125, 130–31, 140, 150; death 152; marriage to James Compton, 3rd Earl of Northampton 96; visit to AC 133–5
Sackville, Lady Margaret (elder daughter of AC) 63, 123, *129*, 167, 178, 206, 218; as child 15, 31, 32, 33, 35, 38, 42n, 43, 55, 57, 60, 67, 76, 78, 80, 85, illnesses as a child

47, 48, 49+n, 62, 65n, 81n; births of children 92, 95, 108, 122; correspondence with AC 232–63 *passim*; marriage to John Tufton, 2nd Earl of Thanet 88; remembered as a child by AC 235–54 *passim*; visits to AC 119–225 *passim*
Sackville, Lady Mary 61n
Sackville, Mr Richard 213
Sackville, Richard, Lord Buckhurst, 3rd Earl of Dorset (first husband of AC) x, xii, 15–18, 21n, *34*, 49, 69, 79+n, 239, 246, 250; character and death 85; relations with AC 45, 53, 76n, 81, 242, 255; will 40n
Sackville, Robert, 2nd Earl of Dorset 50n
Sackville, Sir Edward, later 4th Earl of Dorset ('Brother Sackville') 28n, 29, 51, 53, 59+n, 60n, 61, 62, 65, 69n, 70n, 72, 75+n, 80n, 85, 87, 114
Sackville, Thomas, 1st Earl of Dorset 85
Sackville, Thomas (infant son of AC) 246
Sackville College affair 168+n
Sackville-West, Vita: *The Diary of the Lady Anne Clifford* xiv
St Albans, First Battle of 8
St Anne's Almshouses, Appleby 101, 110, 116, 151–2, 249, 270
St Augustine: *Of the City of God* 68
St Austin (Augustine) Friars 62n, 64, 72–3, 262
St Bartholomew's Priory 87
St David's, Bishop of 28, 31, 36
St John, Lady 42, 45, 64, 72
St John, Oliver, Lord Chief Justice 127, 130, 133
St Nicholas (lands near Appleby) 110, 152
St Lawrence's Church, Appleby 18, 97, 124, 133, 269
Salisbury, Lord 39n
Salkeld, John 132
Samford, Mr Thomas 231
Samford, Mrs 235
Sandford, Sir Richard and Lady 191
Sandford, Mr 40
Sandys, Mr (author) 45
Saragol, Mr: *Of the Supplication of the Saints* 70
Saul, Mrs 243, 244
Saunders, Mr Thomas 199
Sedgwick, Mr George 114, 126, 133, 203, 231, 235

Index

Selby, Lady 36+n, 67, 76, 79
Selby, Sir William 36, 67, 80
Sellinger, Thomas 27
Sevenoaks Church 60n
Seymore, Lady Jane 160
Seymore, Lady Marie 160
Seymour, Miss Anne 67
Seymour, Mr William 49n
Sheffield, Lady 55
Sheffield, Lord 69; daughters 42
Sheppey, Isle of 92
Sherborne, Mr 74
Shrewsbury, Countess of 64, 73
Shrewsbury, Earl of 258–9
Sidney, Barbara 61, 62
Sidney, Lady Dorothy 60n, 61
Sidney, Lady Mary see under Herbert
Sidney, Sir Henry 105
Sidney, Sir Philip 61+n, 105+n
Sidney, Sir Robert 60n
Sillesden Manor 120
Sittin, Abraham 242
Skinnie (servant) and Sara Skinnie 74
Skipton Castle 1, 3, 6, 10, 96, 97, 100, 106,
    125, 133, 142, 162, *163*, 184 and *passim* in
    'Kendal Diary'
Skipton Church 125
Slidall, Jane 242
Slingsby, Mary 80
Slingsby, Sir Francis 80, 81
smallpox epidemic 199
Smallwood, Dr 227
Smallwood, Mrs 235
Smith, Mr 47, 69, 70n
Smith, Mr Leonard 267
Somerset, Frances Ker (*or* Carr), Countess
    of 29, 30n, 35, 36, 38n, 44+n, 56, 57, 72, 73
Somerset, Robert Ker (*or* Carr), Earl of
    44+n
Somerset House 43, 44, 71
Sort, Edmund 242
Southampton, Lady 24
Southampton, Lord 22, 73
Southfield, maps of 243
Spedding, Margaret 249
Spedding, William (farmer) and wife
    232–68 *passim*
Spencer, Anne, Countess Dowager of
    Dorset 15

Spencer, Lord 24
Spencer, Sir John, of Althorpe 50n
Spenser, Edmund (poet) 2, 48+n
Stanley, Charles, Earl of Derby 128
Stanley, Mr Robert 223
Steele, Lord Chief Baron 124
Stiddolph, 'Cousin' 25
Stock, Thomas: *A Tragicall Historie of the
    Troubles and Civil Warres of the Low Coun-
    tries* 40n
Straker, James 130
Strickland, Allan 231, 242, 263
Strickland, Thomas 254, 258, 259
Stuart, Mr Walter 79
Suckling, Sir John 69
Suffolk, Earl and Countess of see Howard
Sussex, Lady 51n
Sutton, Mrs 243
Swarton, Sarah 68+n
Swindin, Arthur 242, 252+n, 255, 257, 262
Symondson, John 185
Syslie, Goodwife 57

Talbot, Gilbert, Earl of Shrewsbury 105
Talbot, Mary, Countess of Pembroke 92,
    105
Taxley, Sir Robert 81
Taylor, Sir John 64, 74, 76
Taylour, Mrs Anne (governess of AC) 25,
    97
Temple Sowerby 101–2; map of 239
tenants: disputes with AC 106–8, 116, 119,
    120, 122, 127, 130, 132, 133; disputes with
    Earl of Cumberland 73, 74, 75n, dispute
    between Earl of Cumberland's tenants
    and AC's servants 39; good relations
    with AC 231–70 *passim*
Thanet, Earls of see Tufton
Thanet House (London) *170*, 171, 183
Thatcher, 'Cousin' 72
Theobalds ('Tibbalds') 22+n, 73
Thorpe, Judge Francis 109, 141
Threlkeld, Sir Lancelot 9
Thwaite, Mr John 263
Tilliburne, Lord 25
Todd, Thomas 40
Toeni, Margaret de 5
Toeni, Ralph de 5
Tothill Street (London), house in 87

Towton, Battle of 8
Trenchard, Lady 51
Tufton, Anne (gr of Ac) 118, 122, 123, 218
Tufton, Cecily (*or* Cecilia) (gr of AC) 188, 191–2, 202, 215–16
Tufton, Frances (gr of AC) 125, 133, 137, 139, 176, 178, 180
Tufton, George (gr of AC) 108, 175, 181, 195, 206, 207
Tufton, John, 2nd Earl of Thanet (son-in-law of AC) 42n, 88, 119, 168, 171
Tufton, John, 4th Earl of Thanet (gr of AC) 114, 116, 122, 126, 133, 137, 139, 149, *167*, 256, 269 and *passim* in 'Kendal Diary'
Tufton, Margaret (daughter of AC) *see* Sackville, Lady Margaret
Tufton, Margaret (gr of AC) *see* Coventry, Margaret
Tufton, Mary (gr of AC) 115, 206, 210, 217, 218, 221
Tufton, Mr Cecil 206
Tufton, Nicholas, 3rd Earl of Thanet (gr of AC) 88, 108, 118, 119, 125, 130, 137, 142, 161, 171
Tufton, Richard, 5th Earl of Thanet (gr of AC) 149
Tufton, Sackville (gr of AC) 175, 181
Tufton, Thomas, 6th Earl of Thanet (gr of AC) xiii, 95, 149, 188, 203–4, 222, 227
Turner, Elizabeth 135, 164
Turner, Judge Sir Christopher 151, 159, 166, 169, 174, 182–3, 187, 190, 196, 204–5
Turner, Mr John 132, 135, 164, 188, 242, 243
Tuscany, Prince of 193
Tutty, Penelope 40
Twentyman, John 245, 259
Twisden, Judge Sir Thomas 147, 166, 174

Vane, Sir Henry 78
Vane, Walter 79
Van Somer (*or* Vansommer), 78+n, 79
Vaux, Lord 36
Vavasour, Anne (aunt of AC) 23+n, 24, 26
Vavasour, Sir Peter 76n
Vere, Lady Susan, Countess of Montgomery (first wife of Philip Herbert) 89, 92, 245
Verulam, Lady 66
Villiers, Sir George 28n, 44

Vincent, Gabriell 133, 138, 180, 252
Viteripont, Isabella de (Clifford) 4, 5, 146, 154
Viteripont, John de 4
Viteripont, Robert de 4
Viteripont, Robert II de 4
Vurdale (*or* Uvedale), Sir William 200

Wainman, Lord 210
Wakefield, Battle of 8
Walker, Isaac 242
Walker, James 132
Walker, John 188
Waller, Thomas (serjeant-at-law) 196
Wallop, Sir Humphrey 26
Walsingham, Lady 23
Walter, Lady Mary *see* Tufton, Mary
Walter, Mr David 206, 210
Walter, Mr William 206, 210, 218
Walter, Sir John 206
Walter, Sir William 206, 218, 221, 225
Walton, Lady 76
Walton, Mr 64
Warburton, Judge 120
Warburton, Sir Richard 26
Warwick, Ambrose, Earl of 70, 71, 72, 75, 244, 248, 255
Warwick, Anne Russell, Countess of ('Aunt Warwick') 1, 21, 22, 23, 24+n, 25, 27, 67, 91, 97, 244, 248, 249–50
Warwick, Lady (Lampwell) 70, 71, 72, 75
Warwick Castle 257
Watson, Mr 37n
Watson, Mrs 53, 64
Watson, Sir Edward and Lady 23
Watson, Sir Thomas 76
Waugh, Margaret 259
Webster, Isabelle 266
Webster, John 233–68 *passim*
Wells, Dr 206
Westmorland estates 3, 4, 18, 101; *see also* Clifford, Anne, inheritance disputes
Whaley, Thomas 235
Wharton, Edward, Lord 146
Wharton, Lady Margaret (wife of Edward) 146
Wharton, Lady Philadelphia (mother of Philip) 97, 119
Wharton, Mr Hugh 234

Index

Wharton, Philip, Lord 119, 128, 130, 138, 168, 210, 223, 234, 256
Wharton, Sir Thomas 119, 138, 144, 195, 248, 253
Wharton, Thomas II 248
Whitaker, T.D.: *History of Craven* xiii
Whitcher, Alexander 126, 133, 140
Whitehall 66, 91
Whittington, Sir Timothy 30
Wiber, Dorothy 249
Wild (*or* Wilde), Sir William 209, 215, 219
Wildgoose, Lady 79
William the Conqueror, King 5
William of Orange, King 206–7, 207n
William, Lord 33, 38, 49, 52, 69
Williams: *Balaam's Ass* 73, 74
Williamson, Dr G.C.: *Lady Anne Clifford* xiv, 230; *George Clifford, Third Earl of Cumberland* 11
Willison, Mr Robert 234, 241, 250, 261
Willison, Mrs 260
Willoughby (servant) 30, 37, 38, 51, 80n
Willoughby, Lady 29, 32
Willoughby, William, 3rd Lord 29n, 30, 33, 53n, 62, 67n
Wilton House 91, 92, *93*
Winch, Mrs 231
Winchester, Marchioness of 24
Windham (*or* Wyndham), Judge Hugh 122, 127, 130, 133
Windsor, Lady 72, 73

Windsor Castle 24–5
Winter, Dorothy 249
Wismar (Germany) 232+n
Withy Pole, Lady 42
Woburn House 87
Wood (servant) 75
Woodgate, Thomas 43
Woodstock, Court at 26
Woodyat, Thomas 31, 48
Woolrich, Mr 36, 37, 56, 57
Wootton (*or* Wotten), Lady 29, 59, 66, 68
Worcester, Lady 47
Worcester, Lord 28n, 47
Wordsworth, William: 'The Song at the Feast at Brougham Castle'
Work, Thomas 79n
Worleigh, Mr 54
Worth, Lady 60, 61
Wright, Mr Thomas (Quaker) 232, 238, 241, 252, 262, 267
Wright, Rowland 169

Yateley, Sir R. 37n
Yeaksley, Sir Robert 79
Yelverton, Hobart 45n, 47
Yelverton, Mrs (second wife of Lord Charles Hatton) 232
York, James, Duke of (later James II) 144, 176, 201, 208

Zouch, Sir Edward 75